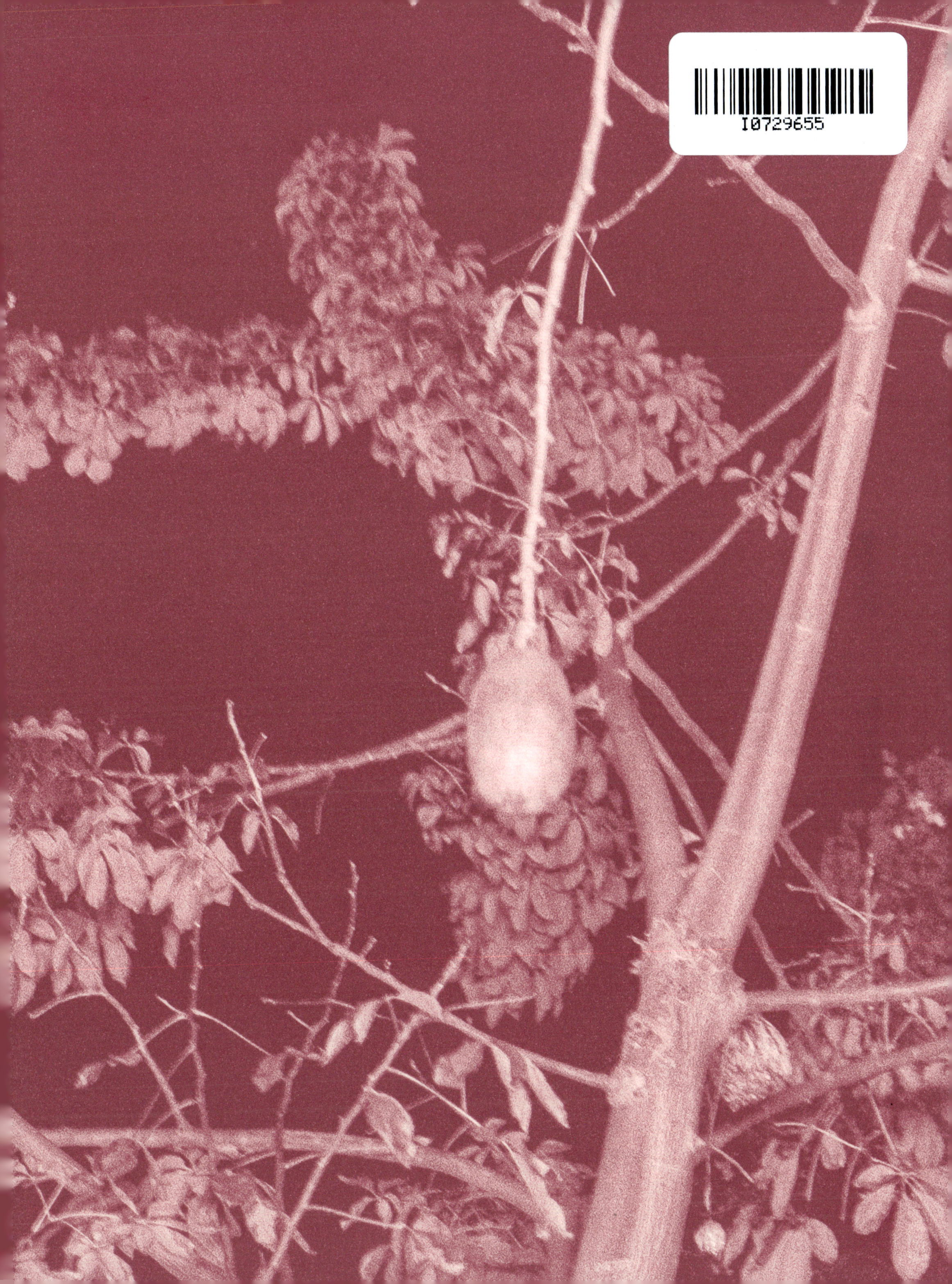

I0729655

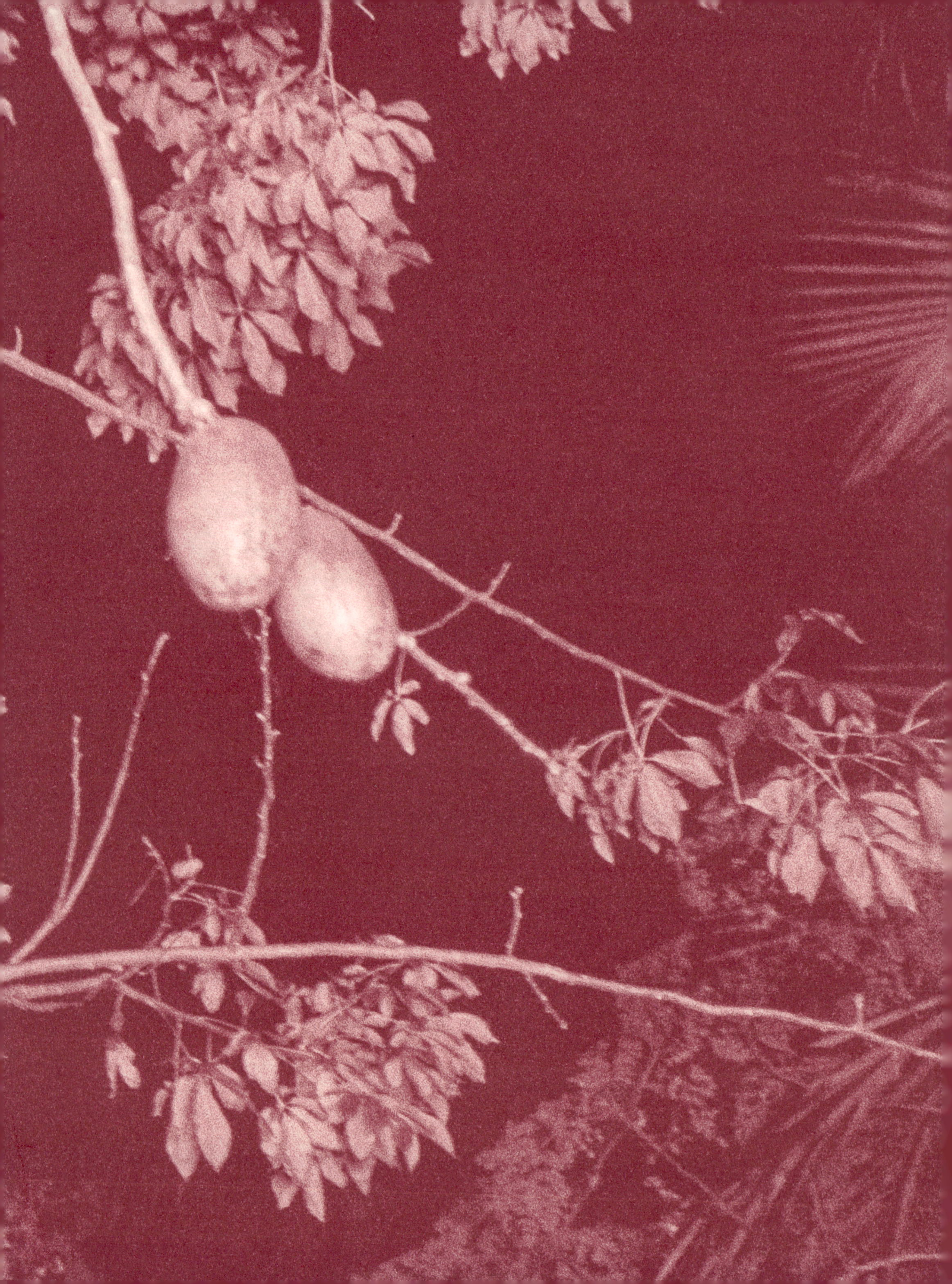

Still Life

Still Life

Photographs & Love Stories

Kate Sterlin

Anthology Editions

New York

This book is dedicated to my family: Marc, for the challenge and power of our love in this crazy world and inside my heart; Adrea, for your beautiful open spirit; Tessa, for this love journey of us that we made together; Zsela, my forever muse, for starting this story with me; and Jody Rome, for always showing me where the light is. Documenting our life together has been a gift. I love you.

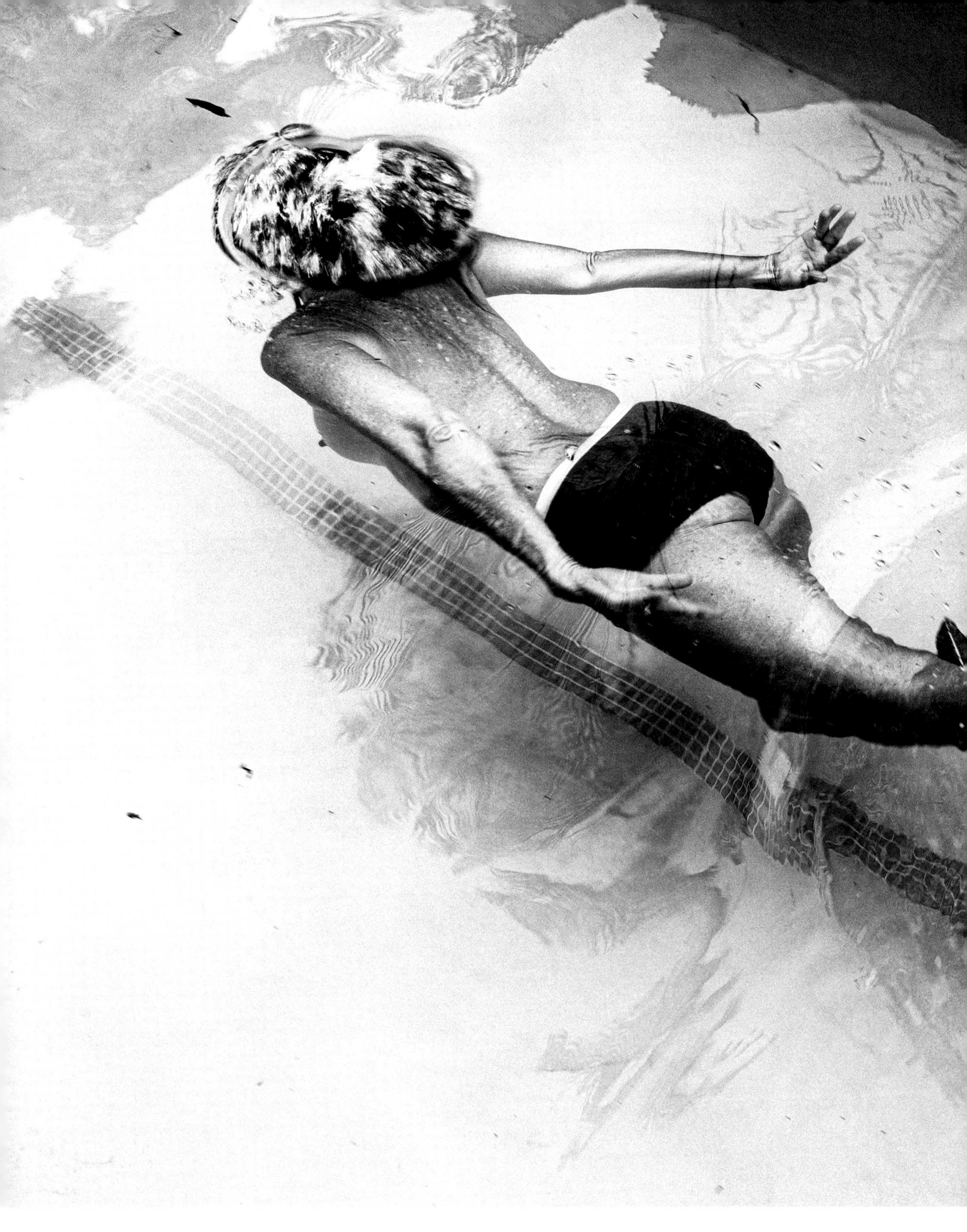

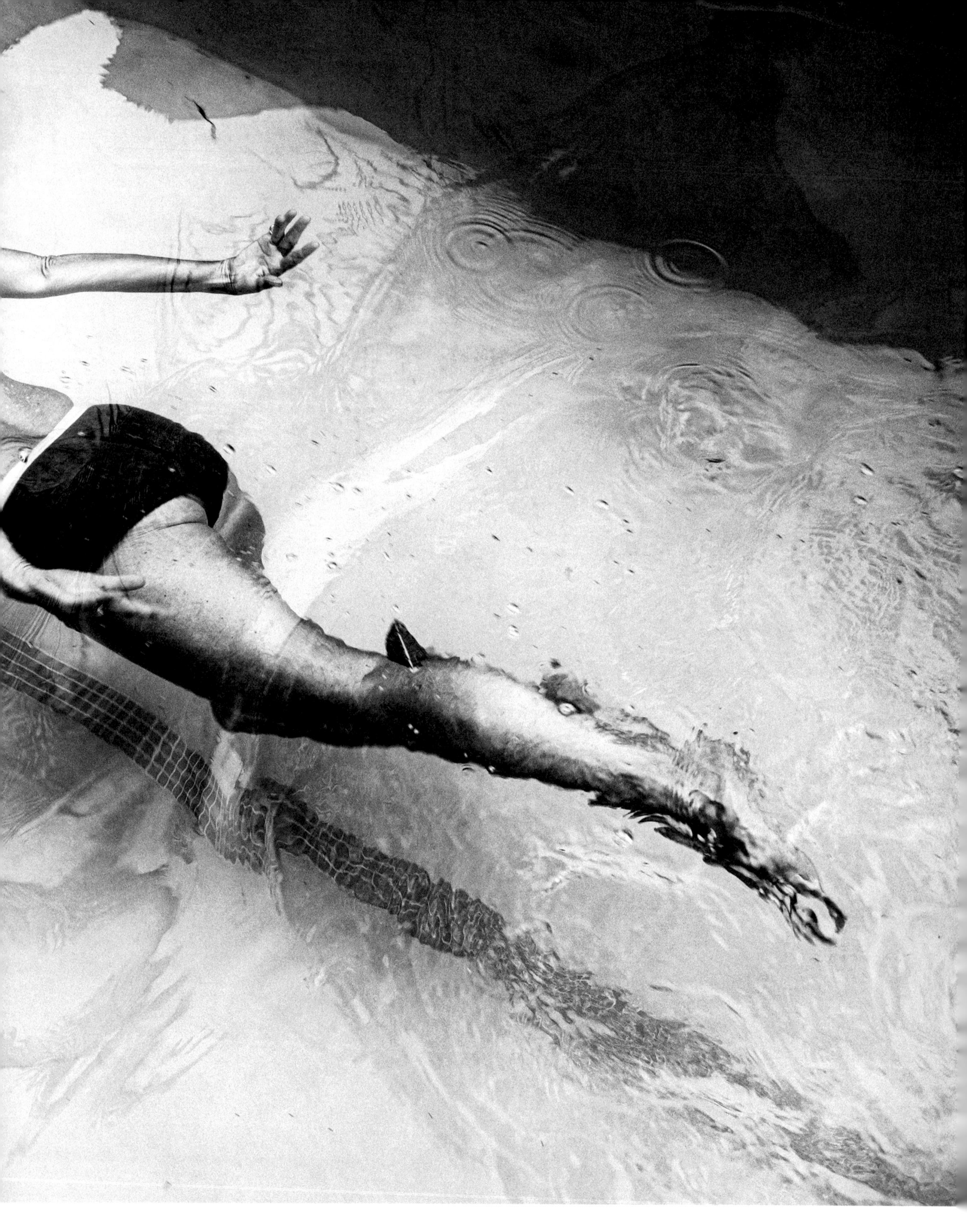

＋＋

You said I had a special something and I needed to keep it alive
by writing. I imagined "it" slowly dying when I was sleeping.
You typed up all my poems and put them in a three-ring binder.
You read me your poems. They were long and full of words I
didn't know.

When I moved away, I would call you. "Wanna hear something?"
You would say read it again and slow down. You said you wanted
to digest it. I imagined you eating it. We talked about words
and sounds and why they mattered.

A nurse held the phone. Your breath was short like you were
climbing. I flew home. I sat next to you at night beside beeping
machines reading softly in blue light. Hoping your own words
might comfort you. I watched you fade into a hospital bed and
surrender to the sounds.

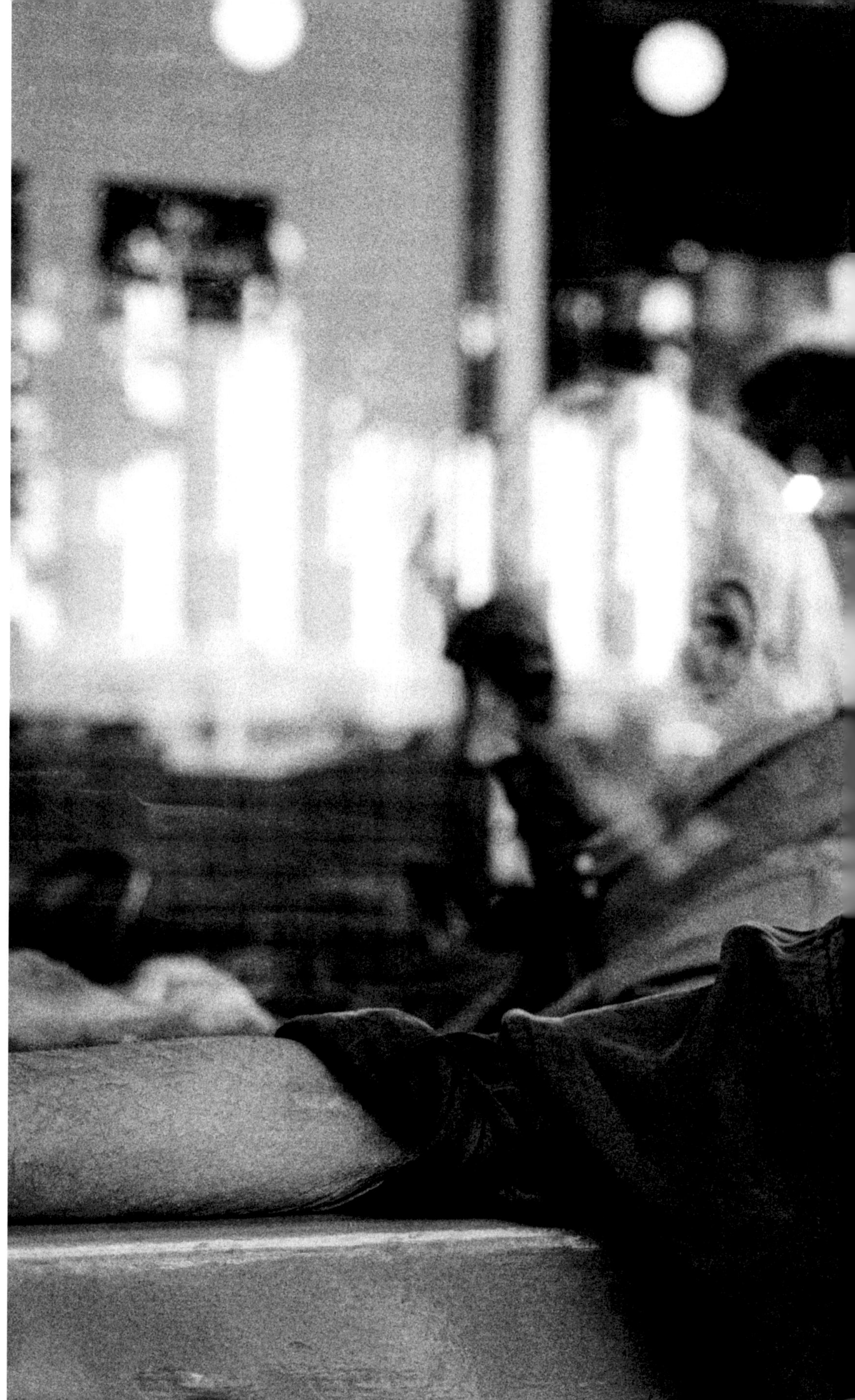

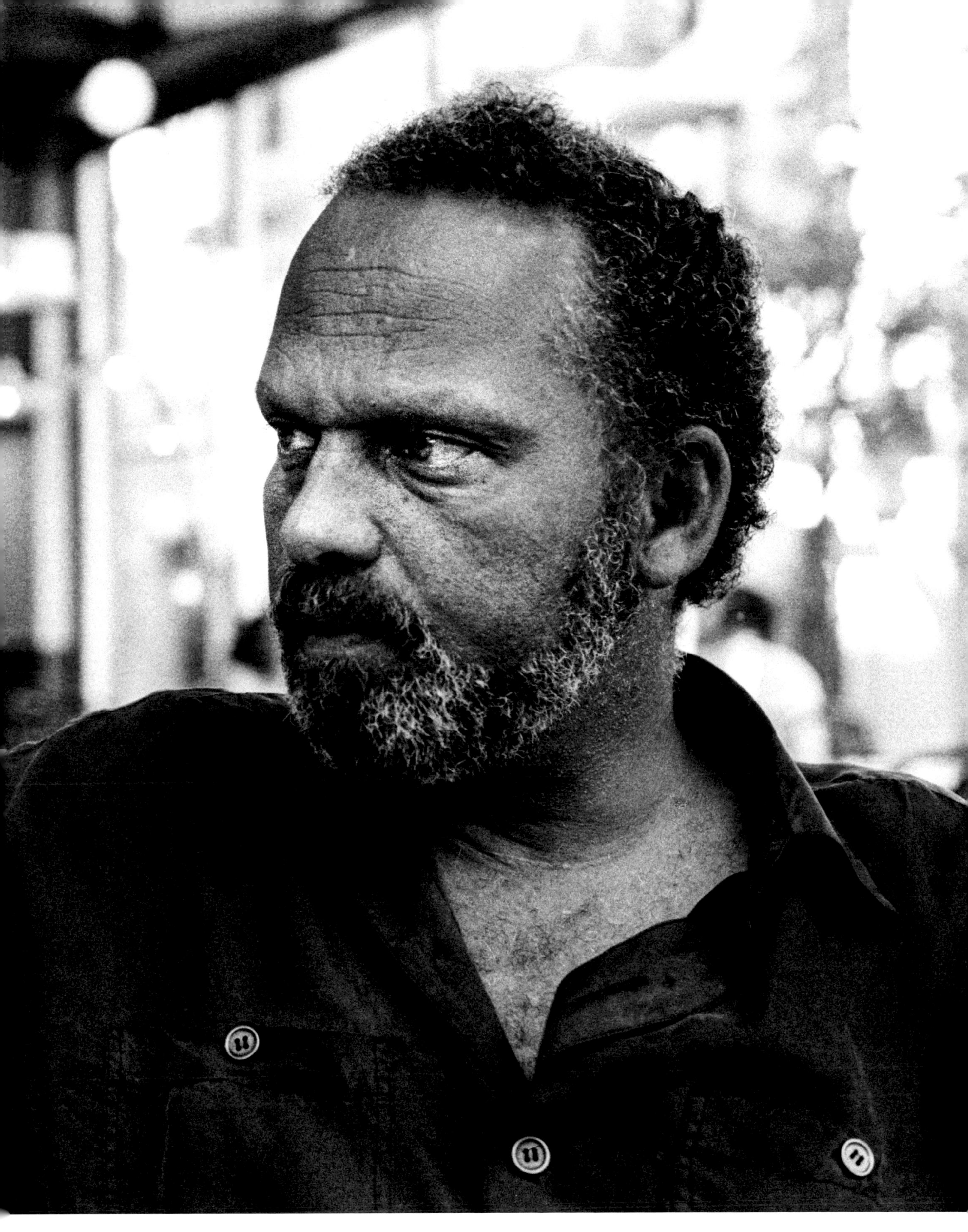

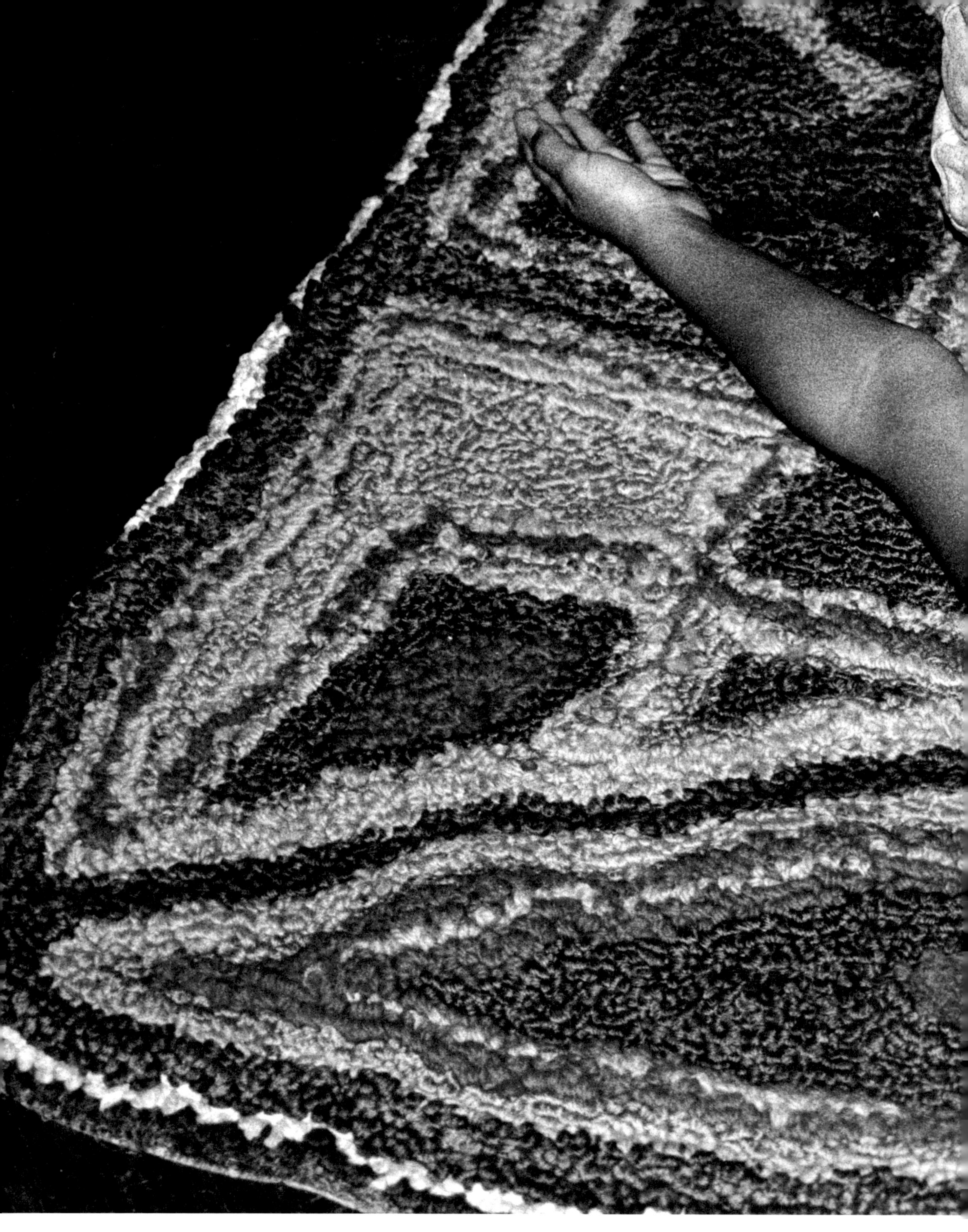

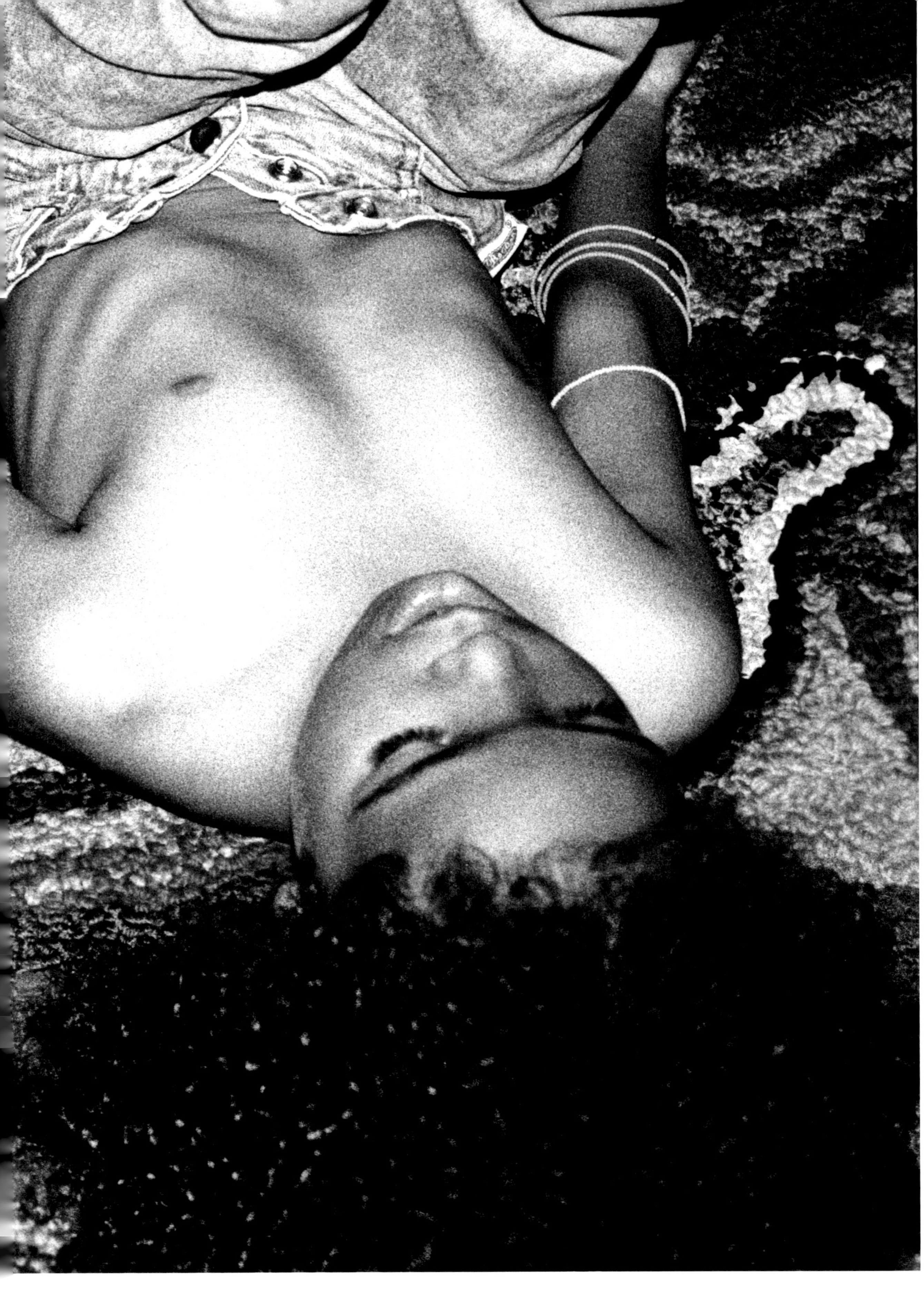

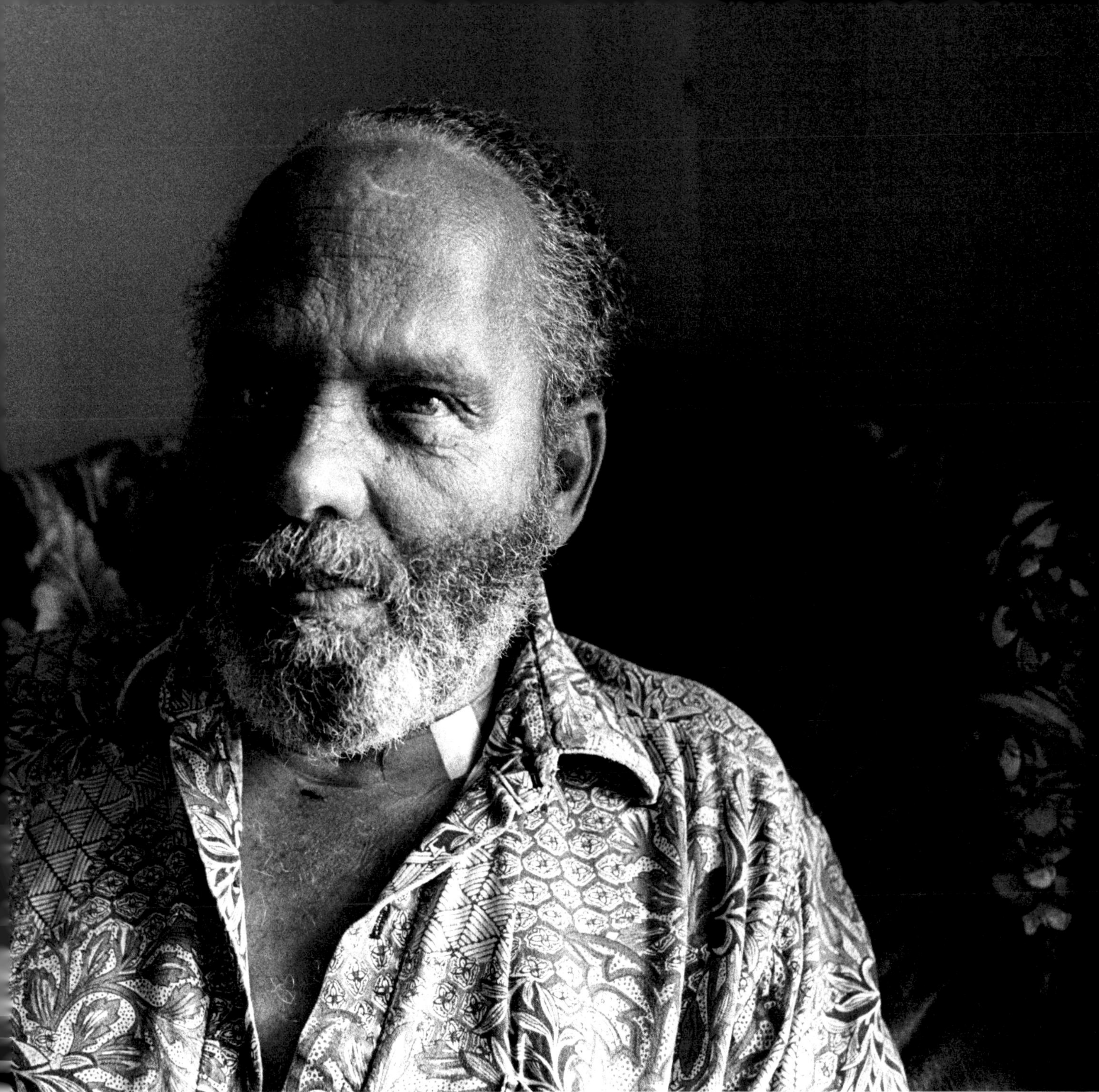

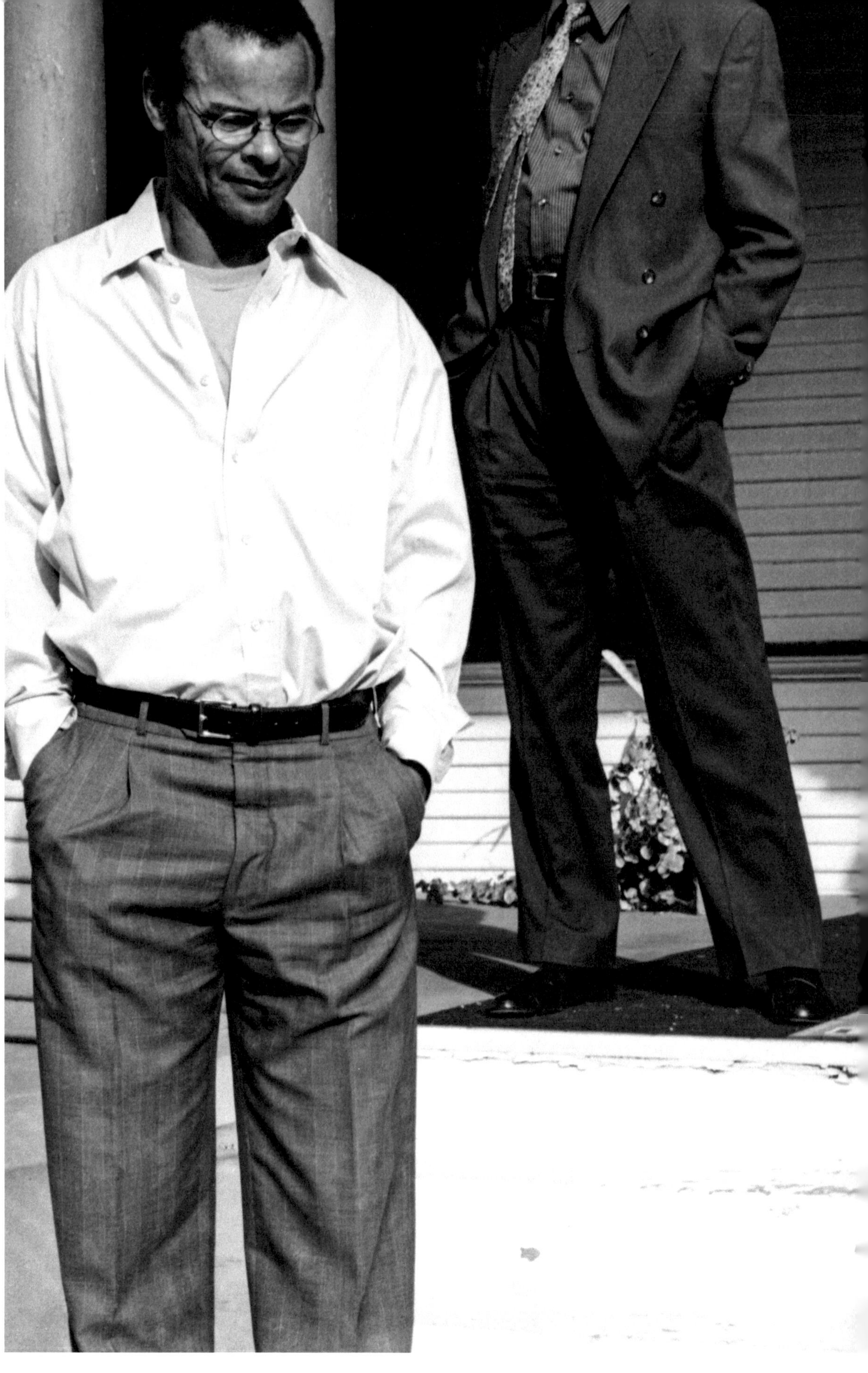

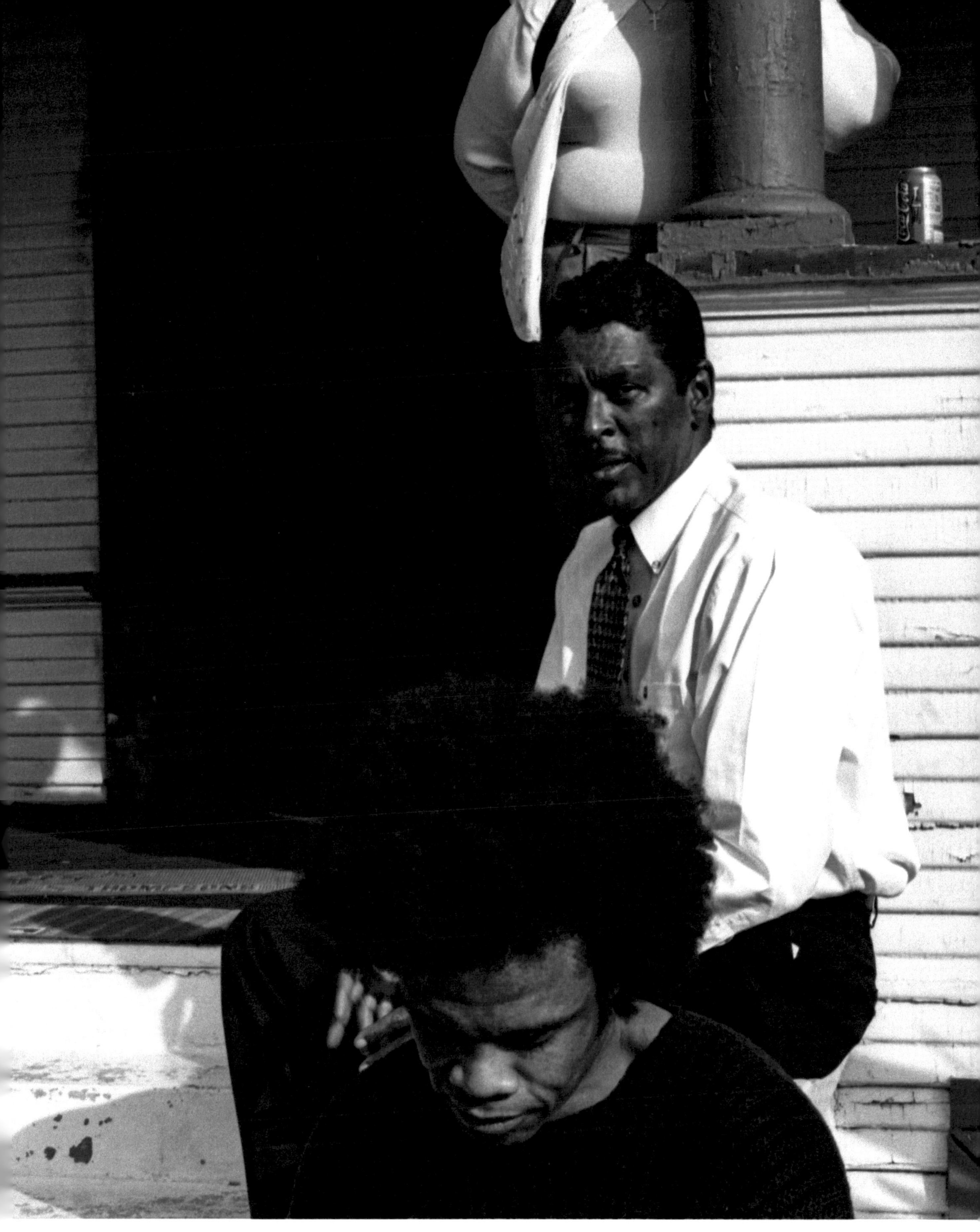

It's never completely quiet even if you lay down underneath. The sour stench of summer baking in black plastic waiting. The early morning haste to be on time. The buses that always come, slowly like whales, exhaling their doors open. Across the bustle of street, the wait and go wait and go. The next day from last night of empties left on the curb and sometimes they're still sleeping on the stoop. The drool making its way down.

The heat already grabbing at your neck. The air thick and still and inside out. Hot cement like powder in your nose. The shifts in faces and colors of before and now. Some are frozen. Locked into yesterday with little left and no shoes. The pleading prayer from the handheld microphone. Working their way back to god. The Blackness retold. Marching through this passage of revival with swagger and grace.

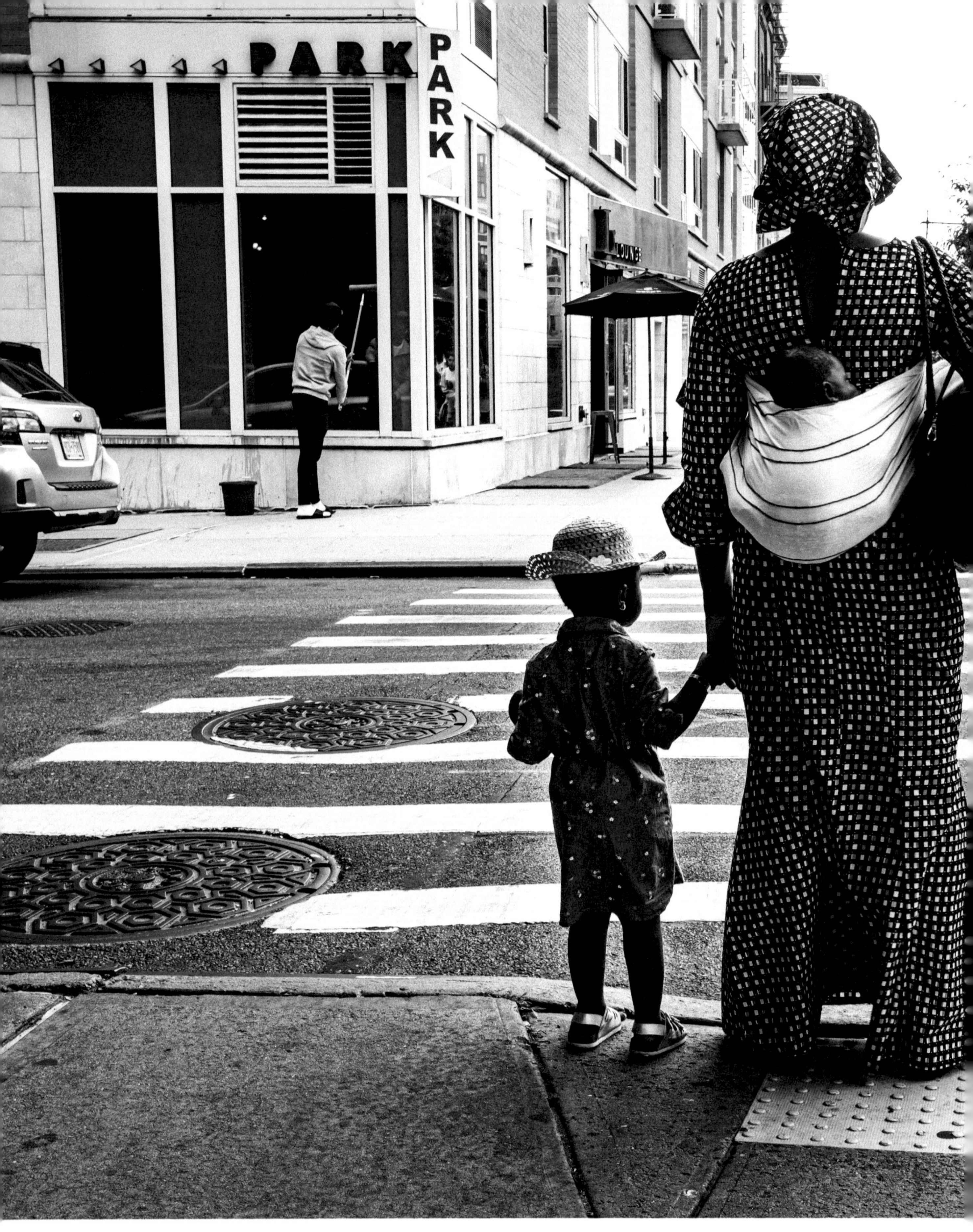
PARK
PARK

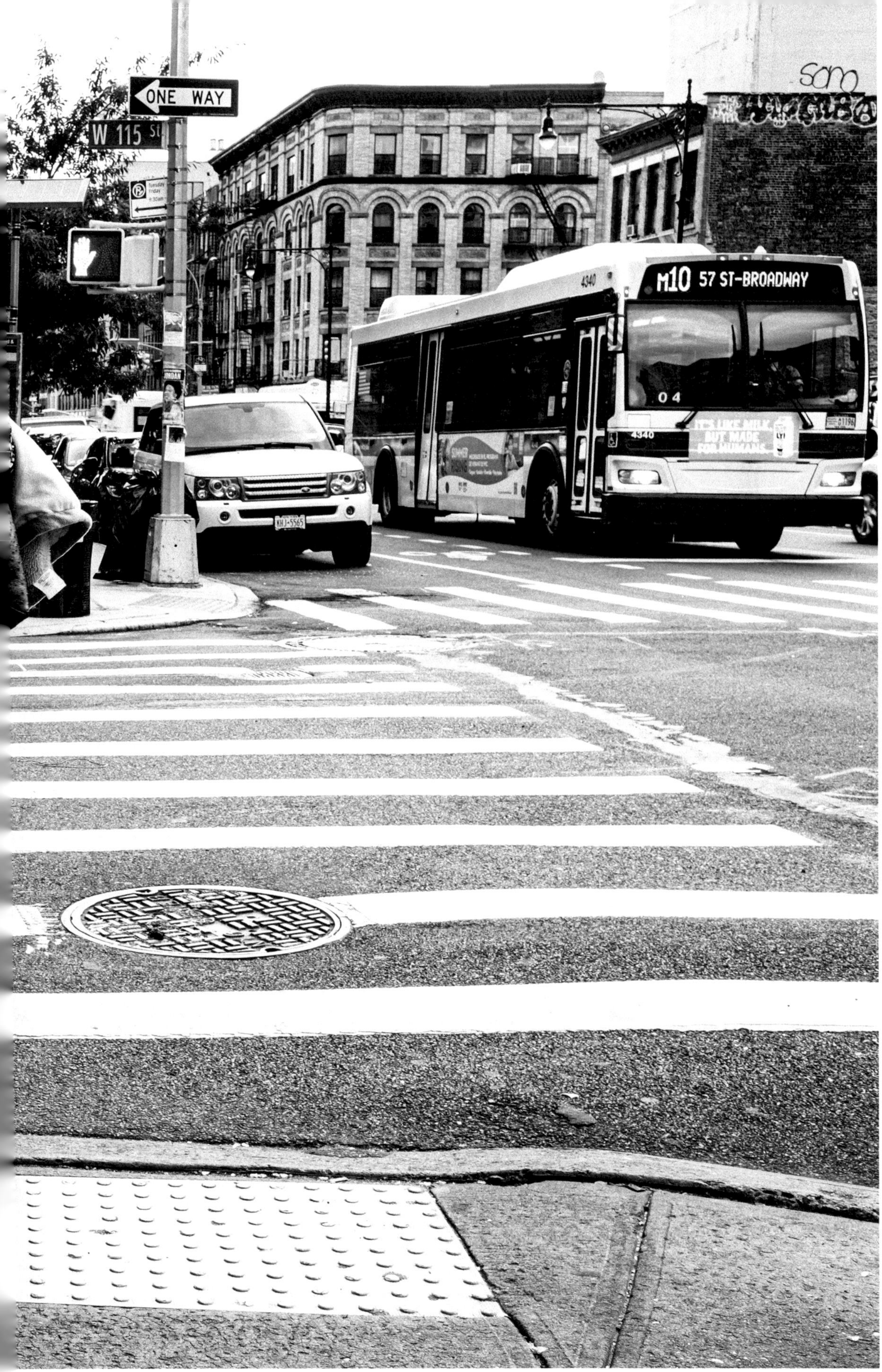

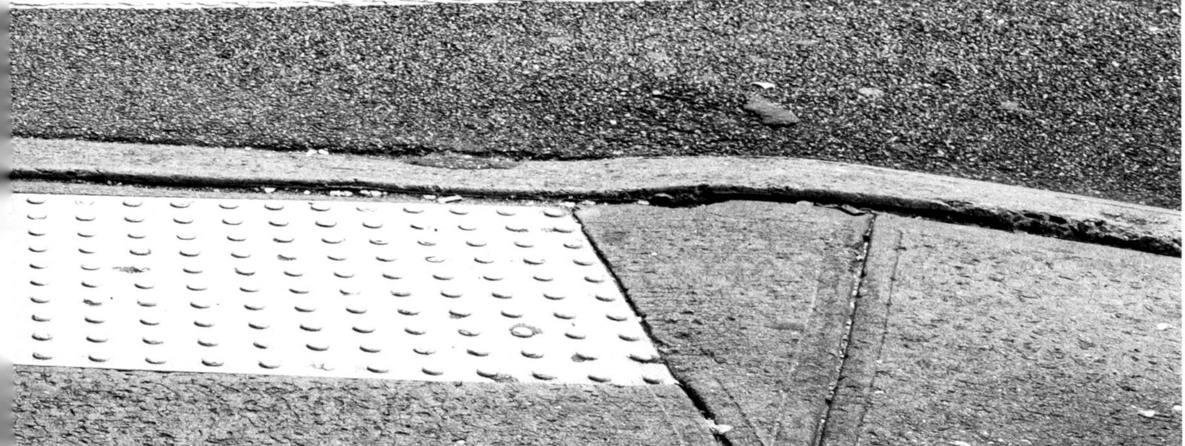

ONE WAY
W 115 St
M10 57 ST-BROADWAY
4340
IT'S LIKE MILK.
BUT MADE
FOR HUMANS.

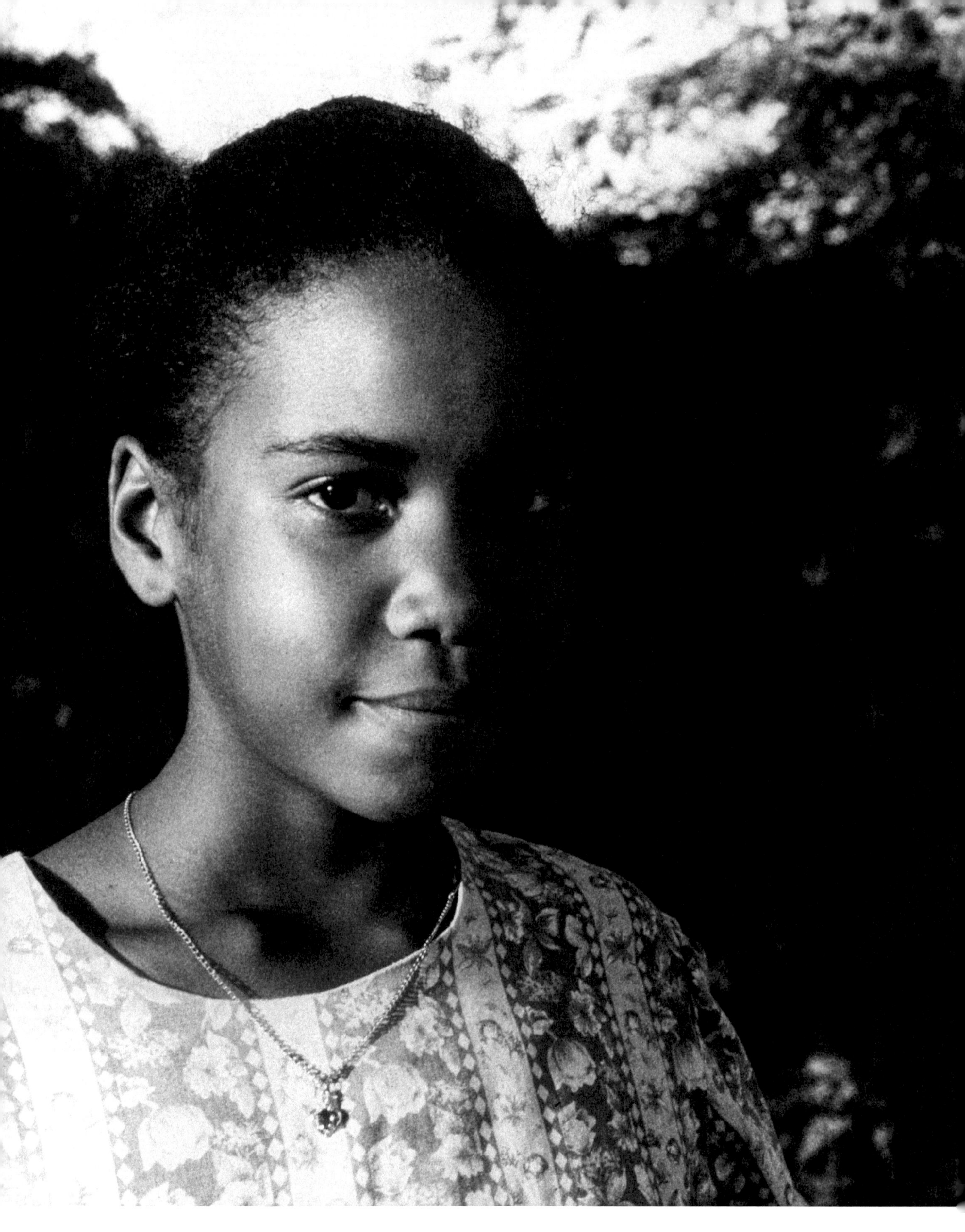

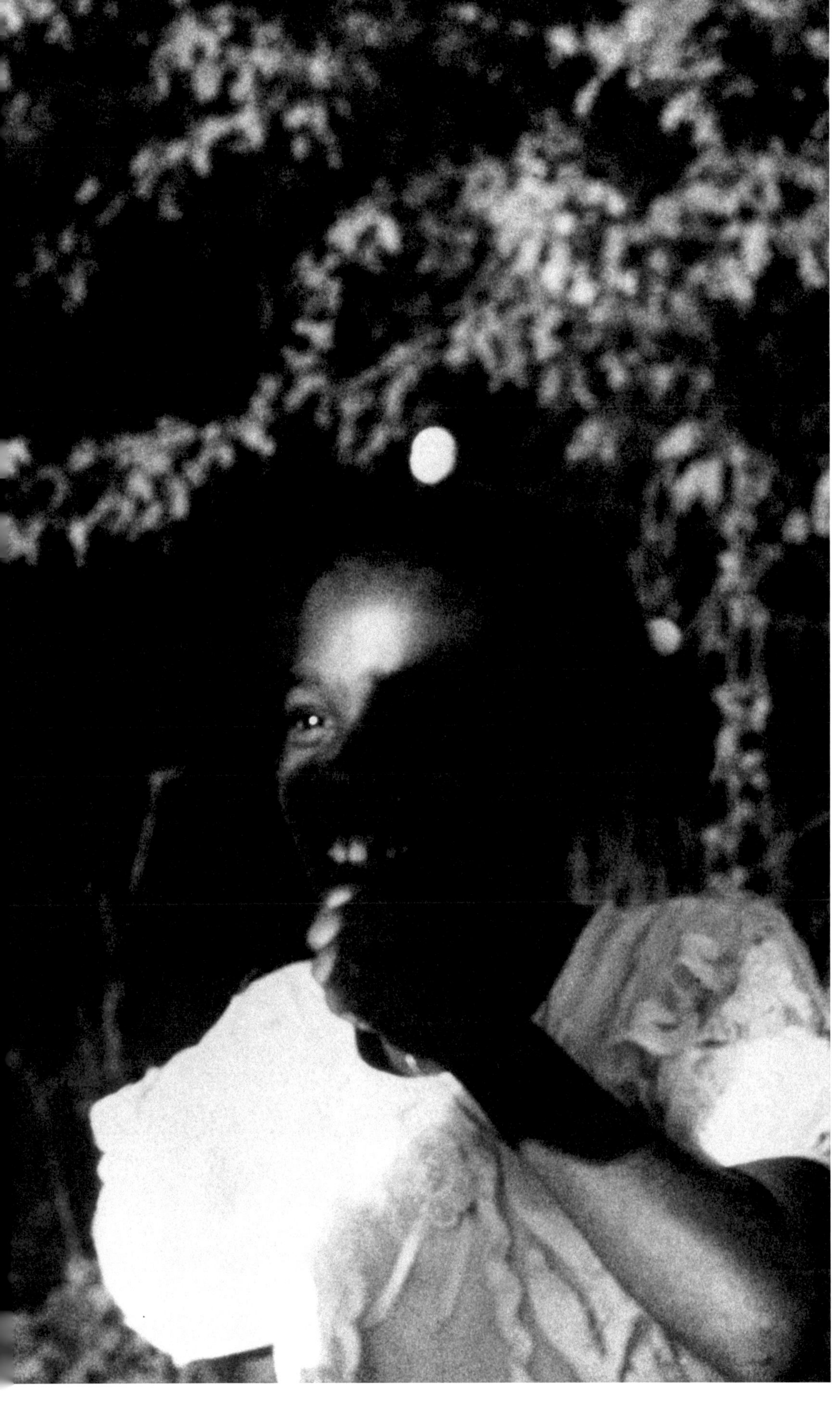

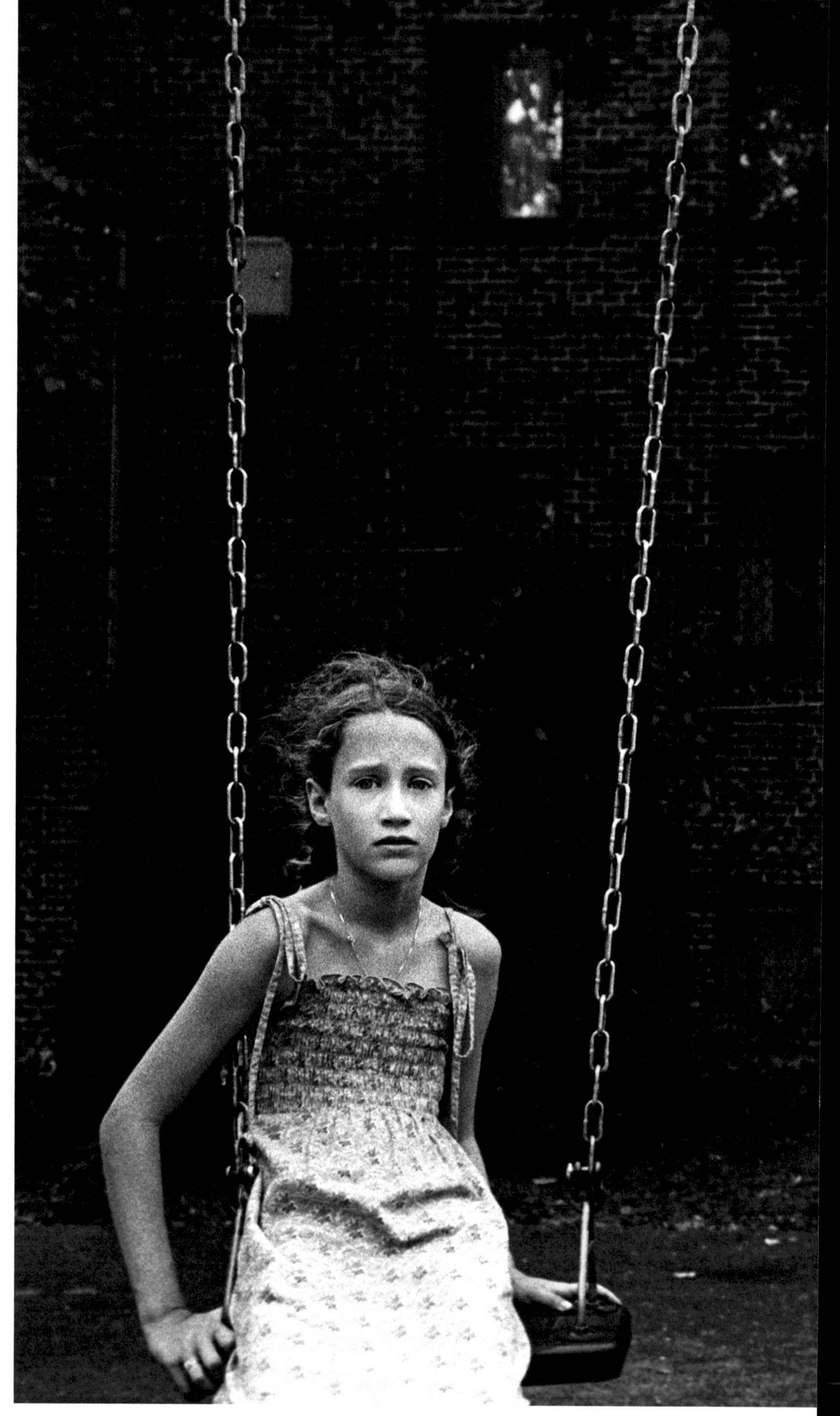

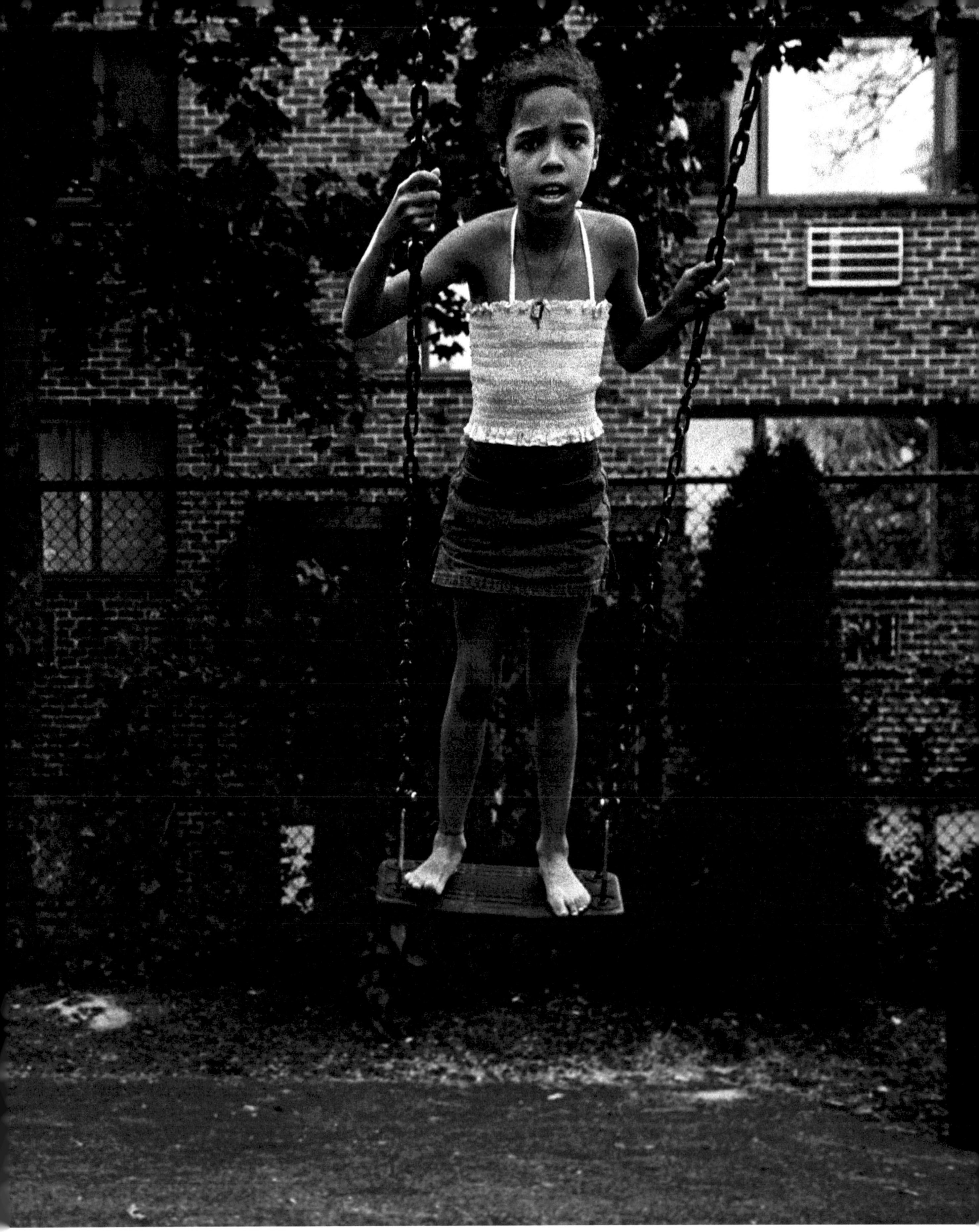

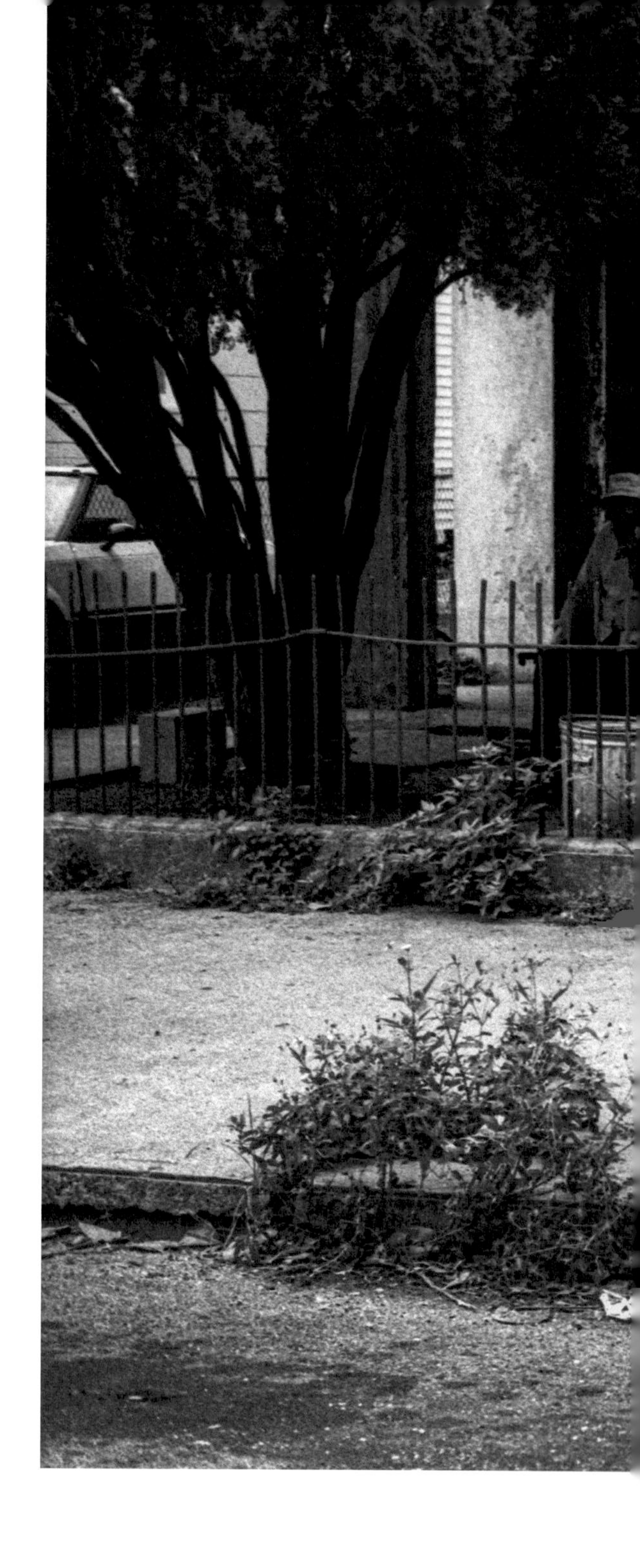

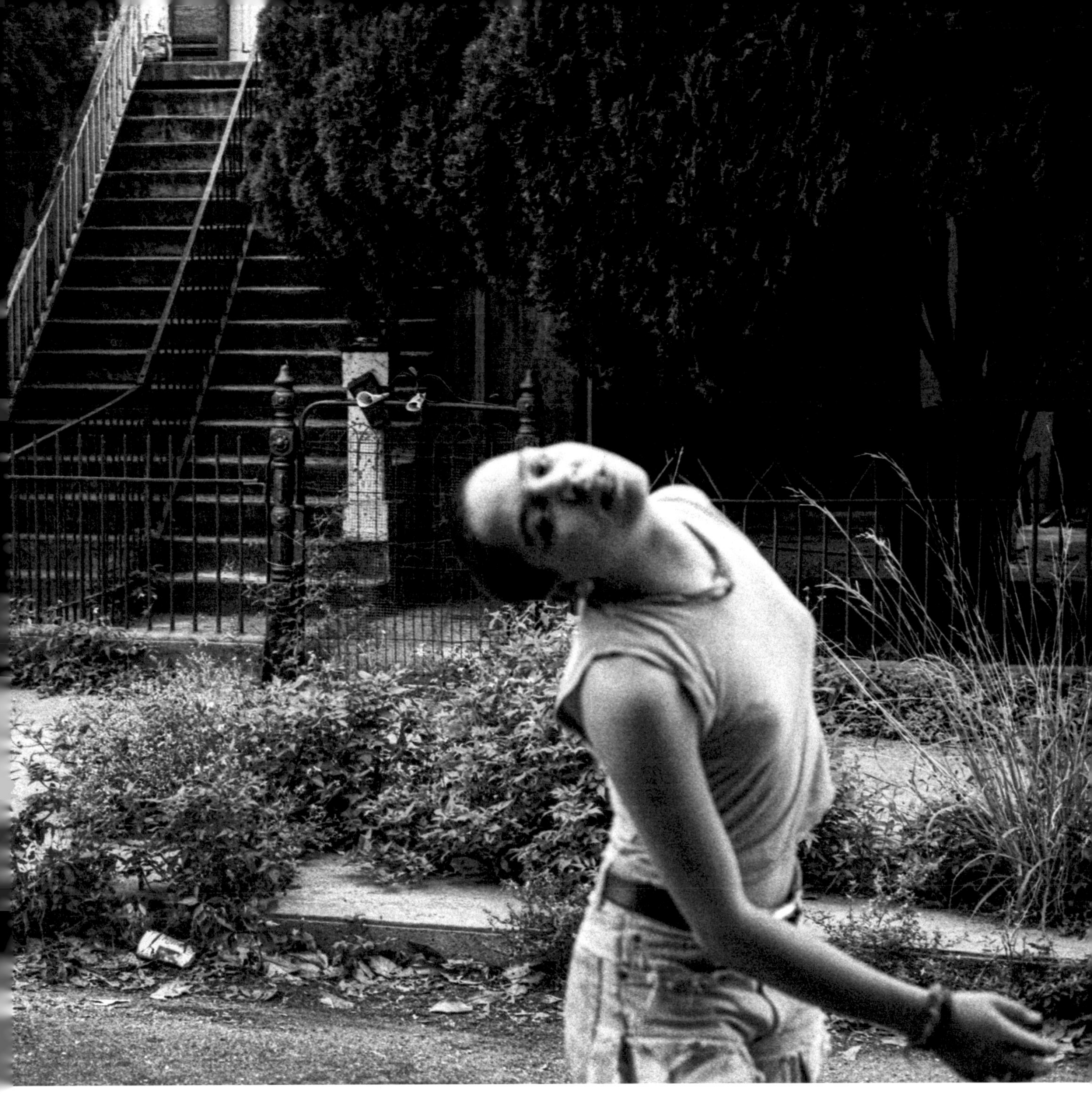

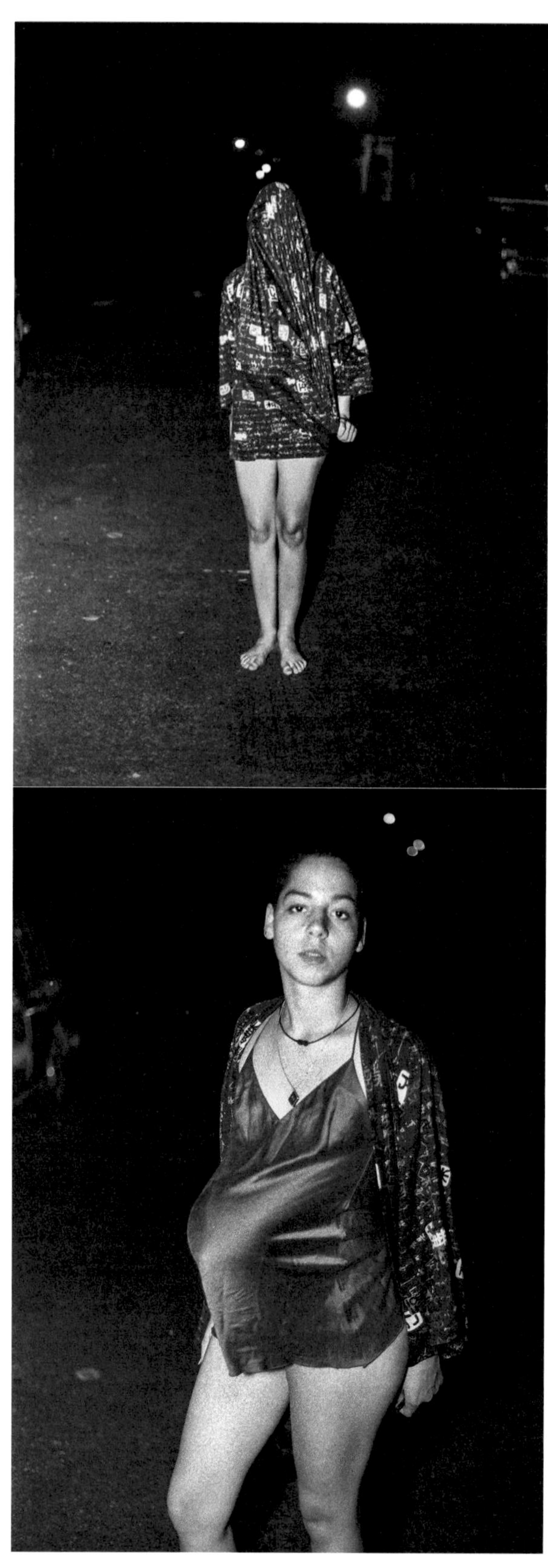

I was still a virgin because he used his fingers. It felt good but he was my father's cousin. My friend, who said he loved me, drove us up from Boston for the weekend to take photos. We went "street shooting" and I wasn't any good. He was in his twenties from Greece with a thick accent and whistled his s's. I slept in my dad's cousin's bed, I thought I was avoiding the awkwardness of my friend who loved me. It happened both nights. I always wondered if my friend suspected. We pretended like it didn't happen. I was sixteen.

He was my favorite of Dad's cousins. He had a raspy voice like he might lose it one day just from talking too much. He made everyone laugh, especially my dad. I wanted to be his favorite. His son died of cancer at fourteen. His wife left him. He would call me drunk and want to know how I was and ramble incoherently in French about the art he was making. He came to my sister's wedding and we had to look for him in the little town. He slept mostly. His sisters became his mothers, whispering. The sad took him. He died in his apartment alone until someone found him.

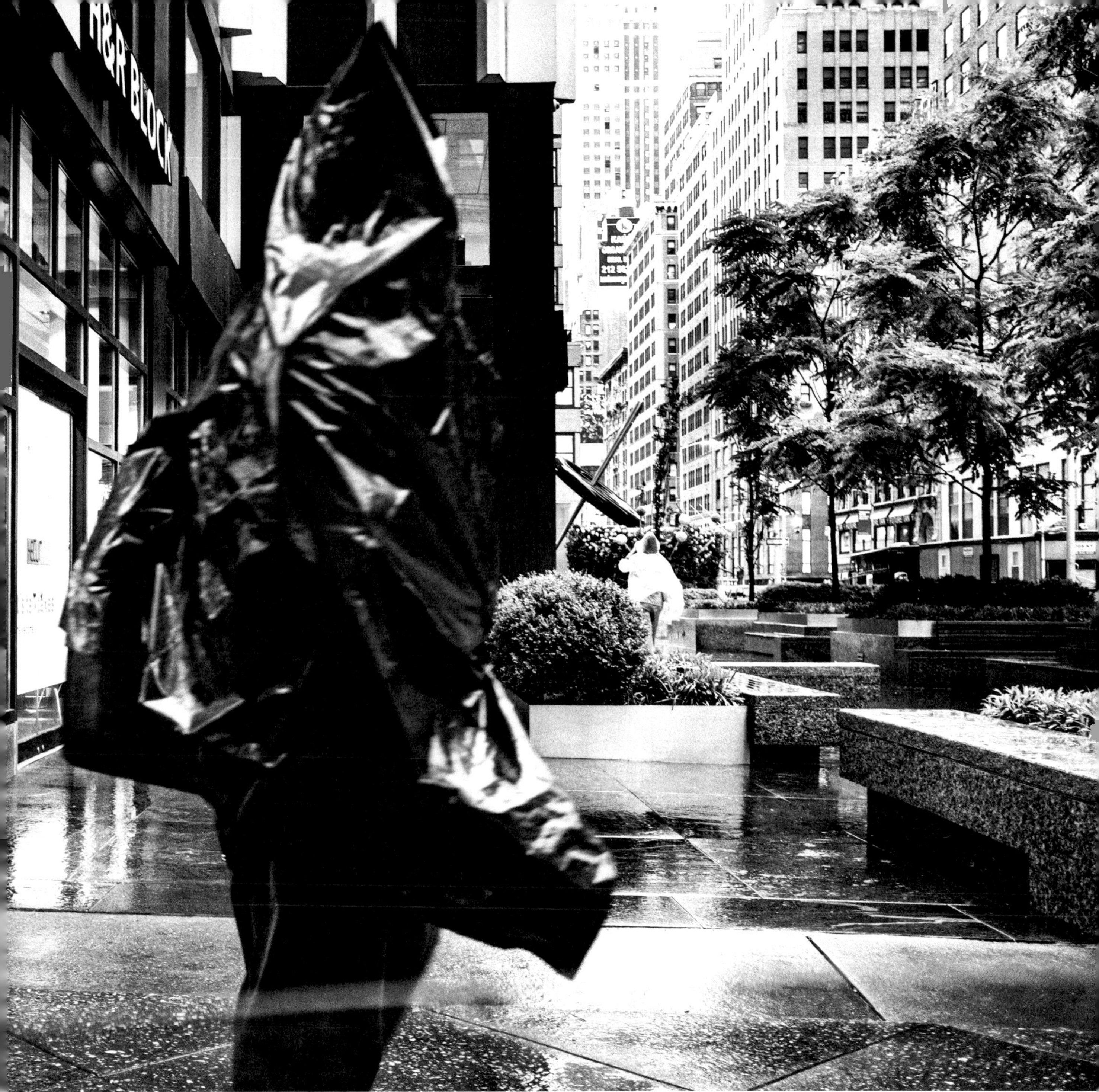

H&R BLOCK

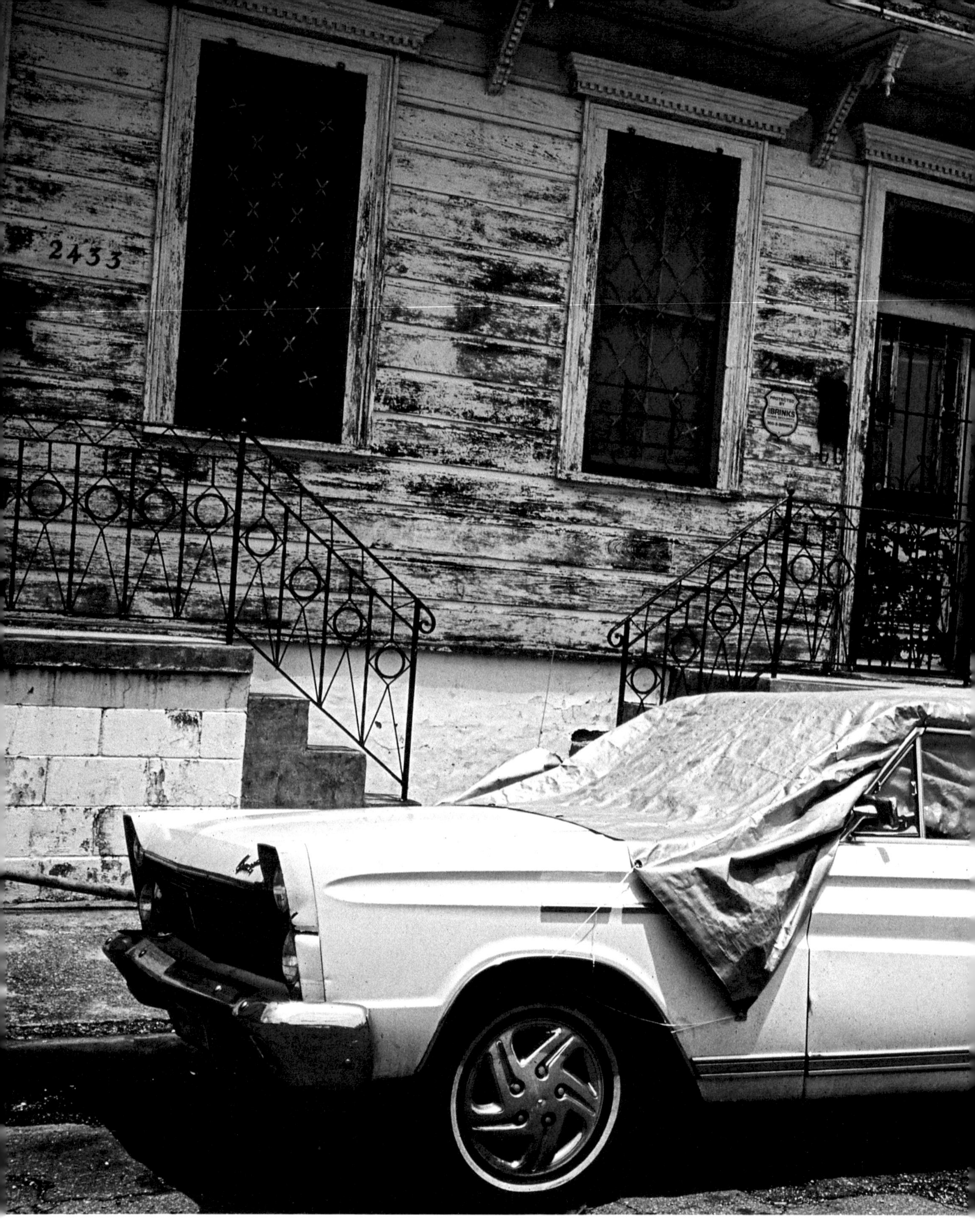

2433
BRINKS

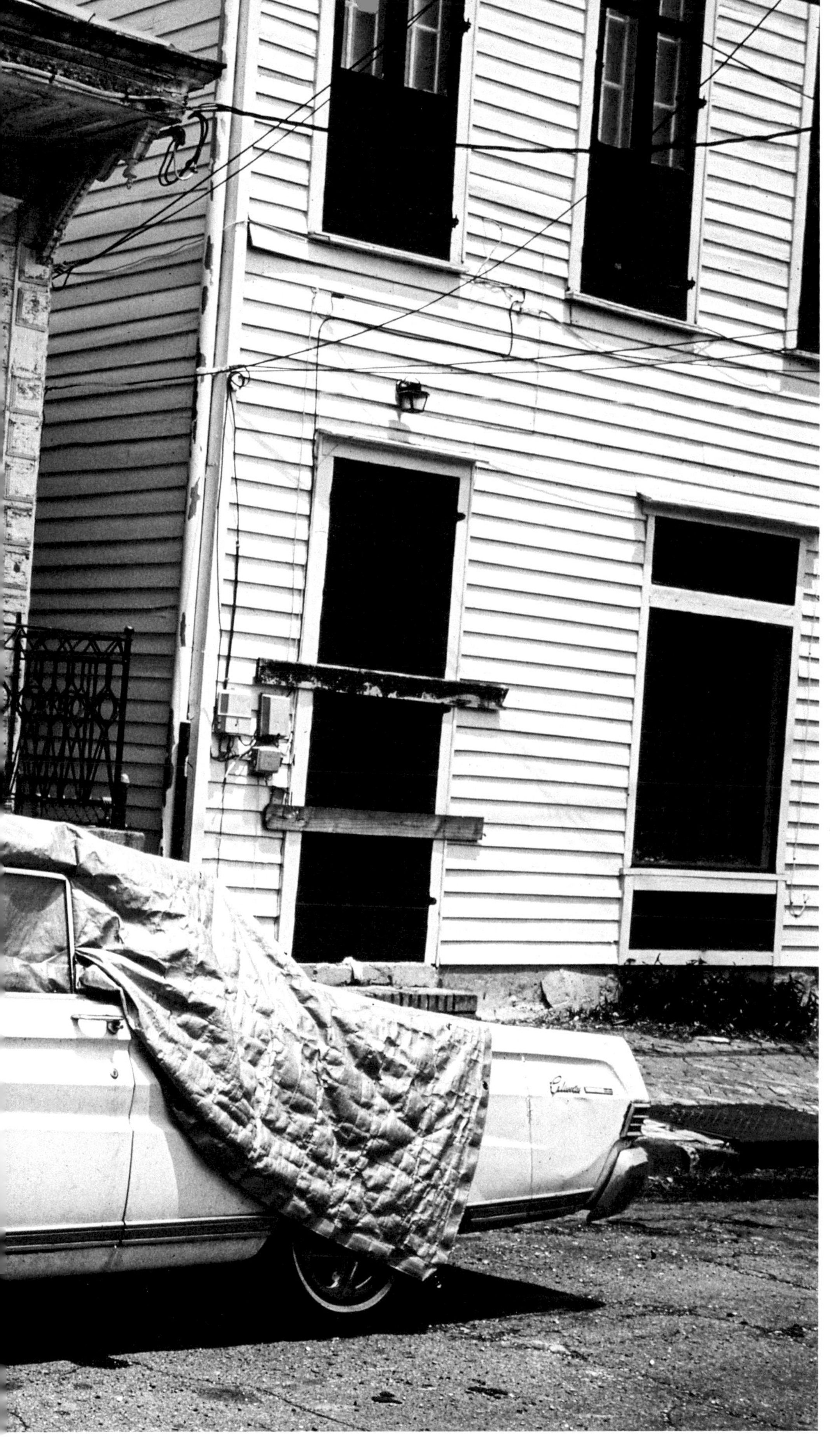

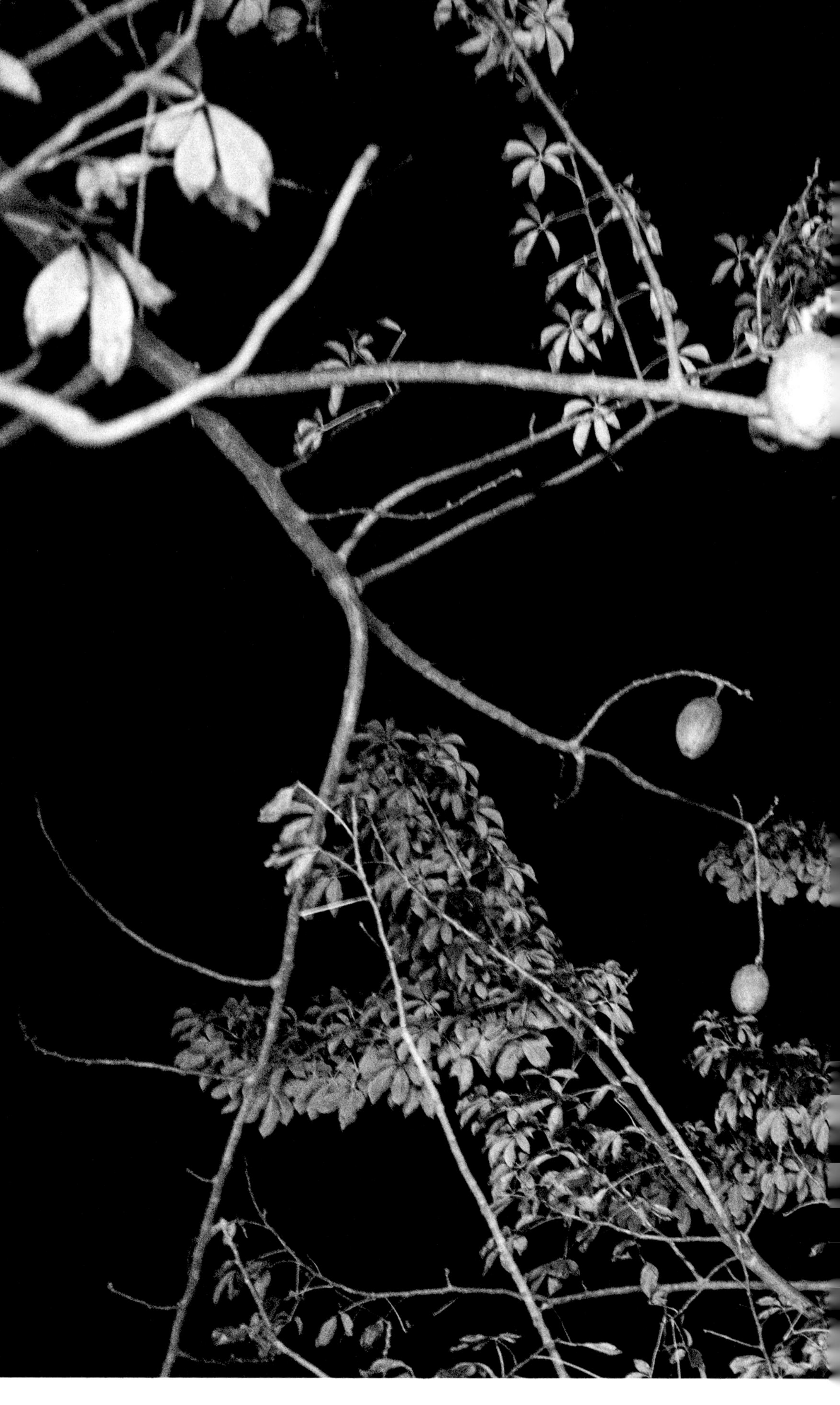

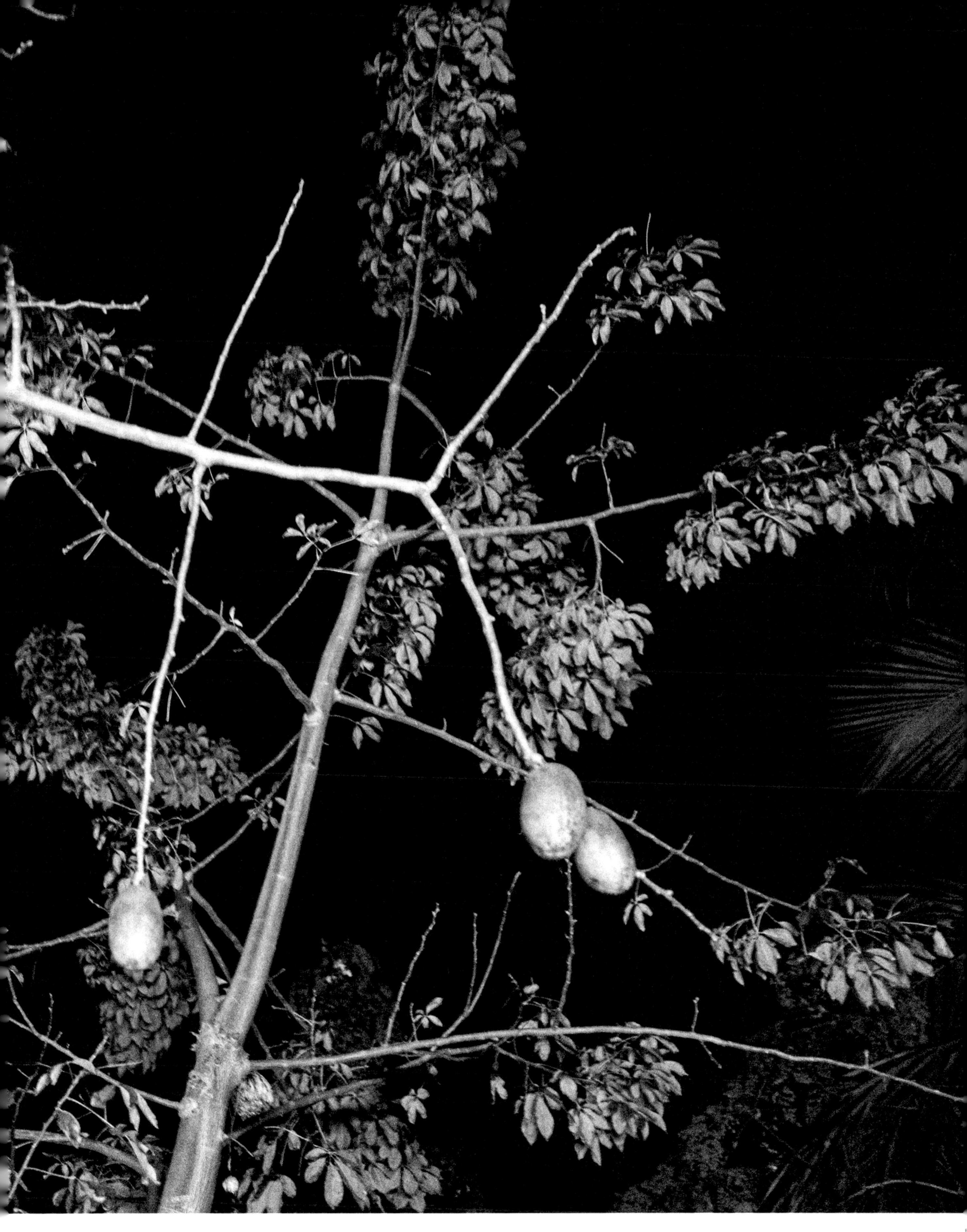

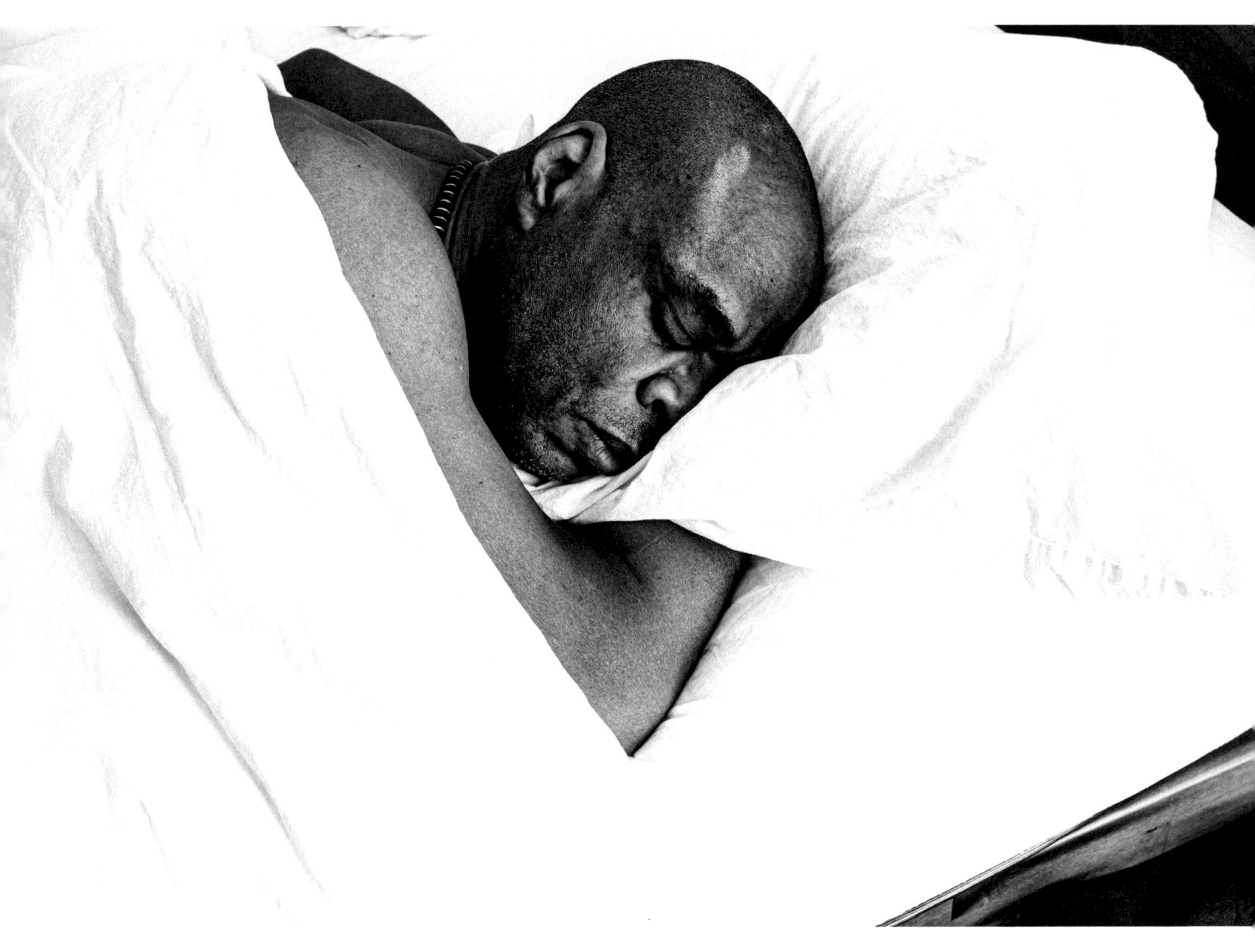

When the familiar becomes the unknown and your body
forgets its own needs, where will we be? I can't think of the
memory but it's safe from melting and falling through the holes
of thought. You noticed the things I tried to save. Toothpaste
split open longways down one side. You said you did that too.
We had sex in the afternoon. You said "good bye sweet girl"
on a sticky note while I was in the bathroom, warm sap dripping
out. We were friends who didn't know each other yet. Honesty
would have to wait.

There isn't enough time to be famous. We never made sense to
anyone else. How will they tell our story? The dry pain of deceit
filling in the cracks and the ache of the unknowing. The kind of
love that makes you look away. Take the truth and squeeze its
hand. The me and the you before me and you. Be free. Tally up
the things we tried to save inside the myth of what we are.

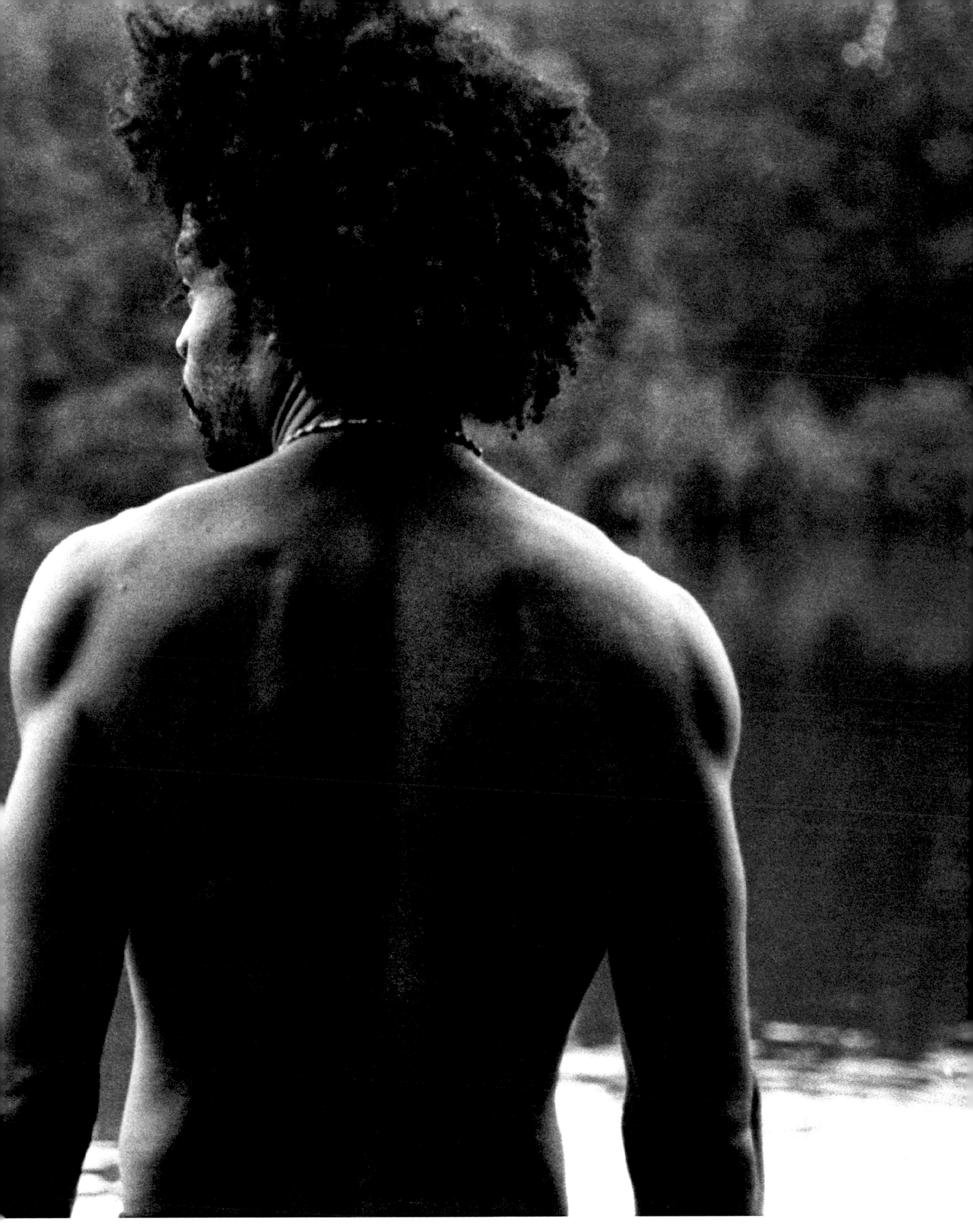

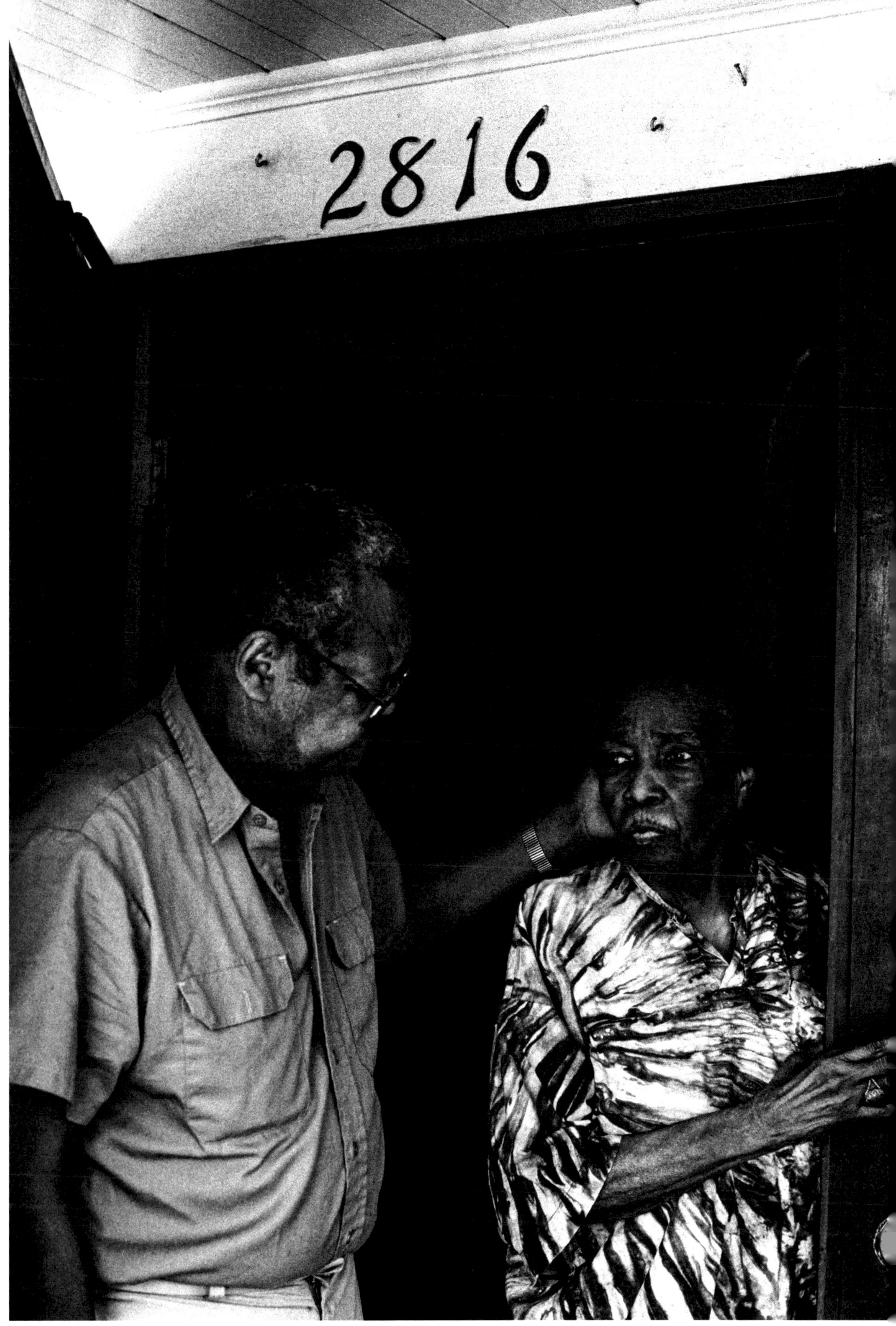
2816

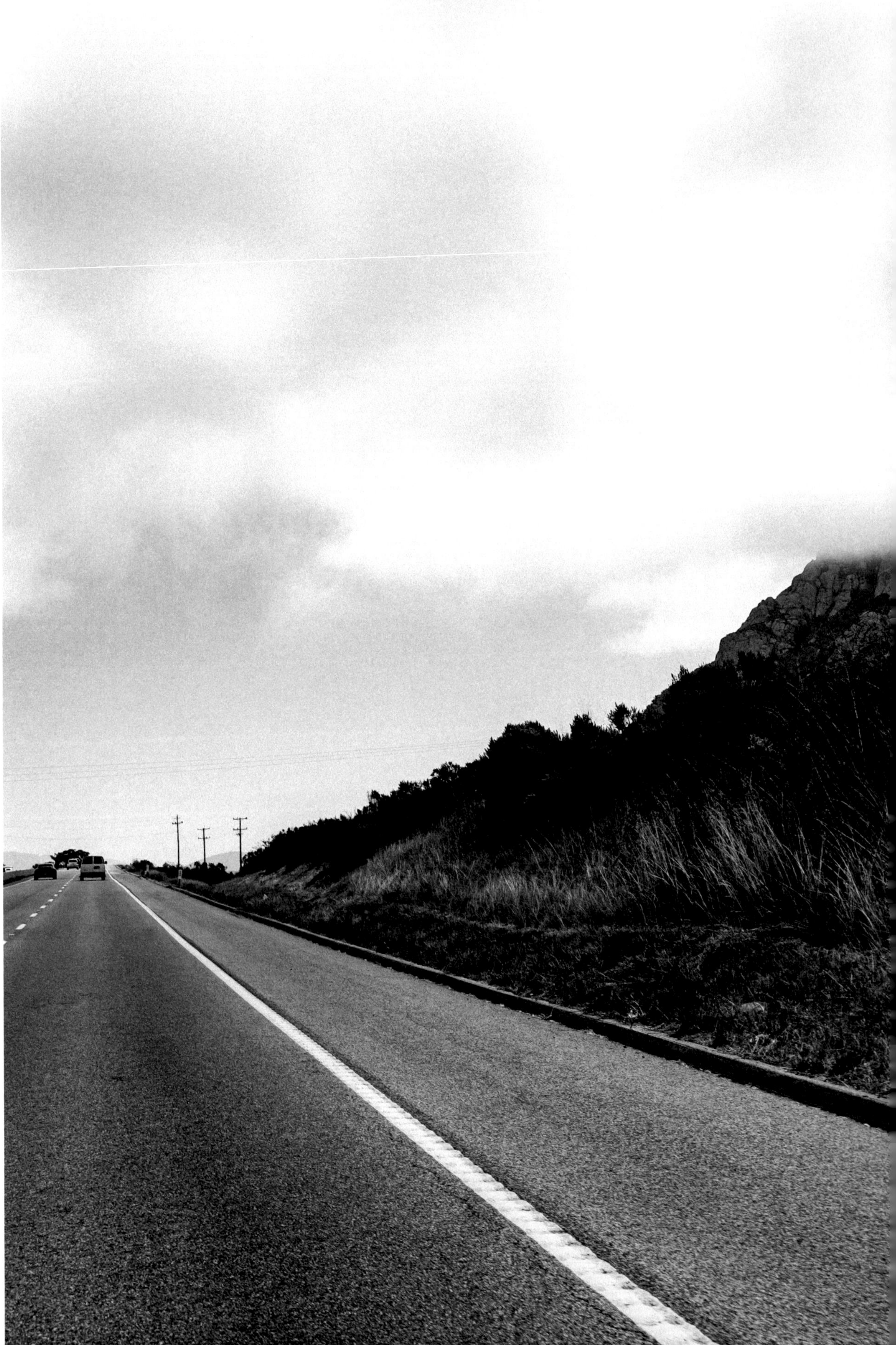

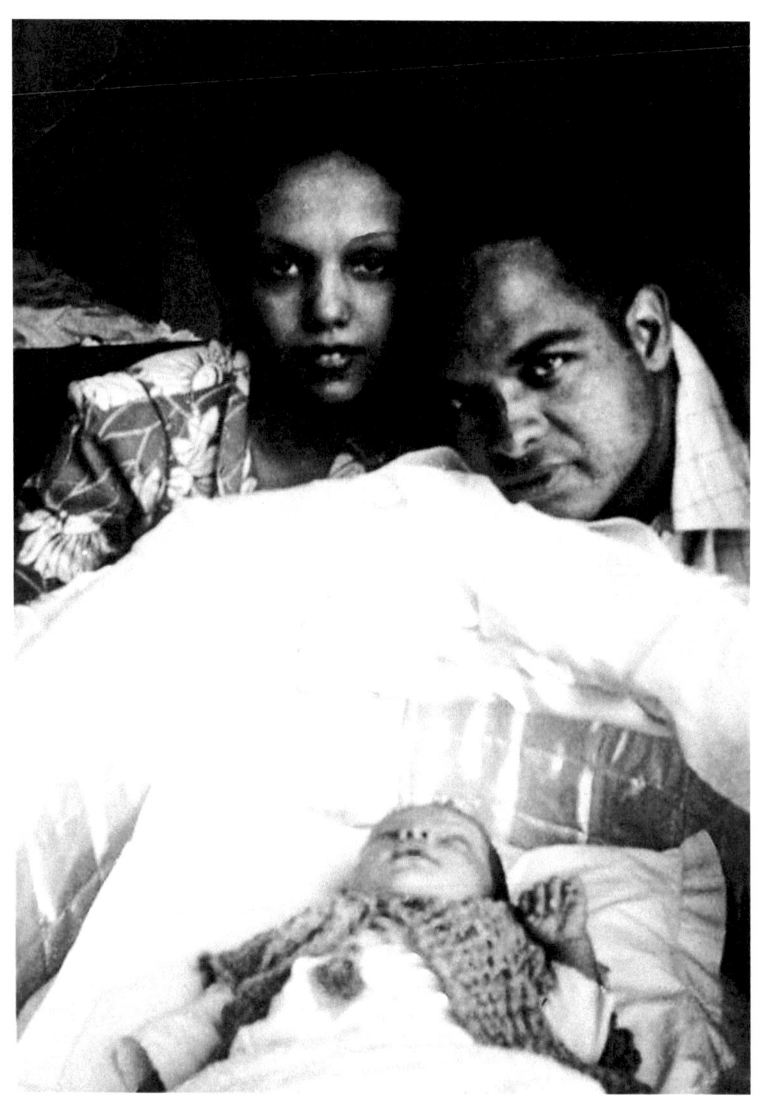

He died broken and afraid. But loved. I taught myself about racial identity without his help, or hers. What it meant to claim Blackness in a light skinned body. Trying to claim it for him. For his fractured family, for the childhood of discrimination he silently swallowed. For the conversations that were squashed or never dared. Unsuccessfully passing through.

He said he felt European. She asked about white pride. My hair was braided and she looked at me with distrust and anger as though I hurt her. She had nightmares that we would be dark. Darker than him. We had the red door in a row of council flats. Tiny clips of memory. Evaporating. Faded square photos with rounded edges. Without them it's too dark to see.

I've never been to Haiti. It always seemed mythical. Magical. Small bright paintings my grandmother would bring when she visited. The interrogation of time, of language. Terms. Words. Whiteness. Half-caste. Mulatto. Quadroon. Octoroon. High Yella. Black blood. Brown paper bag. One drop. They paid us to leave. "A gentleman's agreement" not to return to England. My father was sick and needed better medicine. His kidneys failed. He almost died. California fruit trees and Catholic school. The smell of eucalyptus and baked dirt. The drawl of an accent I quickly wrapped around my terms and words and feelings and my skin browned in the hot pulsing sun.

We stopped saying mulatto. We said "mixed," no embrace. No place. Parts. We were part Black. A part unknown. He didn't help. He didn't know. It was his Blackness but it sat by the door. Unclaimed. In this whiteness. Political correctness. "What are you?"

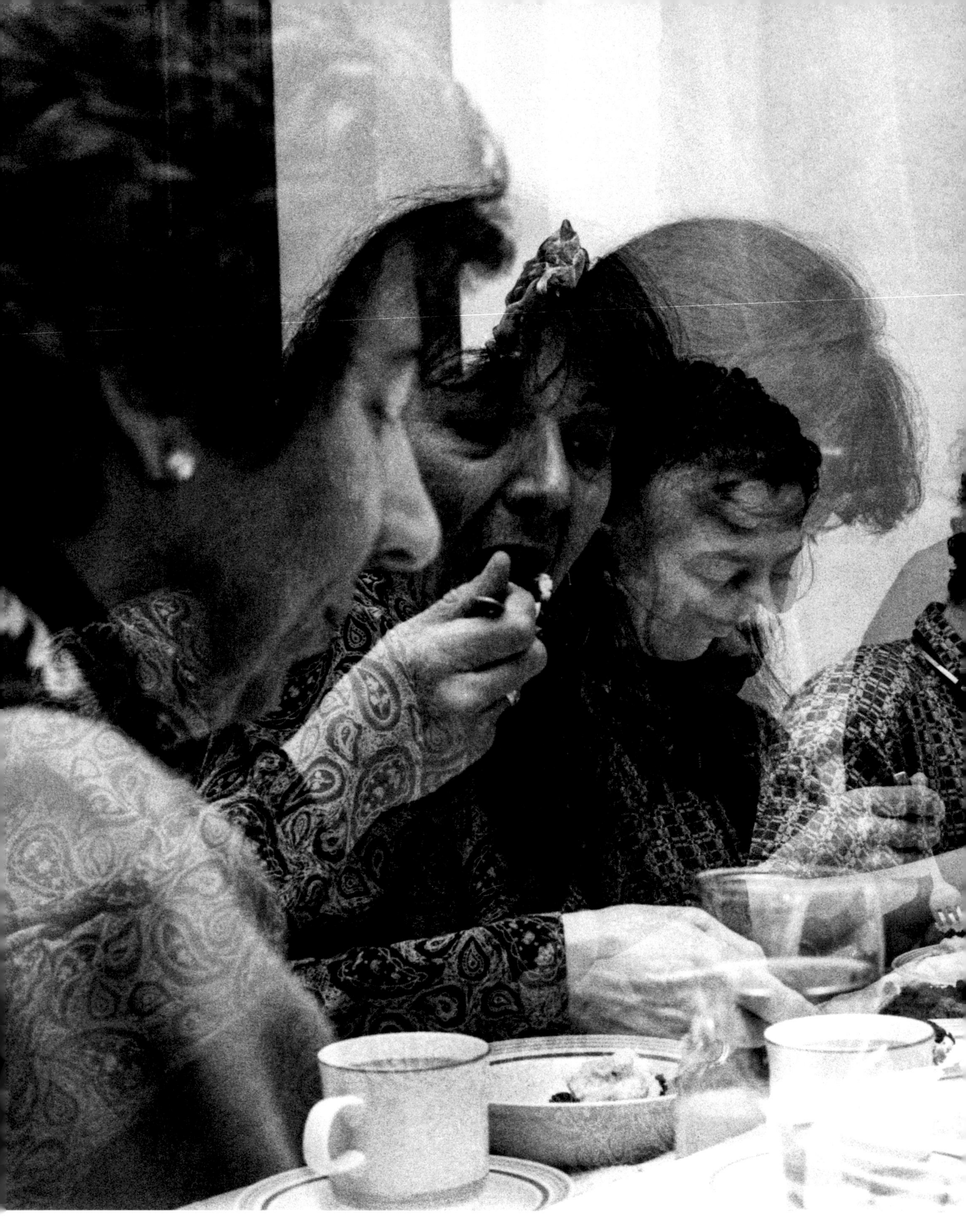

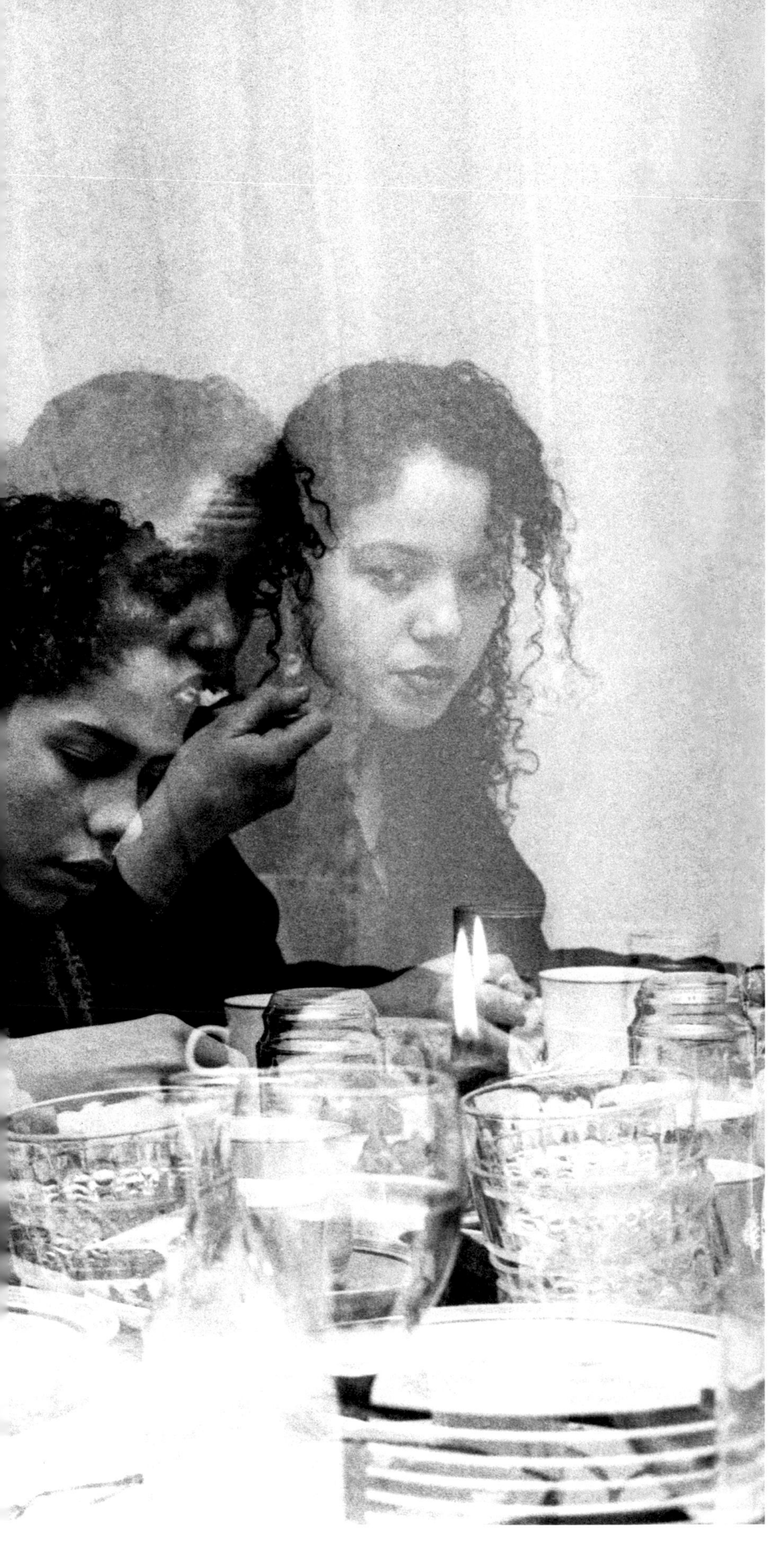

+++

I painted her brittle clawlike toenails while she watched her soap
opera on the rented TV. Her feet were the same square shape
as mine. The sameness made me feel special like I had a secret.
She was fragile and winced when she moved. I see photos of her,
at the age I am now, and I am in her face. In her glare.

I wish I could have that time back without the shyness of not
talking. I wish I asked her all the questions. What did people say,
dare to say? Think to say. In that time. From a brain-drained
tropical island to the 1950s American suburbs. Before my
grandfather died in the driveway. Before she went back to Haiti
and lived a life half broken. Before she lay in the ground next to
him in that unforgivable New England town. Tell me everything.

Light Privilege is a now term. It's what I claim to know. For the
me who taught my confused mixed self about white passing.
About the guilt of claiming Blackness as a choice. Of learning and
relearning about this nuanced navigation in black and white
America. The comfort of the careless white faces as they continue
to spill and stain the ground around me.

Wrapped in muslin and tucked in a straw basket like baby Jesus.
Limbs of a tree, of a ghost. Maybe he would have liked the irony.
We wanted ashes and nature. To return to the mythical. Magical.
But we couldn't convince her through her blank stare hollow
with grief. So we sat in the small empty church sobbing gently
through a meaningless sermon. My sister and I were wearing
matching black pumps we had bought at Marshalls on clearance.

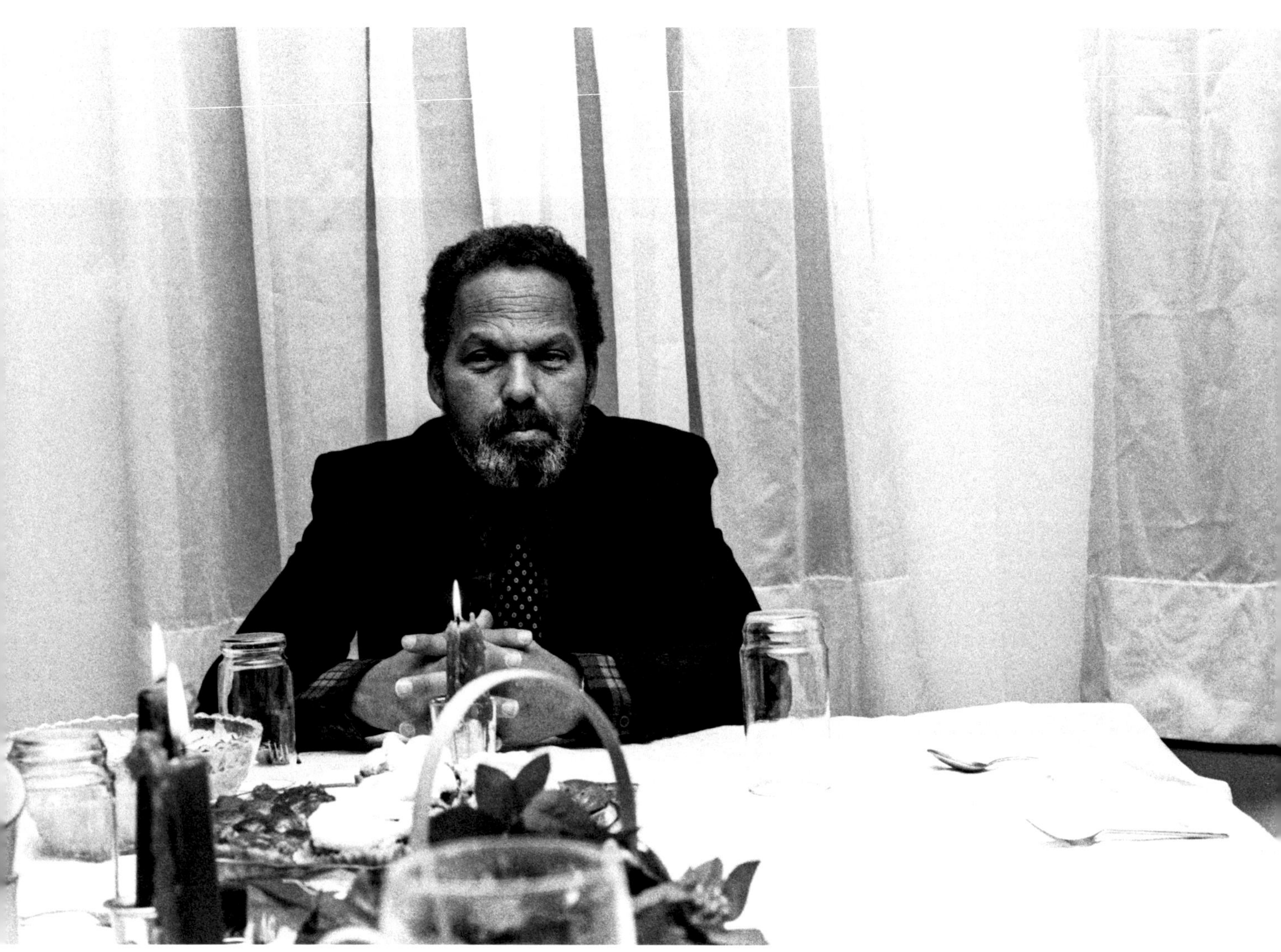

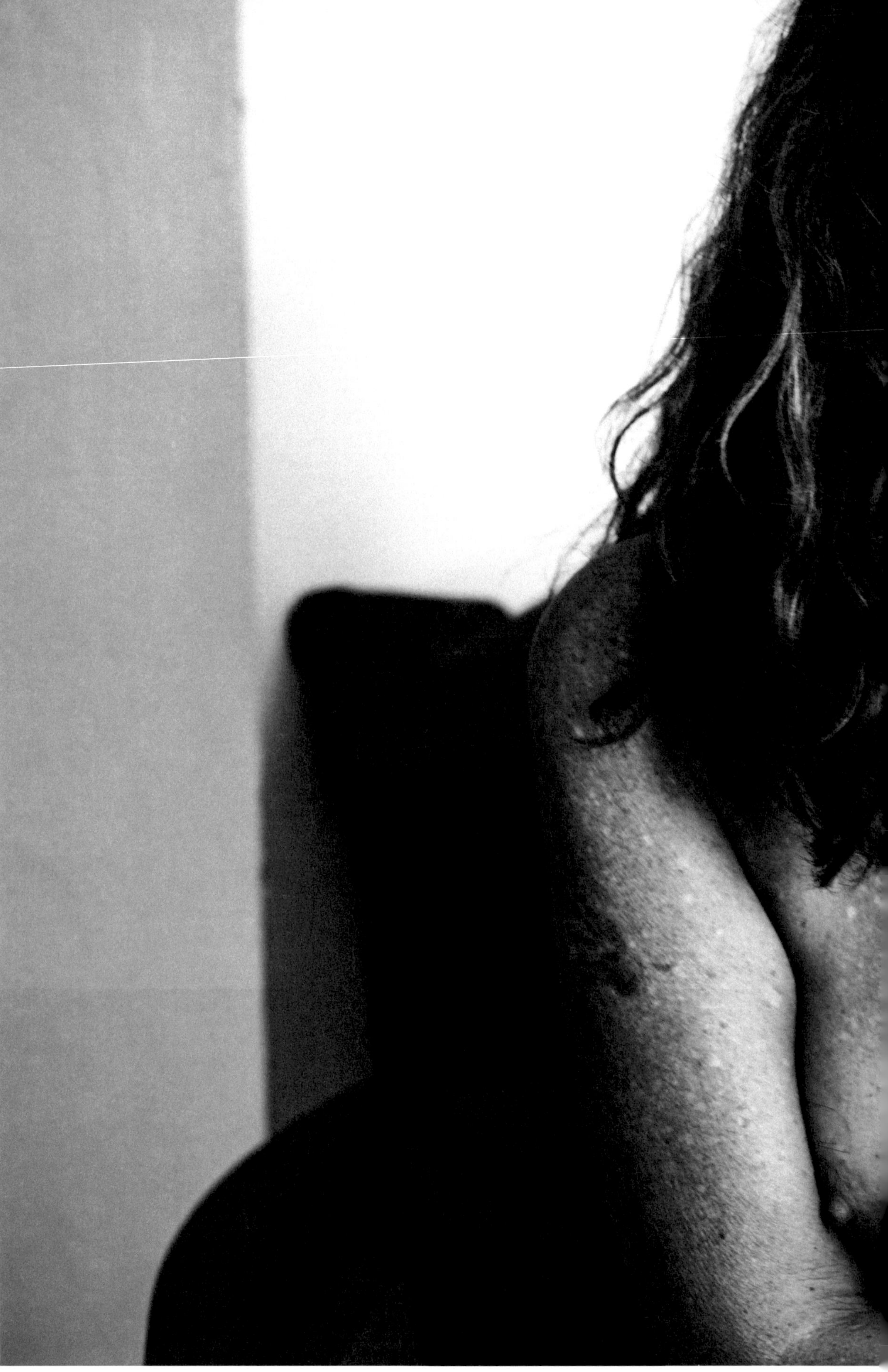

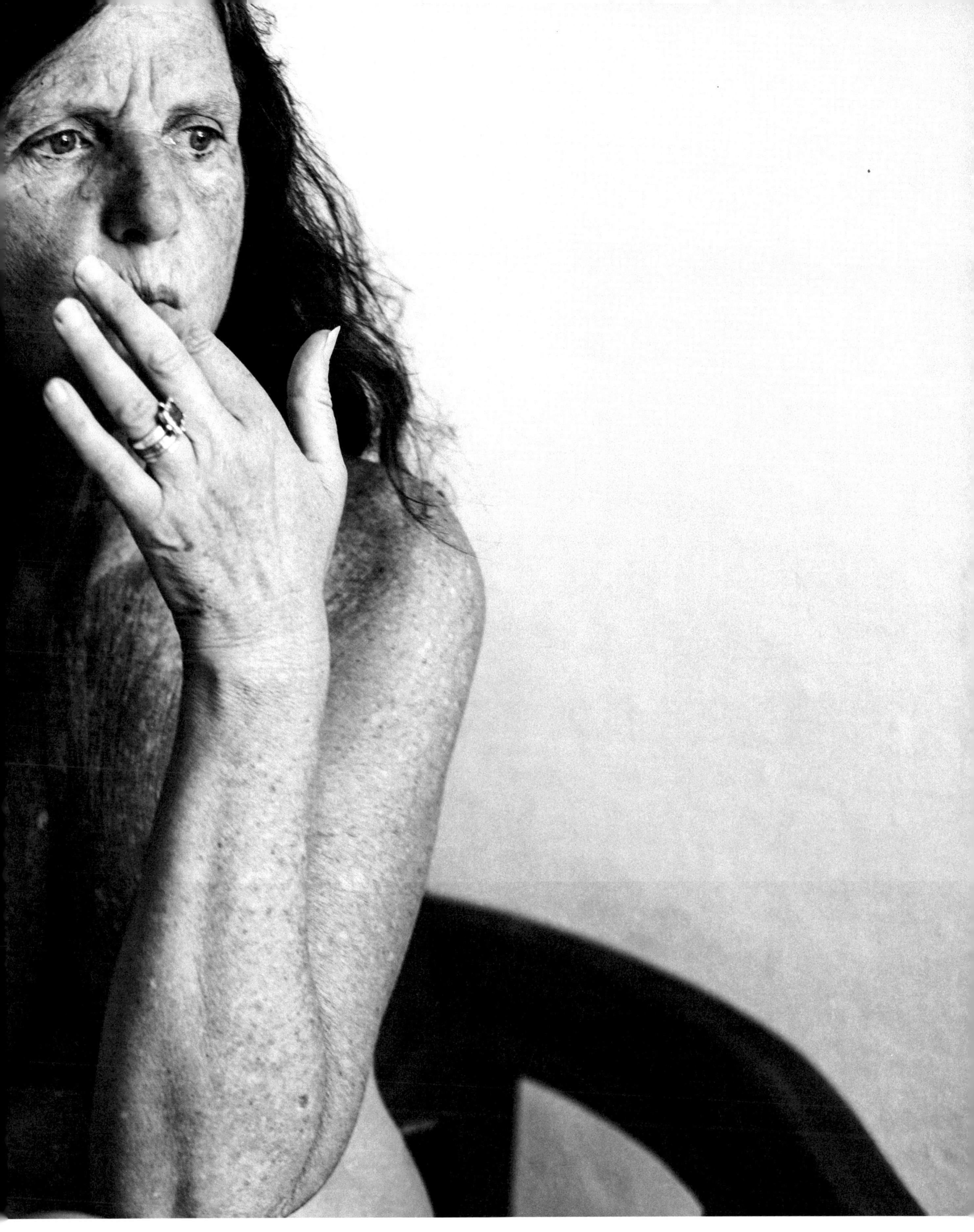

You were married and I was forgiving myself. We convinced ourselves that no one suspected. We were wrong. I knew it was the last time. You were bitter and angry, and I left you at the bar alone in your drink.

The boredom weighs on my neck. Closing my throat as I drag it from the room. The day is brighter than the night as the sun streams in through the sides. The neighbor's security light tricks me and I bury my head and hate them every night. I make lists. Minor accomplishments to cross off, before I crawl under the warmth of stillness and no expectation. Halfway is about where I get. Maybe I've lived half of my life. I'll never be able to know.

Your disappointment finds your face as you look at me and try to smile. We never had enough time to be fully naked. Fucking in the car mostly. Once on your bathroom floor when I stopped by on my way to the airport. You came and groaned loudly. My body was numb, and I could feel the cold tiles harden under the weight of you. Shame and fear were mixed into every moment and made us hurry. We pulled on the clothes that were half-off. I walked out wordless.

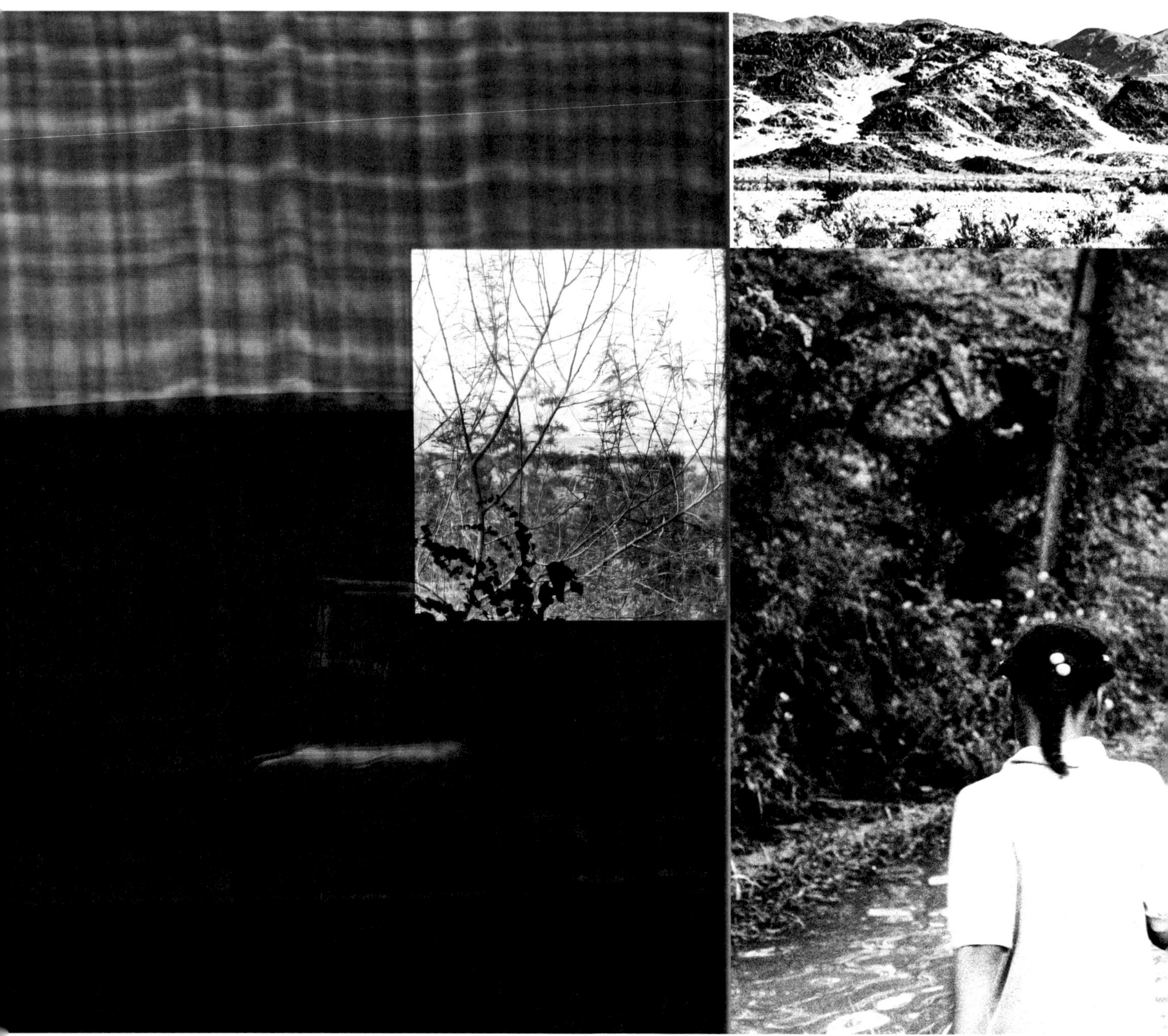

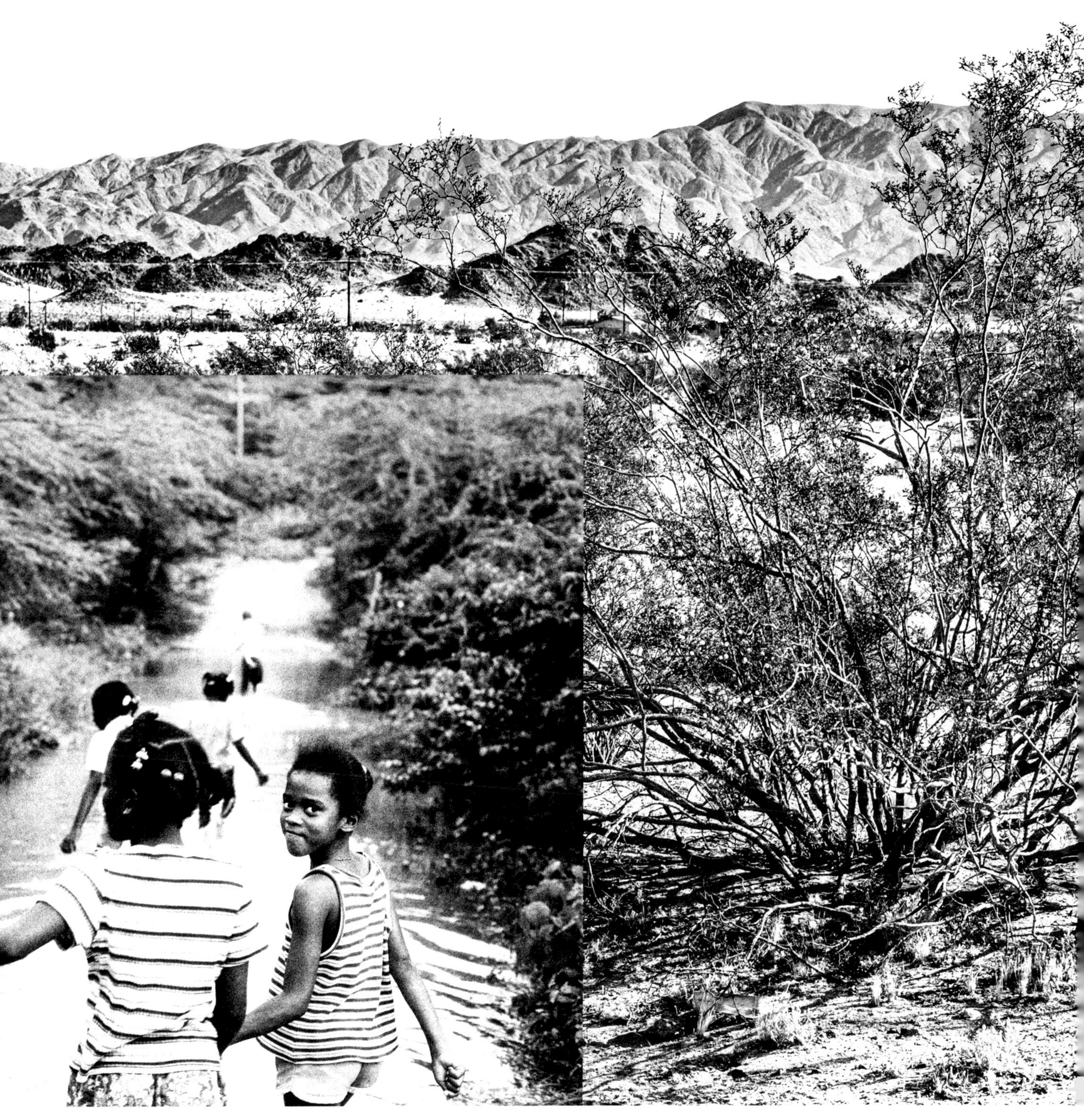

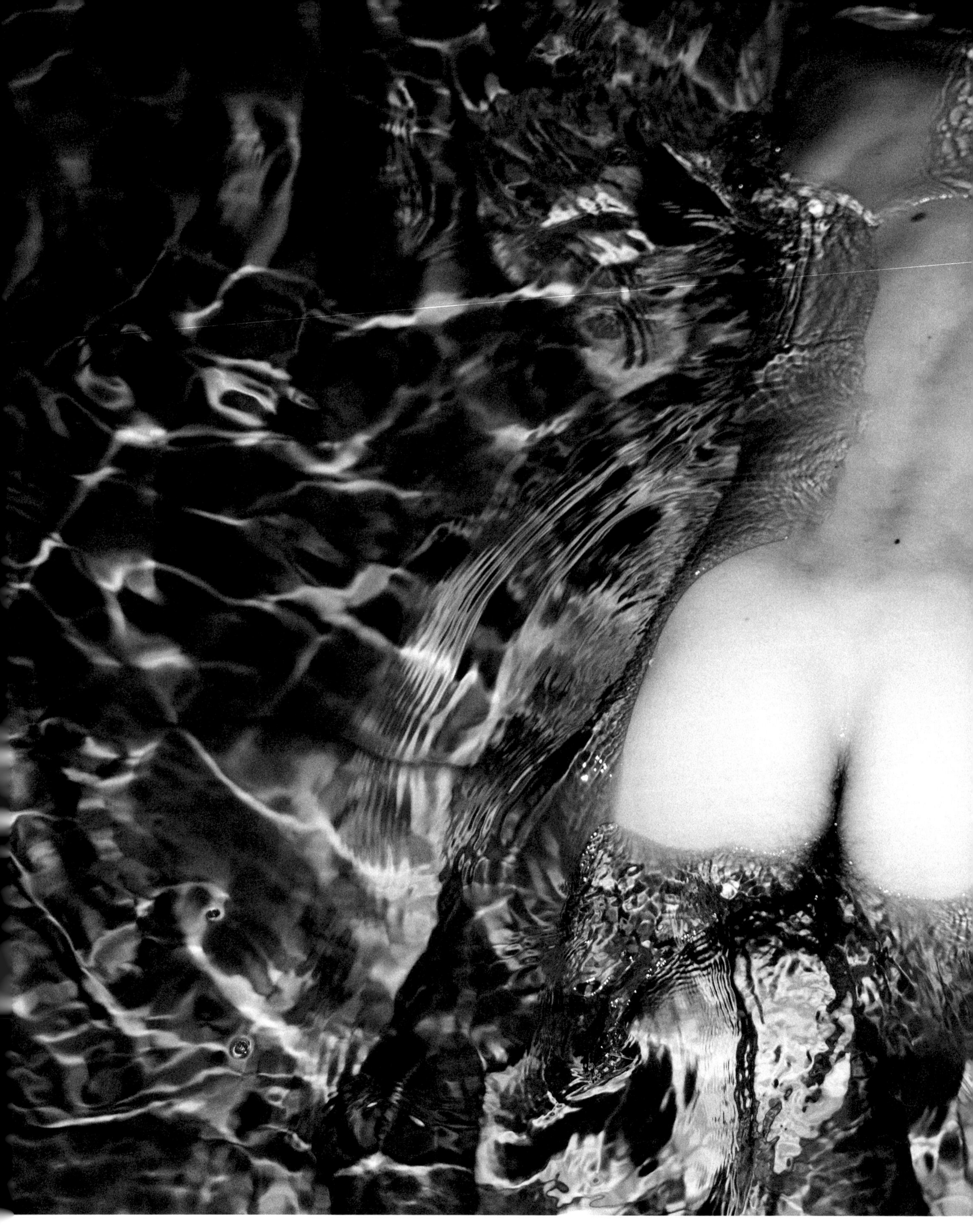

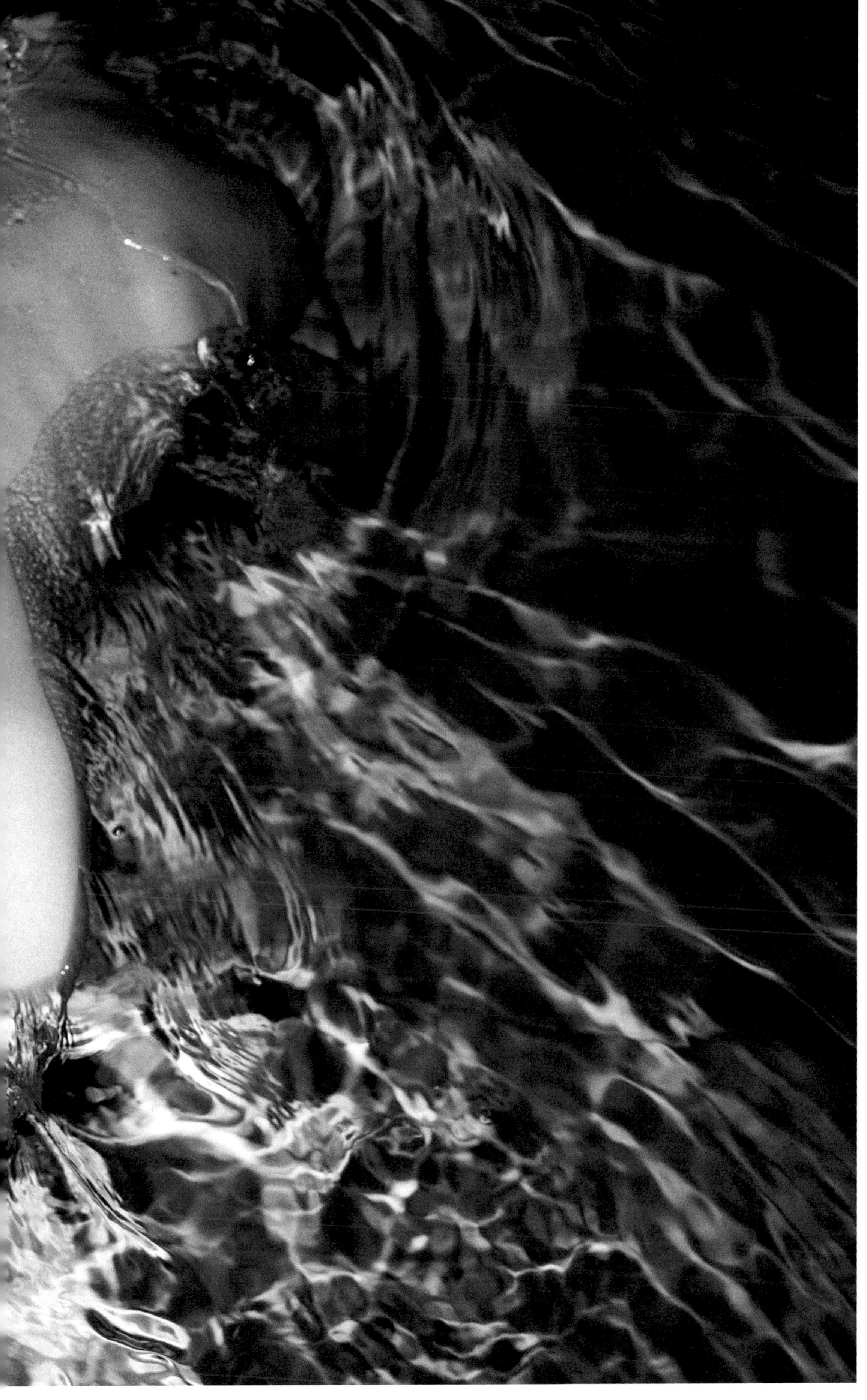

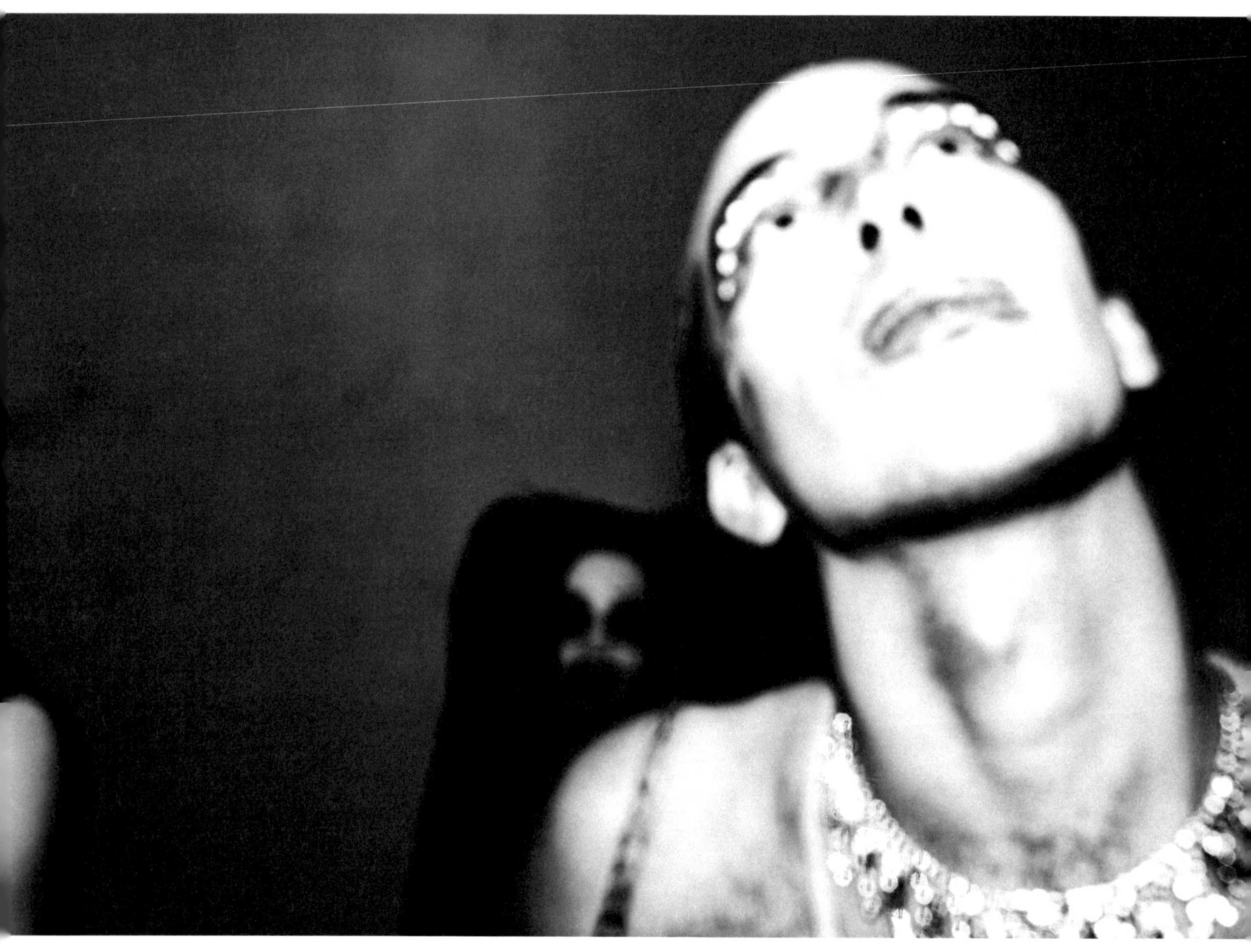

His mother sued the city. She didn't want it to be his fault.
We were sleeping in the empty apartment next door. We had
been evicted and moved into his tiny studio on the third floor.

He was special and seemed like he was floating and not here
for long. He wore capes and long skirts. He talked in riddles
about the other side. About time. About aliens. There were
Xeroxed signs up around town from a girl who wanted to find
him from their brief encounter. She said she loved him and to
please call her.

I was never sure if he died in my arms on the sidewalk or in the
ambulance on the way to the hospital. Holding his head trying
not to move as a woman shouted about him falling out of the
window. Kneeling in my underwear with gravel digging into
my skin. I had been asleep until the explosion. He didn't feel
alive and it made me shake. I thought his death might take me
too and I didn't want to hold his head anymore.

He had talked about explosives and suicide and we knew but
never said. The firefighters soaked everything we had.
A neighbor brought us sweatpants. We weren't allowed back
inside. You had gone in towards the fire and I ran downstairs
towards the screaming. The investigators and lawyers
called me for months with questions I never answered. You
moved away.

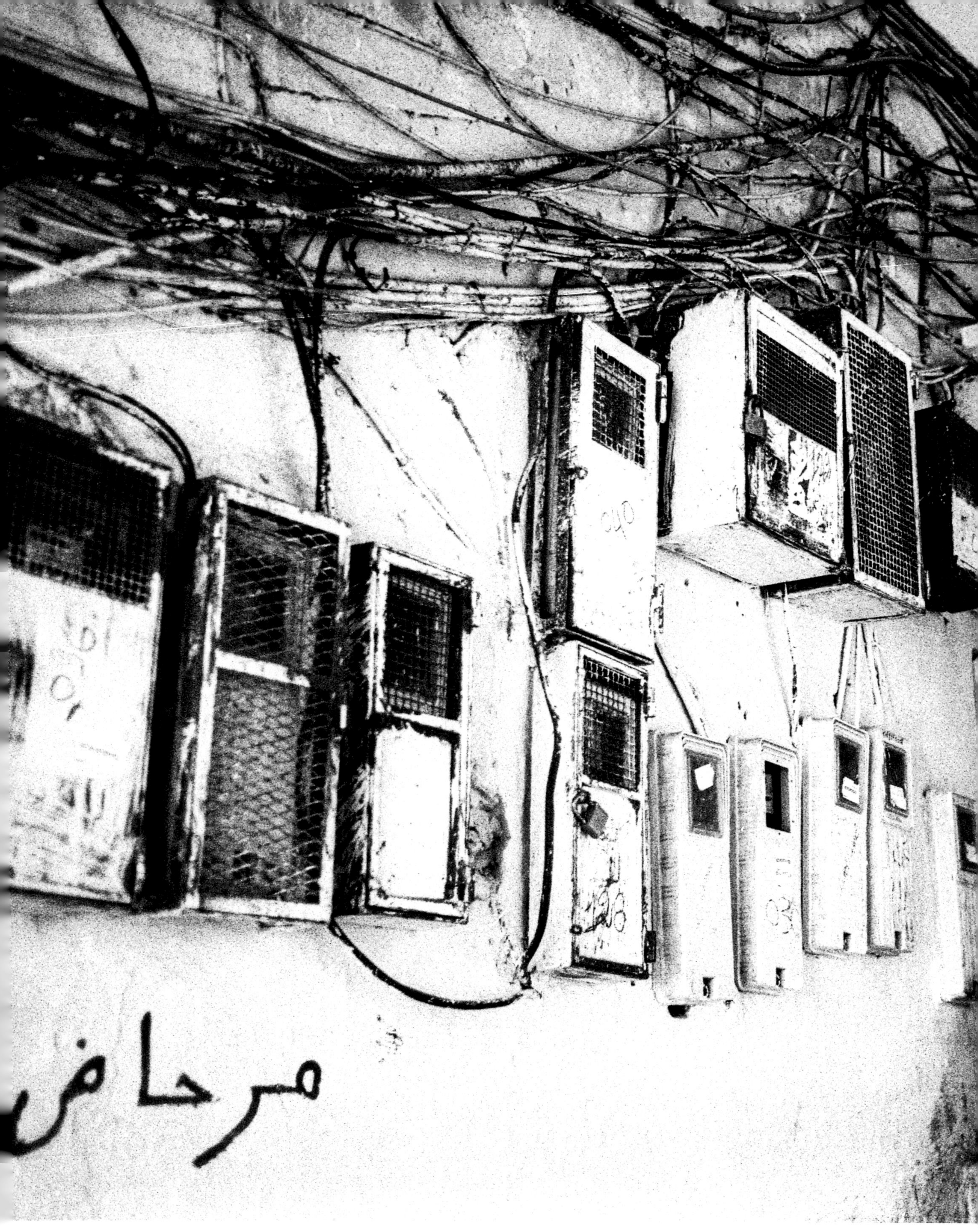
مرحاض

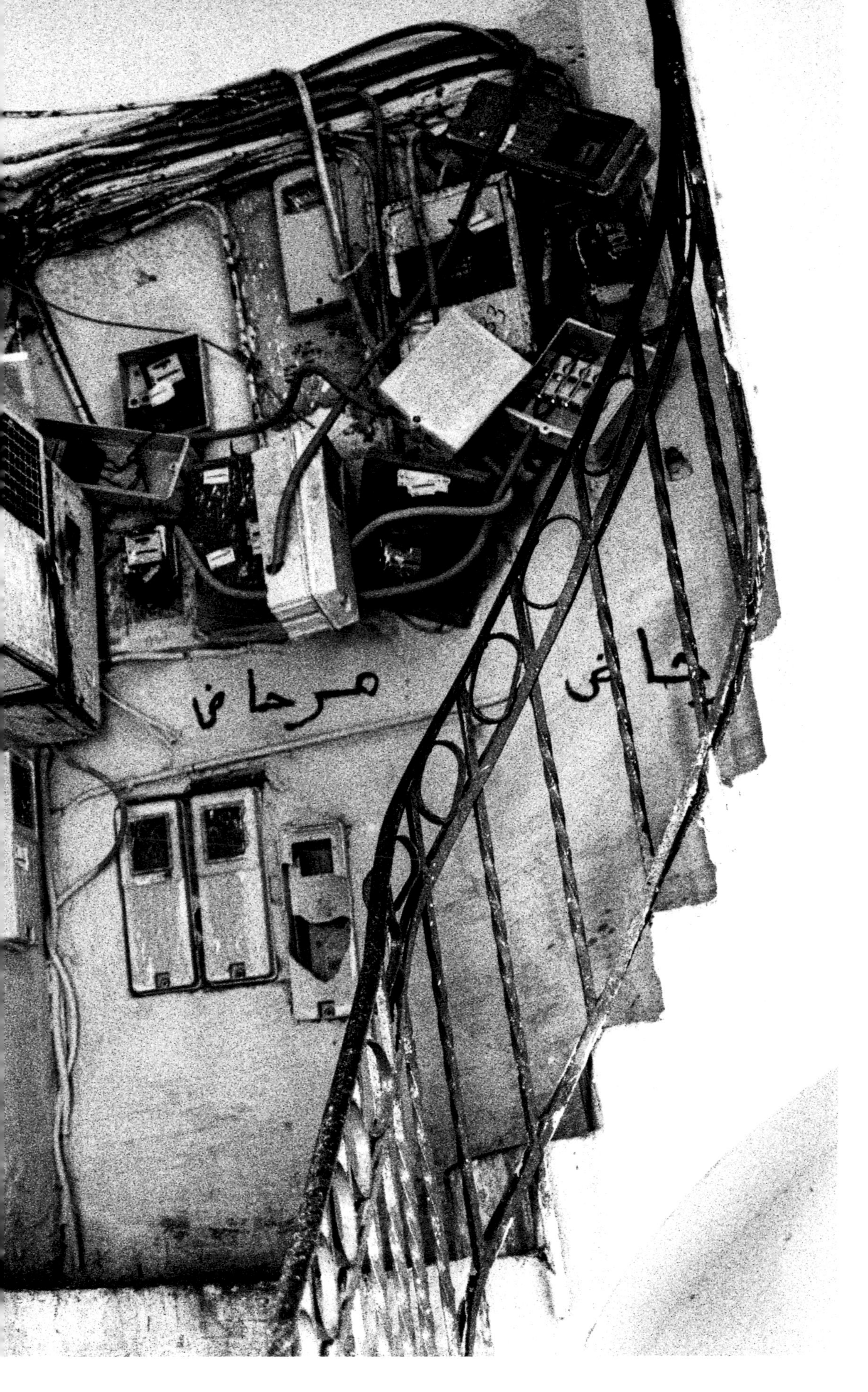

مرحاض
خاص

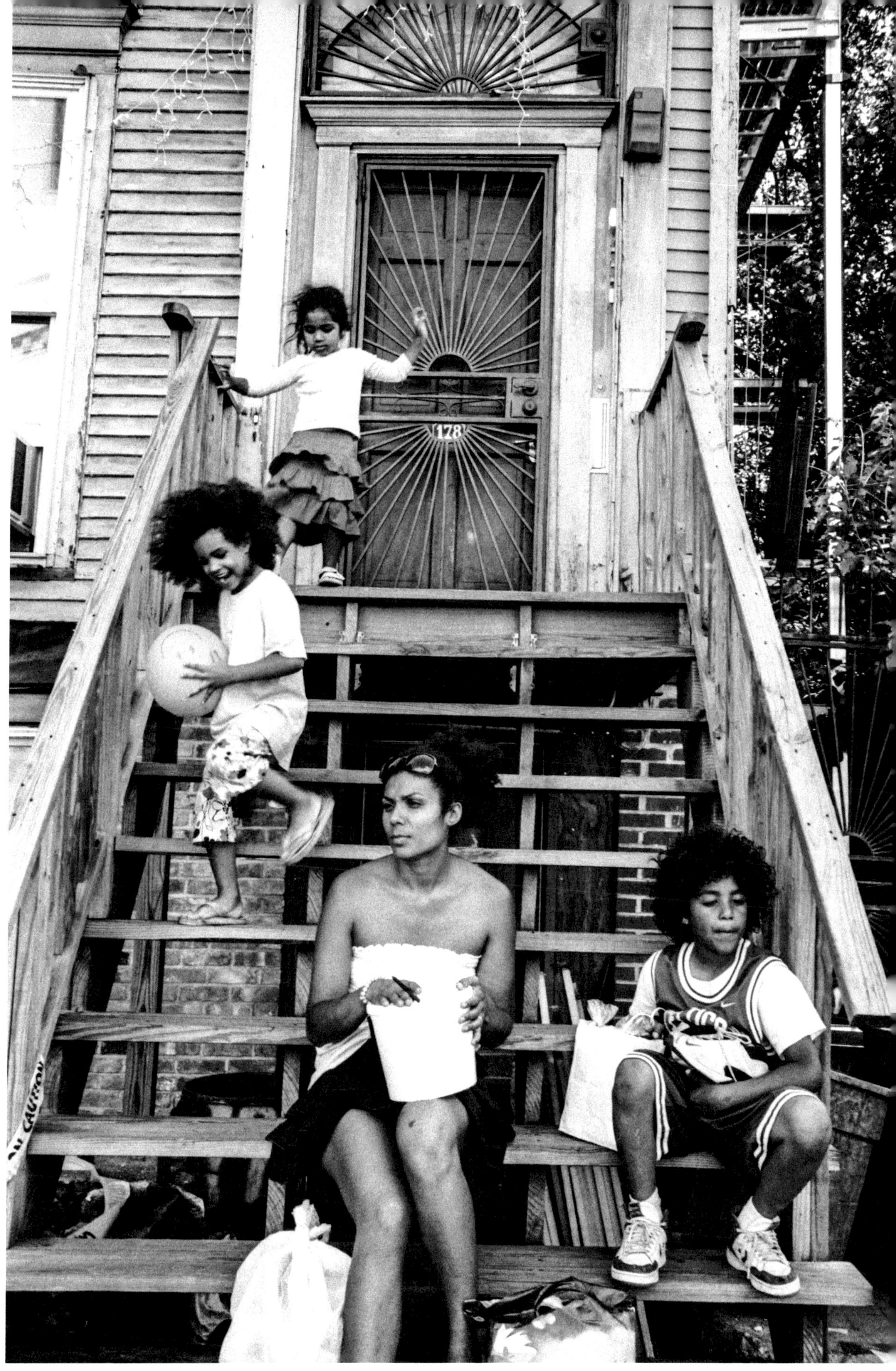

There was always so much blood and shame. The edges of my
thoughts were sharp and kept me still. I held a magazine but
couldn't focus on shiny faces with perfect white teeth. My throat
was dry and tight. Scanning the baseboards for cleanliness,
I waited anxiously for my name. The receptionist ushered me
through the door.

I took everything off and put on the yellow paper gown. Scoot
all the way down and relax, she said. The cold metal clicking.
Holding the warm gloved hand of a nurse shhhing me. The
shine of his balding head through my thighs before they got
thick. He didn't say a word. He never looked up.

That night I went dancing. It was too soon. They all knew.
I was weak and shouldn't drink but I wanted to. I caught a cab
and watched them shove back inside. It was raining and the
tires splashed the curb. I was alone but only just.

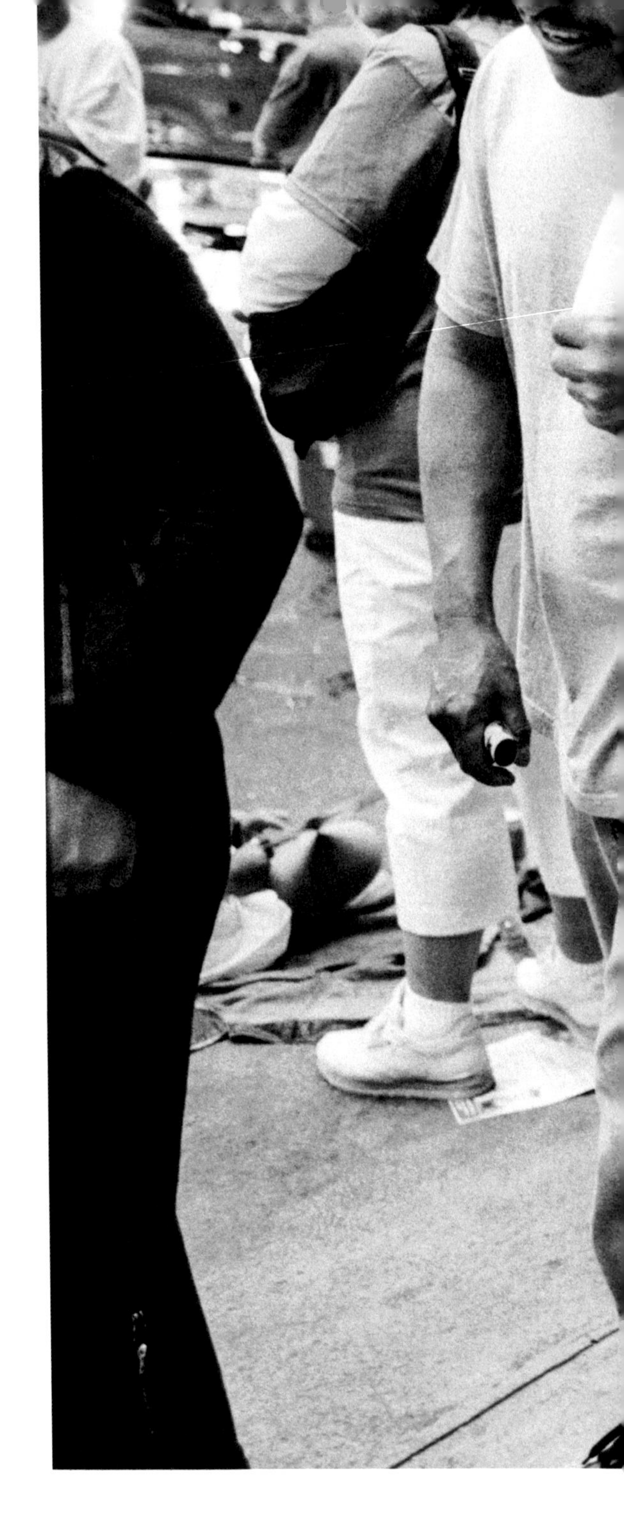

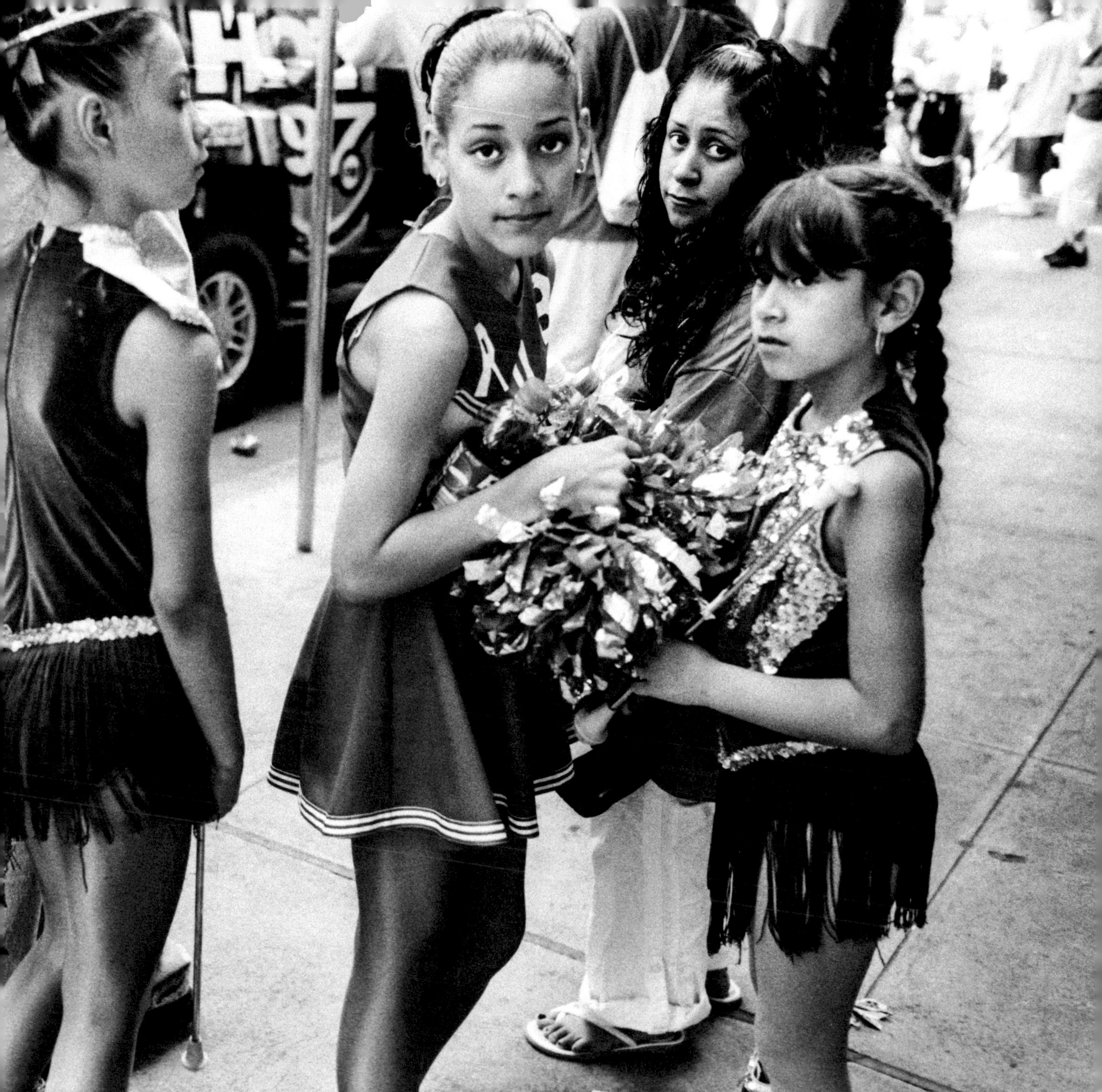

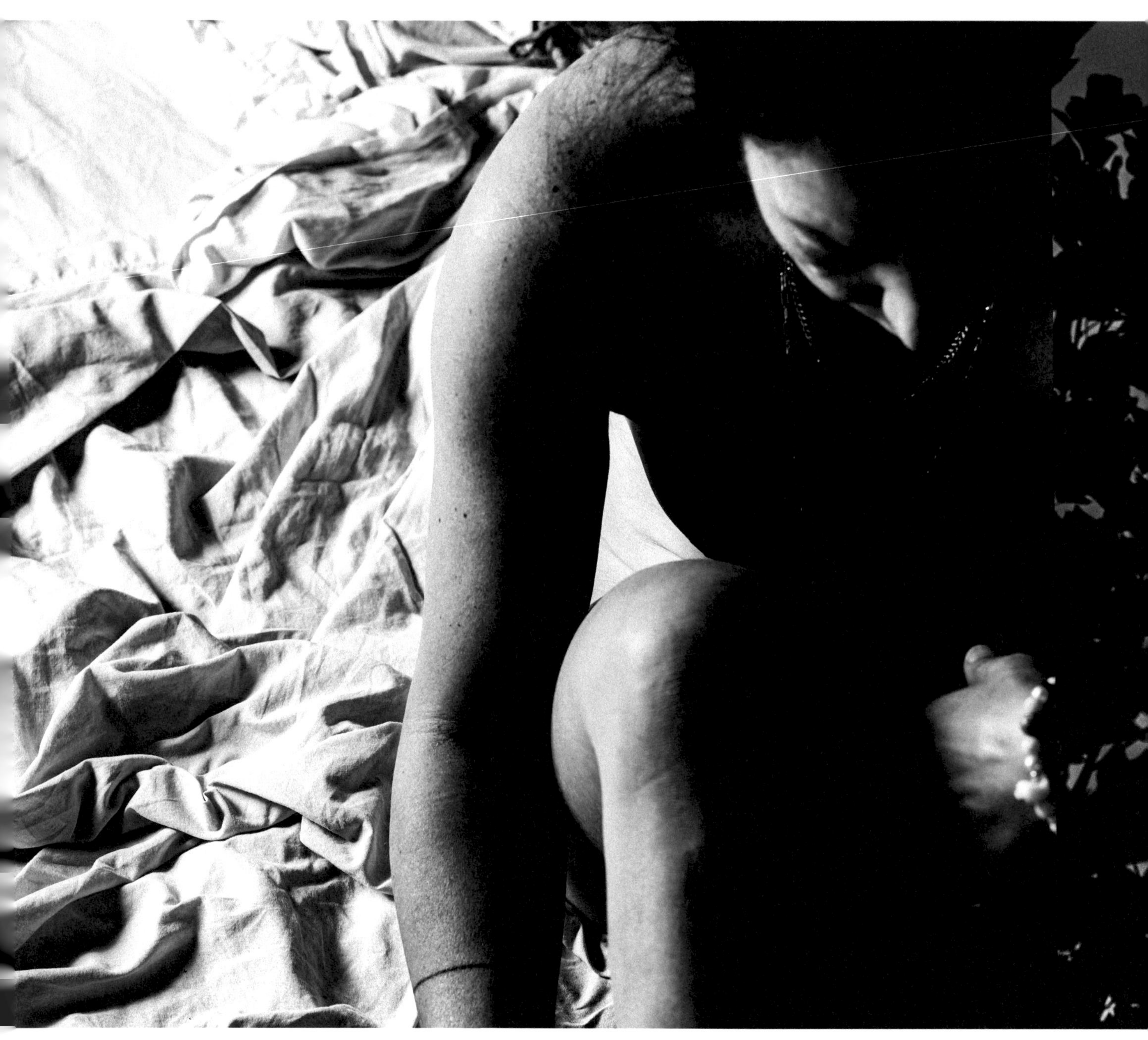

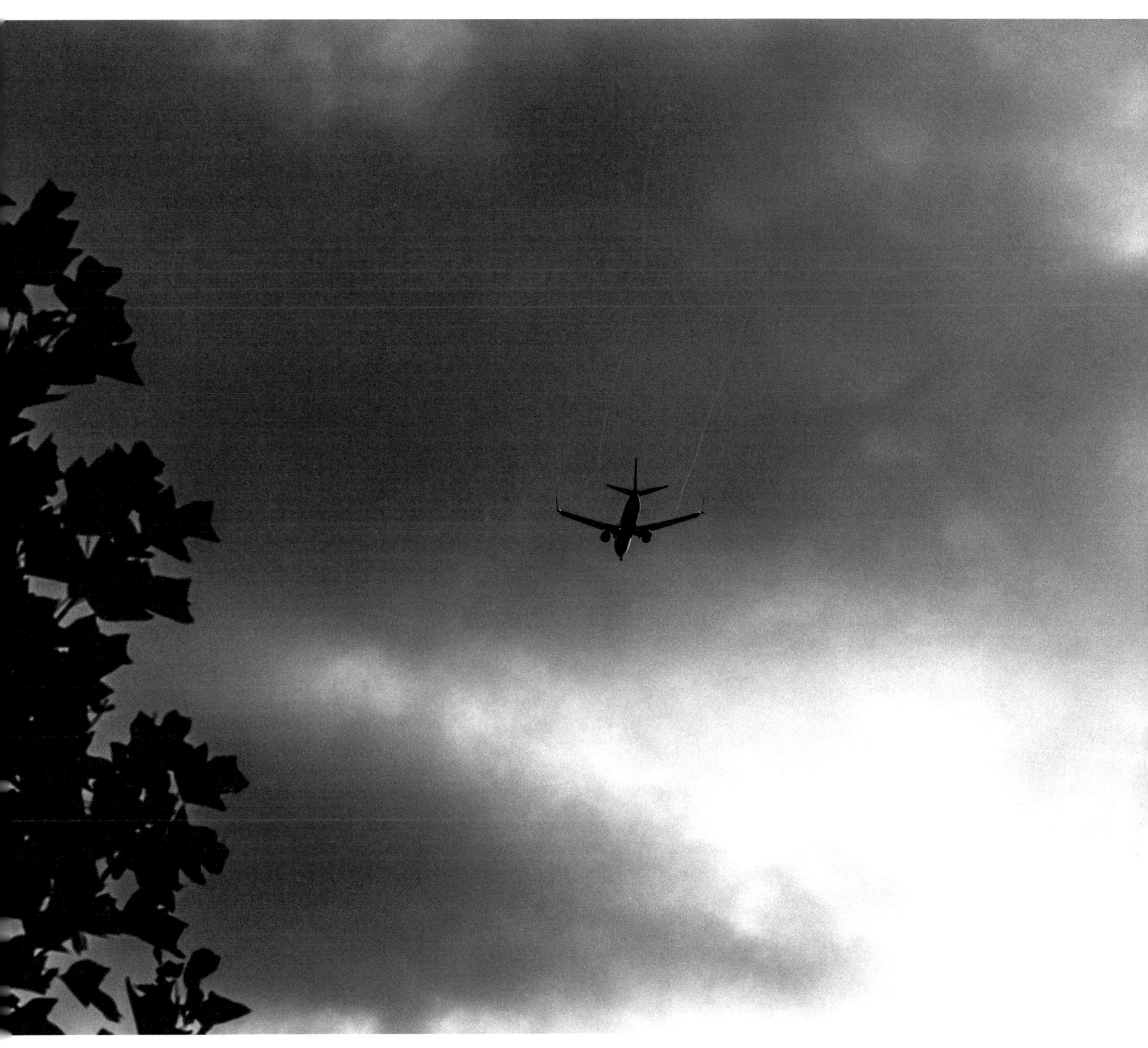

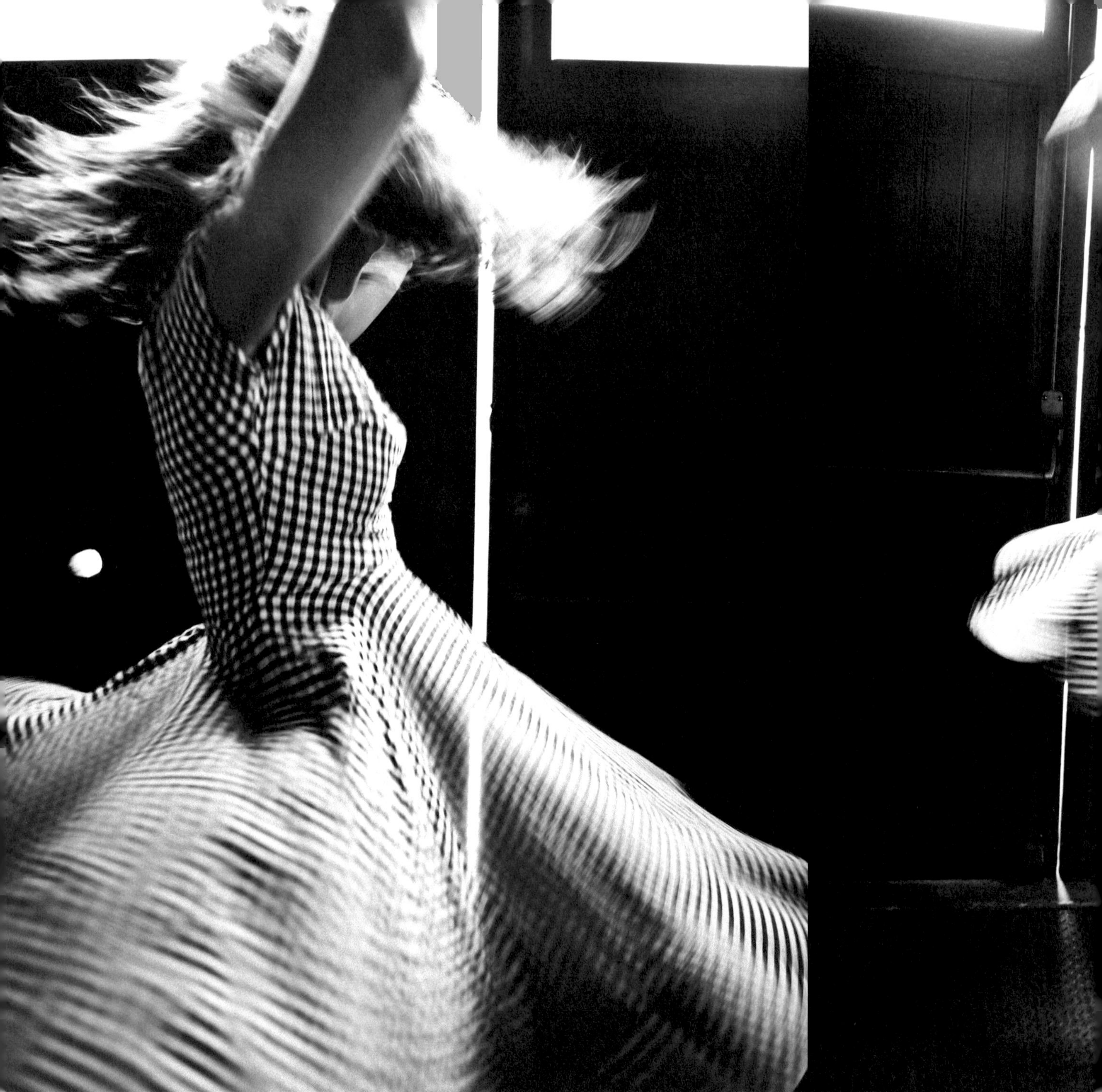

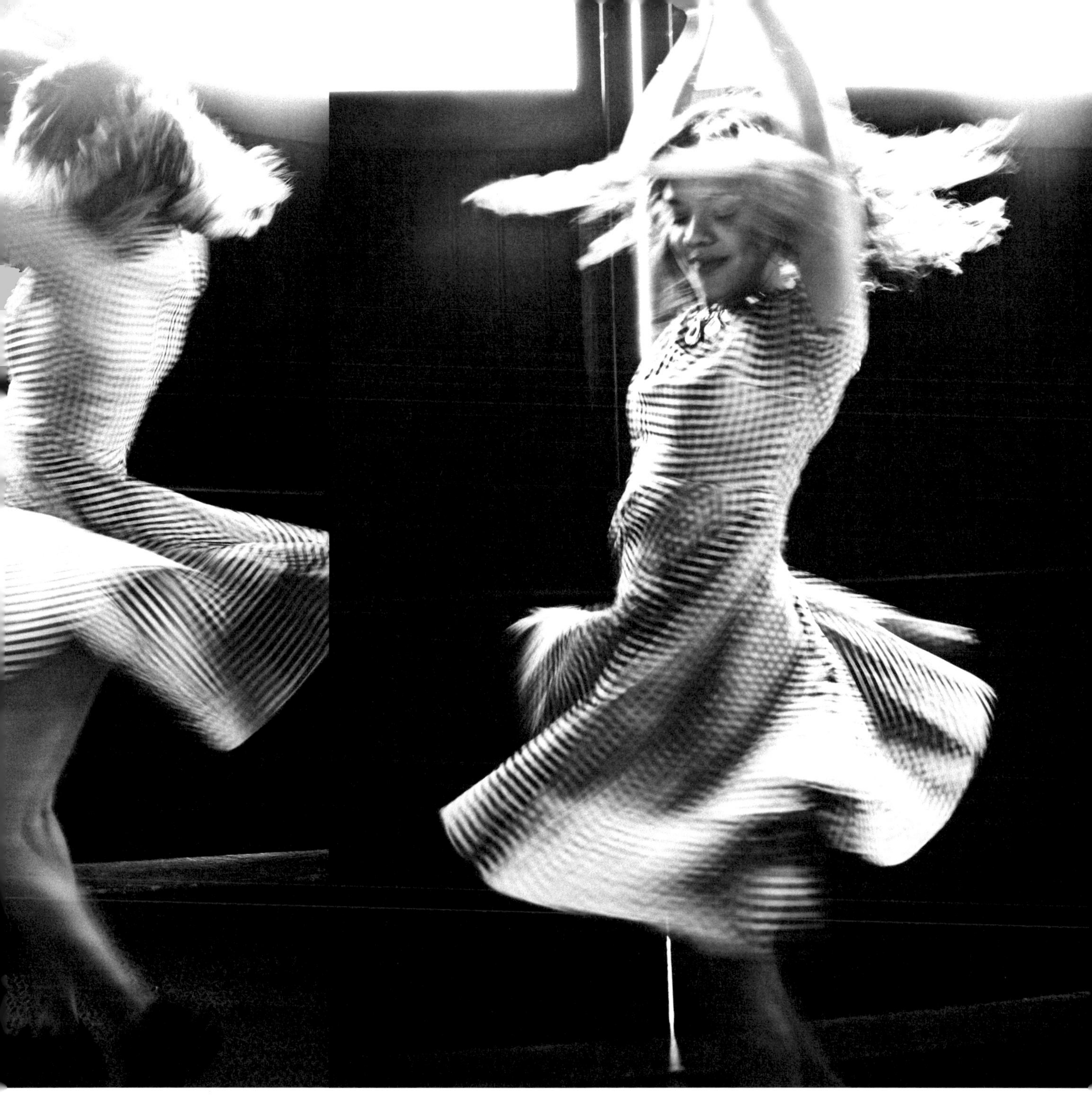

The time I carried you down the stairs. Your limbs gave up and
you said falling felt nice. Your neighbor stared at us with pity but
not surprise. I snarled back as much as I could trying to hold
us both up while going down. You made jokes but I could tell
you were scared. I drove slow and fast. "Steady, breathe, be calm,"
I repeated. Your half-sister next to me squeezing my hand.
Her bottom lip trembling, eyes pinned ahead.

I kept looking in the mirror to make sure you were awake.
My anxious heart thudding in my neck. Stopping and going at
the lights. Rounding the corners to get us home. There was
that time and another. Each seemed like it had to be the last.
I stopped counting. It seemed cruel.

You called once from the hospital and told me stories and
untruths. Rapid talking with no stops. Constructing regrets
and apologies all lined up for later. I pretended not to know
and measured my words, letting the air out between breaths.
I wanted to keep us talking until I figured out your angle.
You said you had to go and would call again but we both knew
you wouldn't.

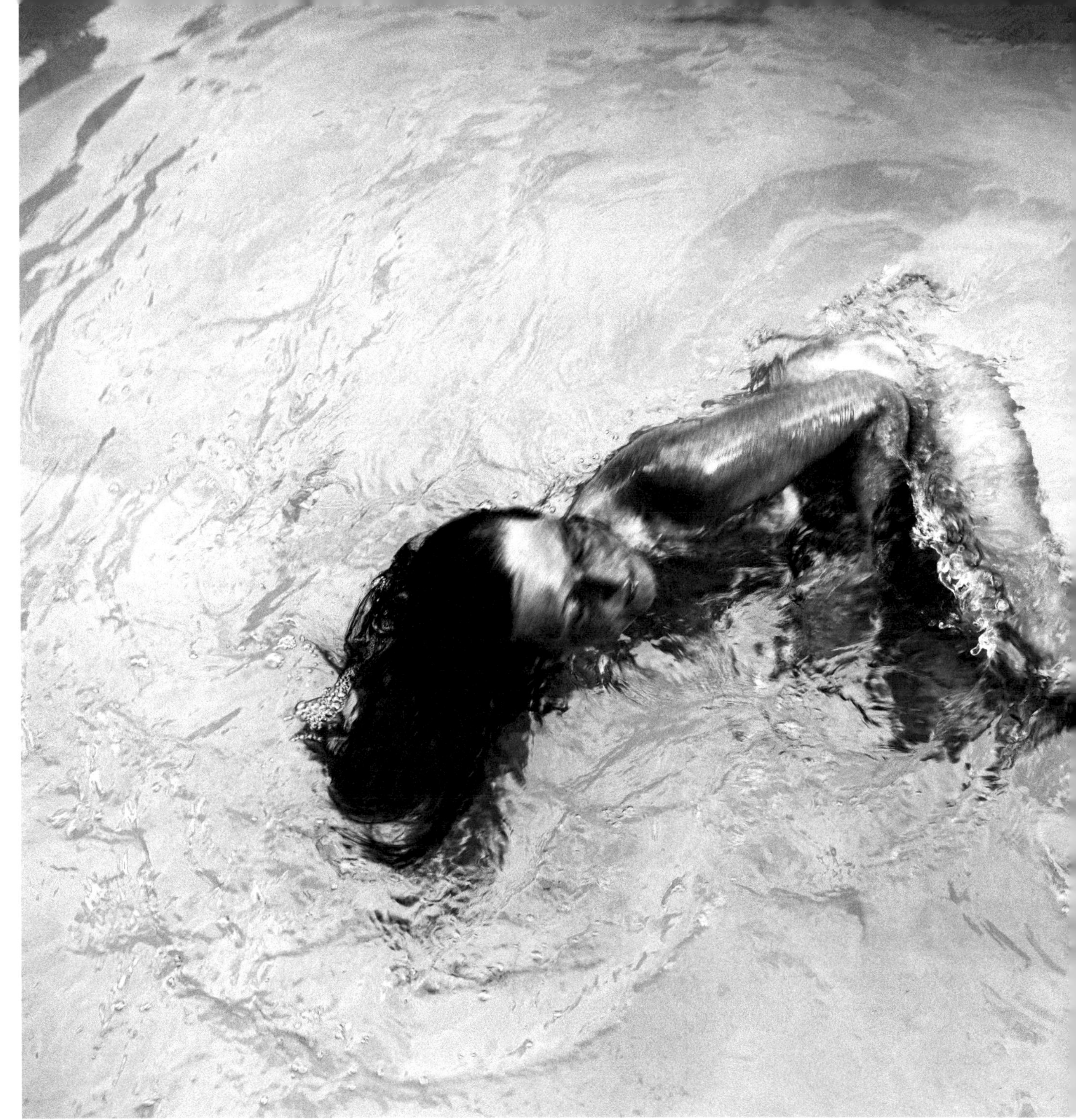

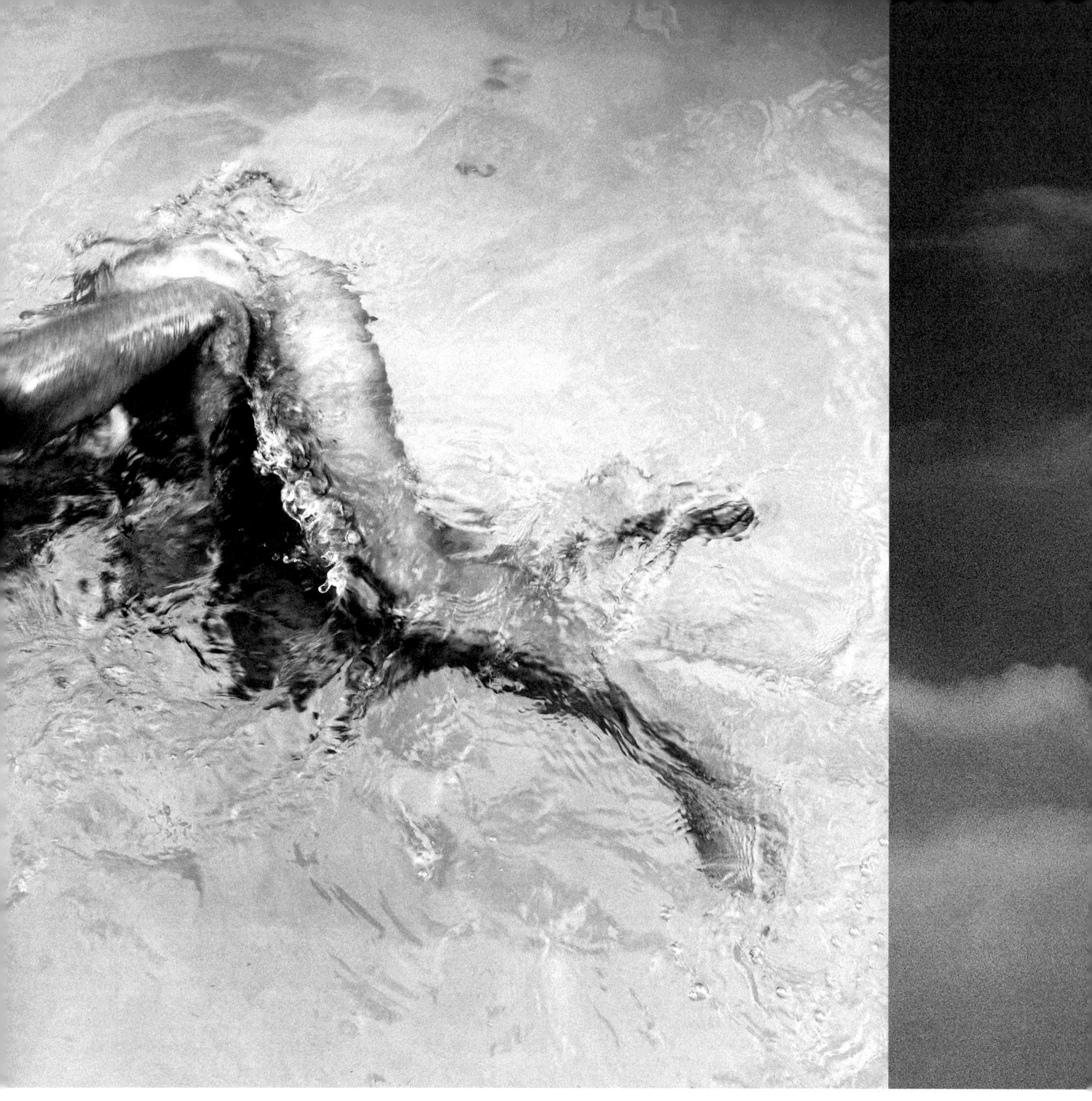

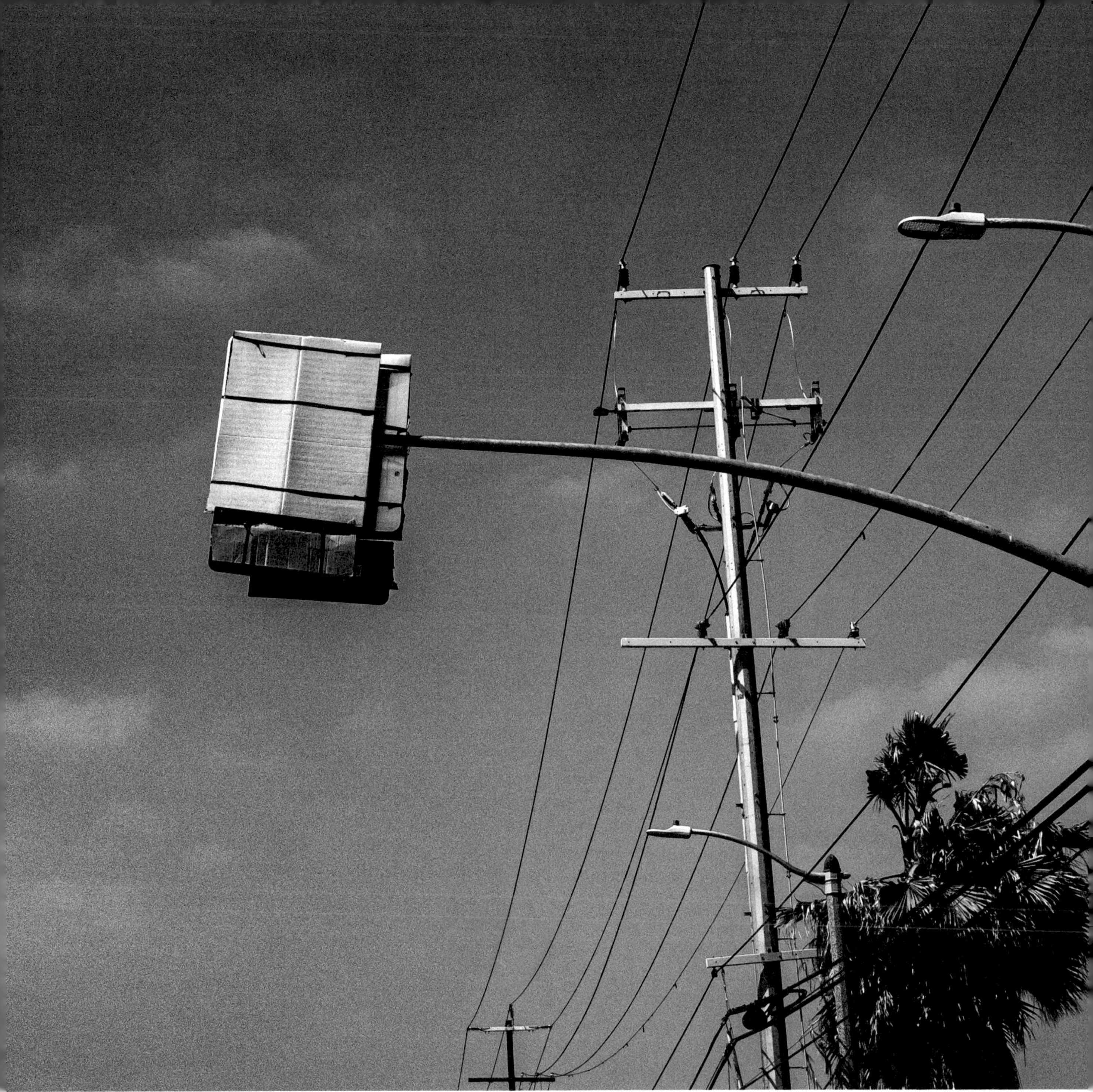

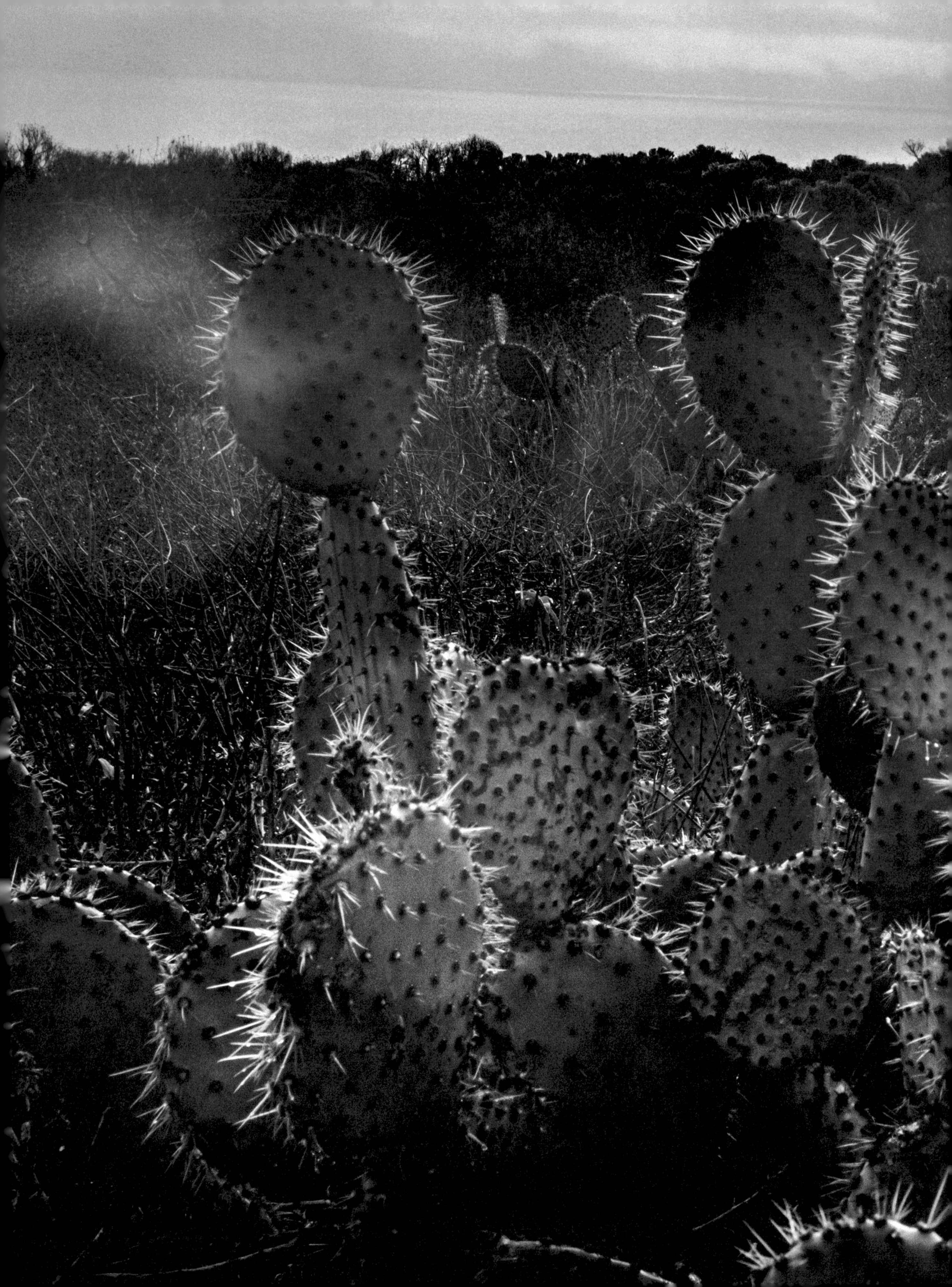

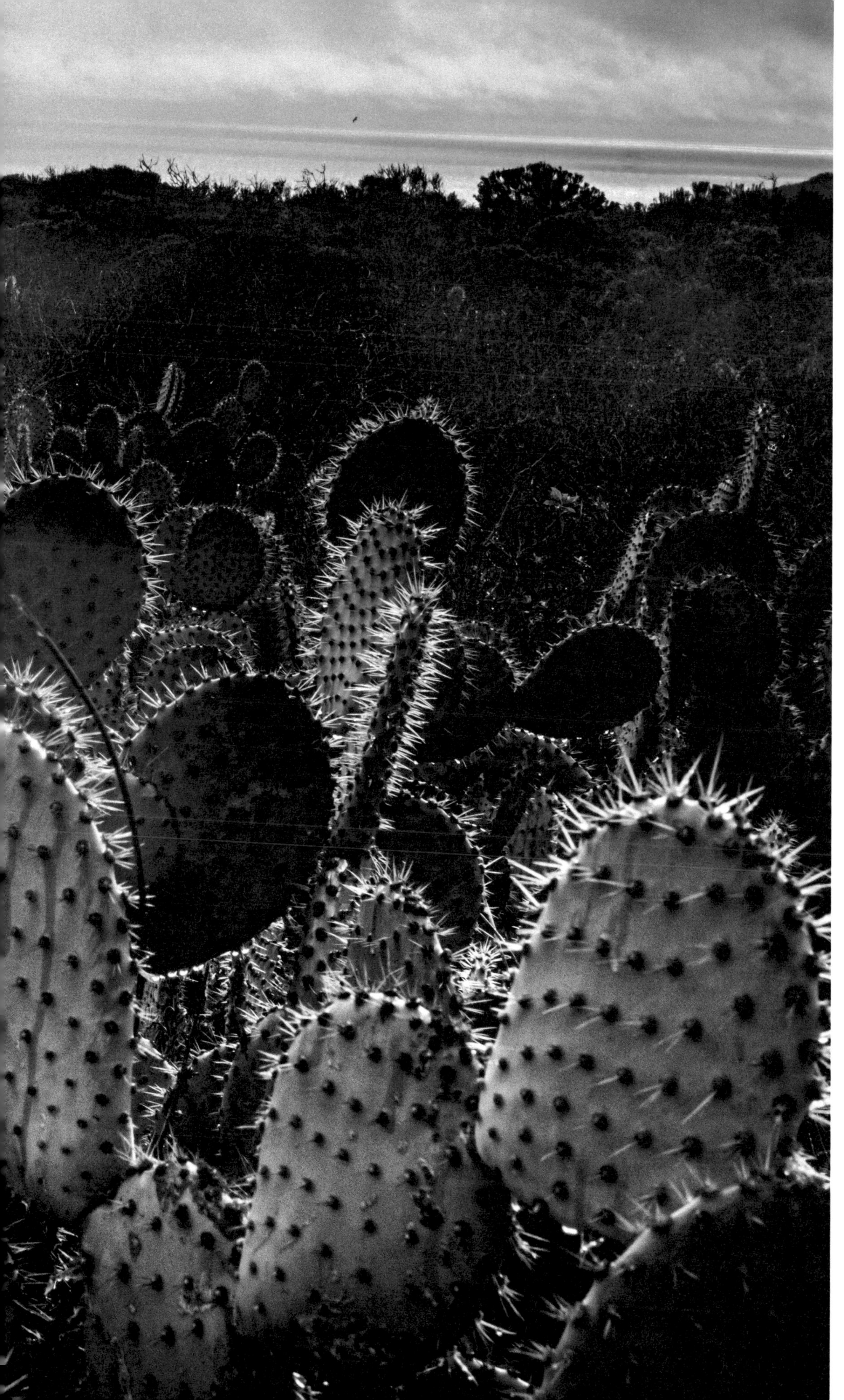

You tried to die in Boston. They said you probably couldn't hear us but we talked to you anyway. We sent for your mom and sat in the room awkwardly shifting through the air. Mostly nodding without words. She seemed scared but also like she had done this before. You were tucked tightly under white sheets motionless.

When you recovered she took you home. I flew to Lisbon. You hadn't answered my calls, but I went anyway. I arrived at your building. Beautiful blues painted everything that wasn't tiled. The doorways were built for giants. They were digging up the sidewalk to uncover an ancient theater. I could see the curved seating raked beneath the barricades. Yellow tape tied to stop people from falling in.

We walked through the city stopping at all your favorite places while I held your hand. It's the most we ever touched. I was happy and didn't have a flight back. You said you loved me but that I should leave. I loved you too but you said I belonged to someone else. I felt like something of value that needed to be returned. I cried and wanted you to see my wet face. We sat in silence waiting for the taxi with sadness in our laps. We said goodbye and meant it. I returned home, and you died in a hospital two years later.

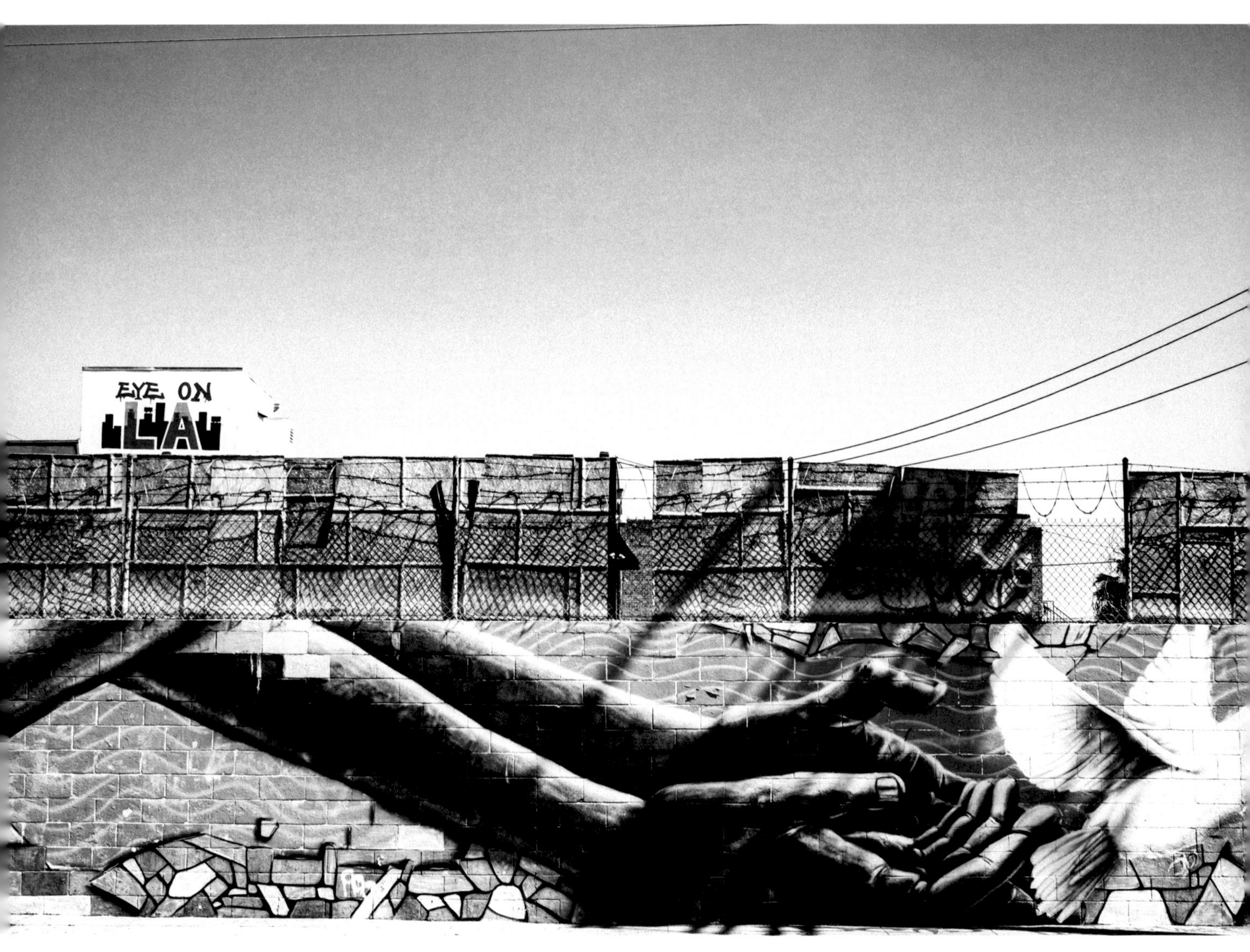
EYE ON
L.A.

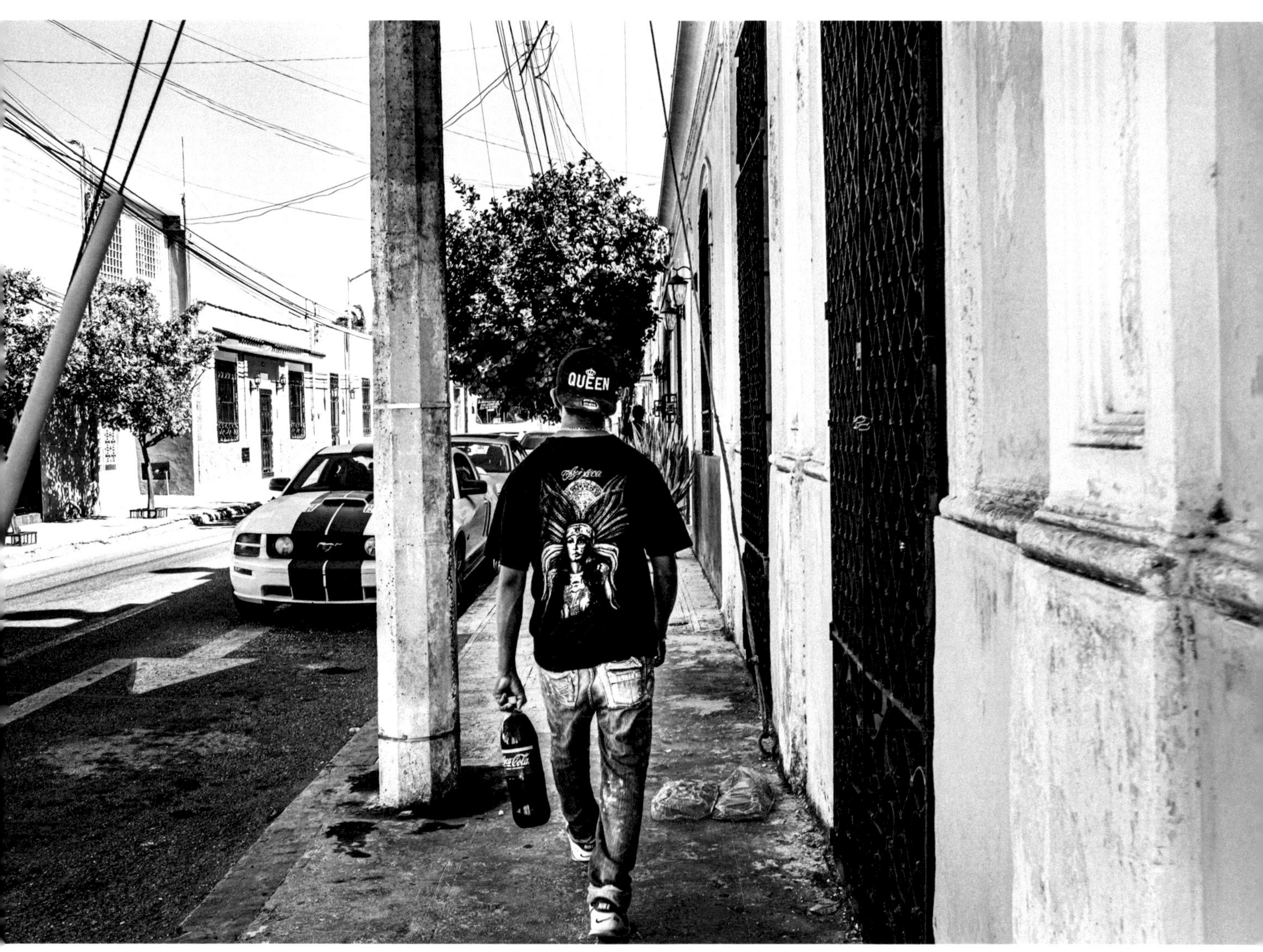

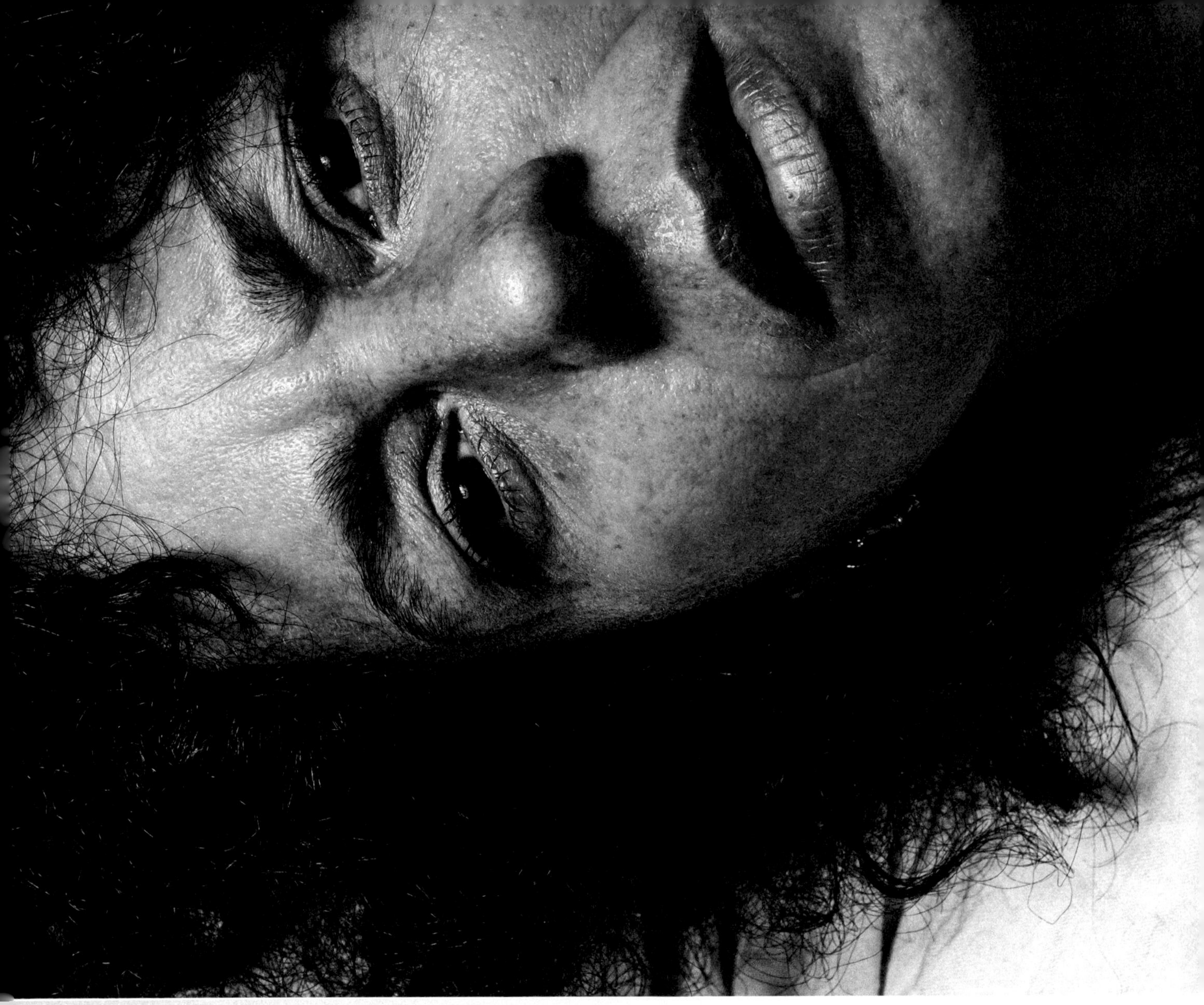

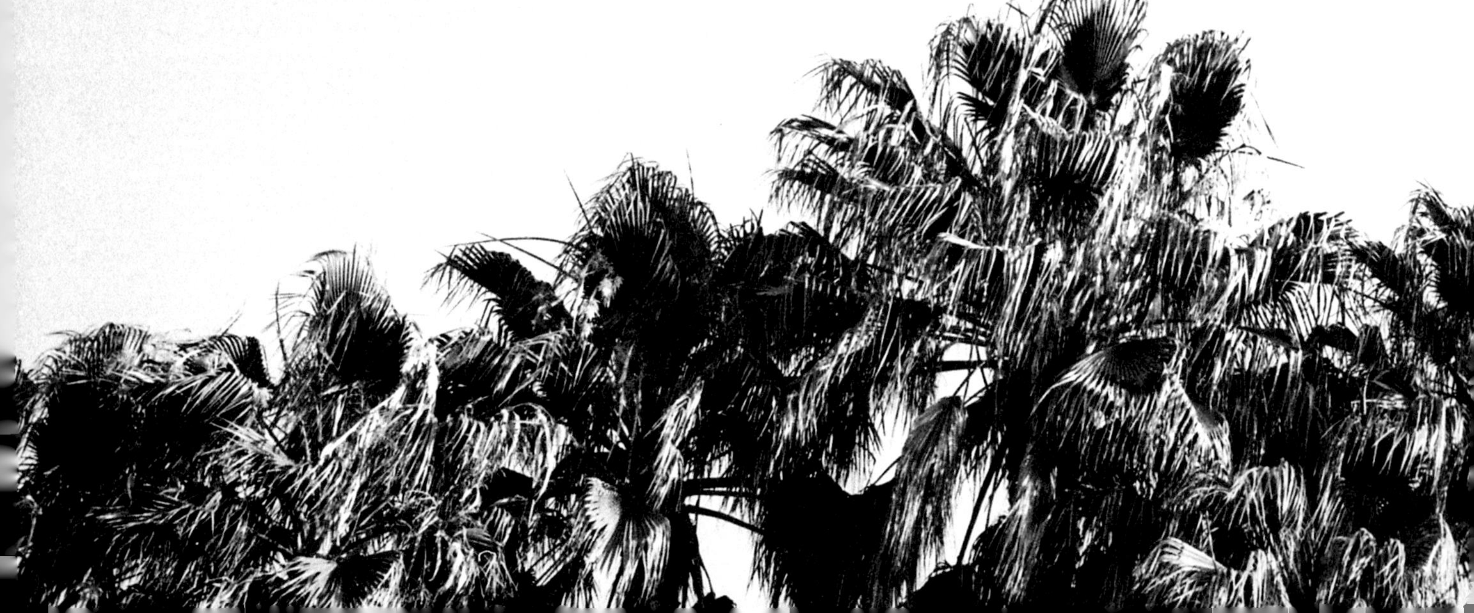

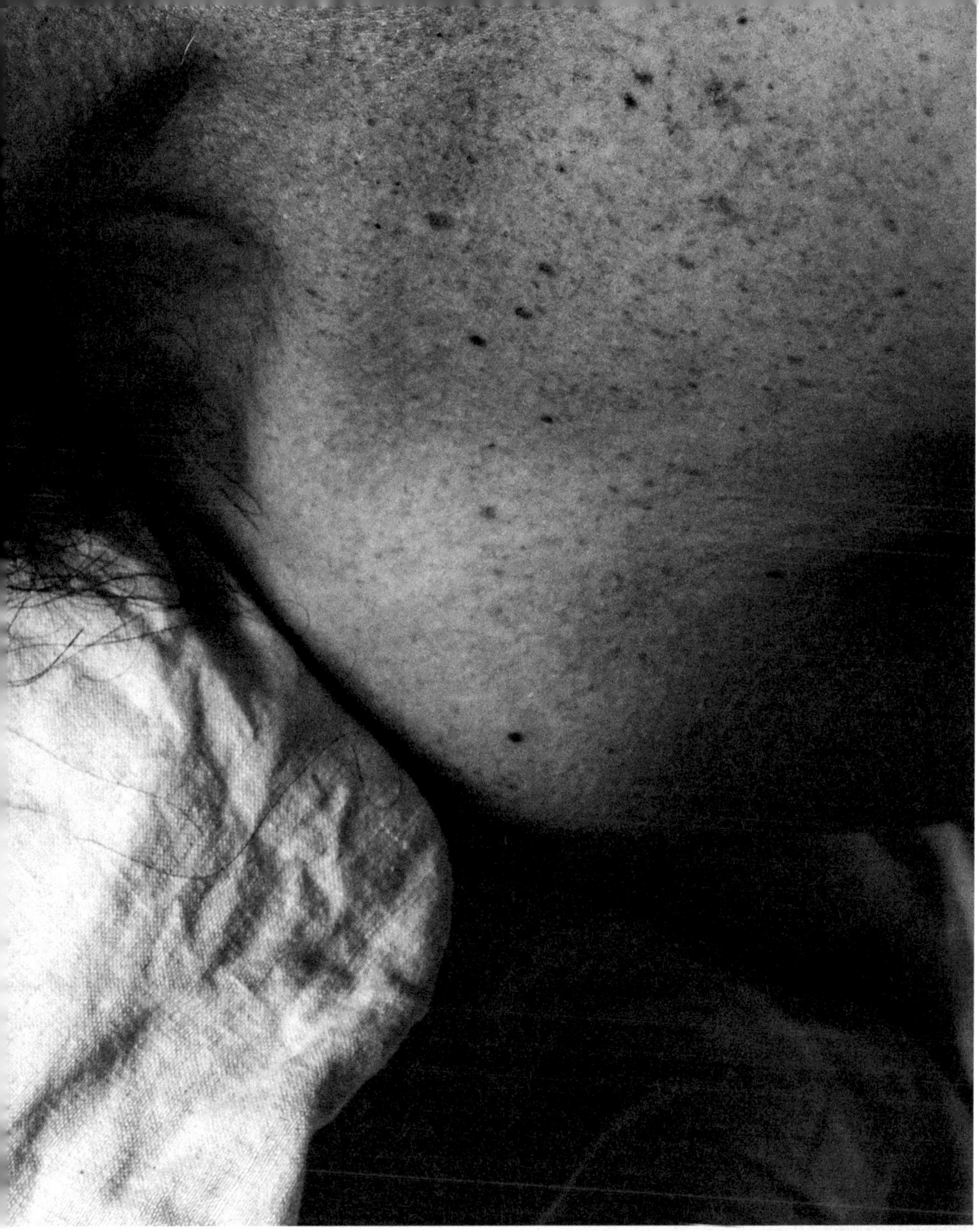

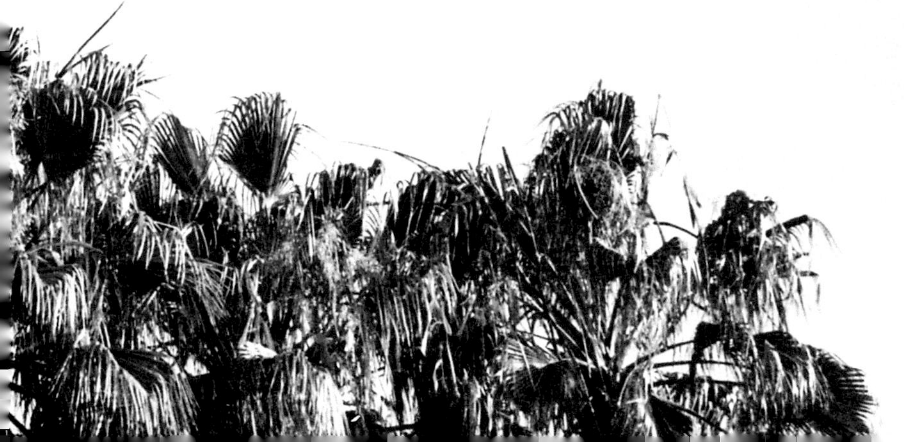

We were up till three am not understanding each other. Not listening. We finally gave up and went to separate beds in separate rooms and my body pretended to sleep. I cried until I couldn't breathe out of my nose. I woke up with a headache and my heart felt flimsy. All the words were piled in the corners. I felt lame and stupid and dramatic and off-balance. I wanted you to say it was ok but you didn't. I wanted the weight of the house to crush me. To stop the racing anxious flimsy heart. To stop all the worry and half thoughts, to stop feeling the dark lonely nowhere. But it didn't. We packed in the quiet. We loaded the dishwasher and washed the sheets. We missed our flight and sat drinking bad wine, waiting for the air between us to thaw.

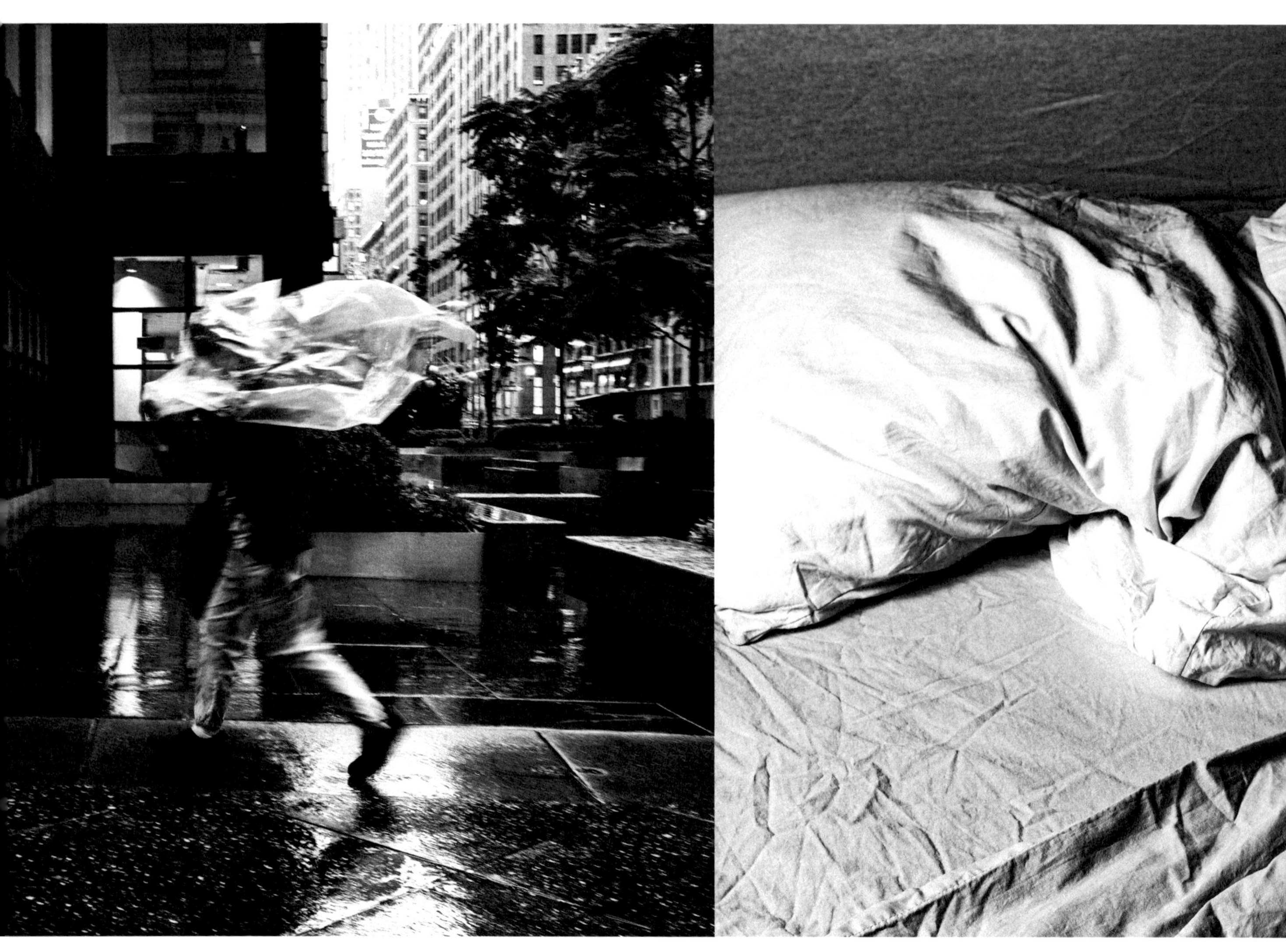

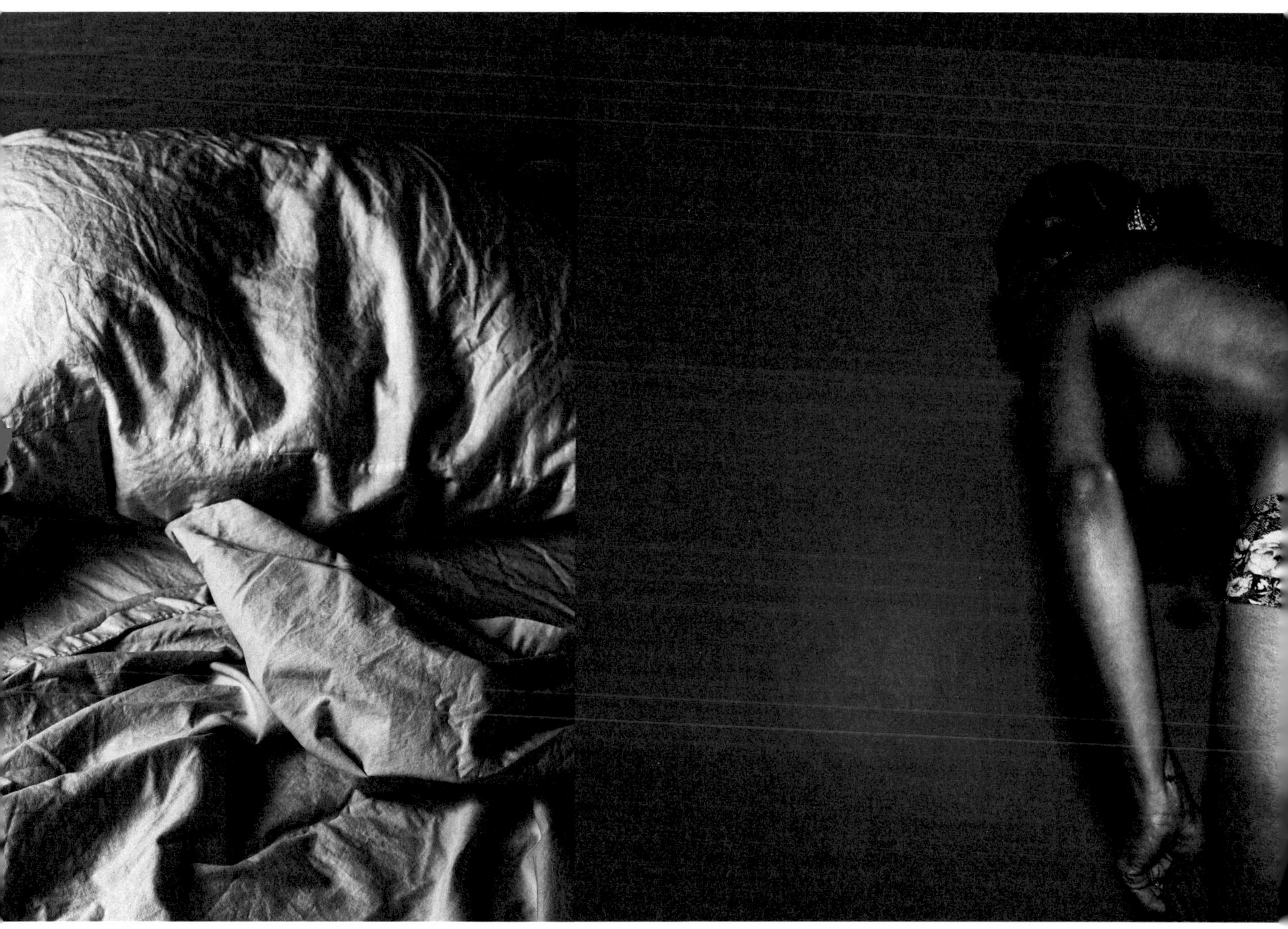

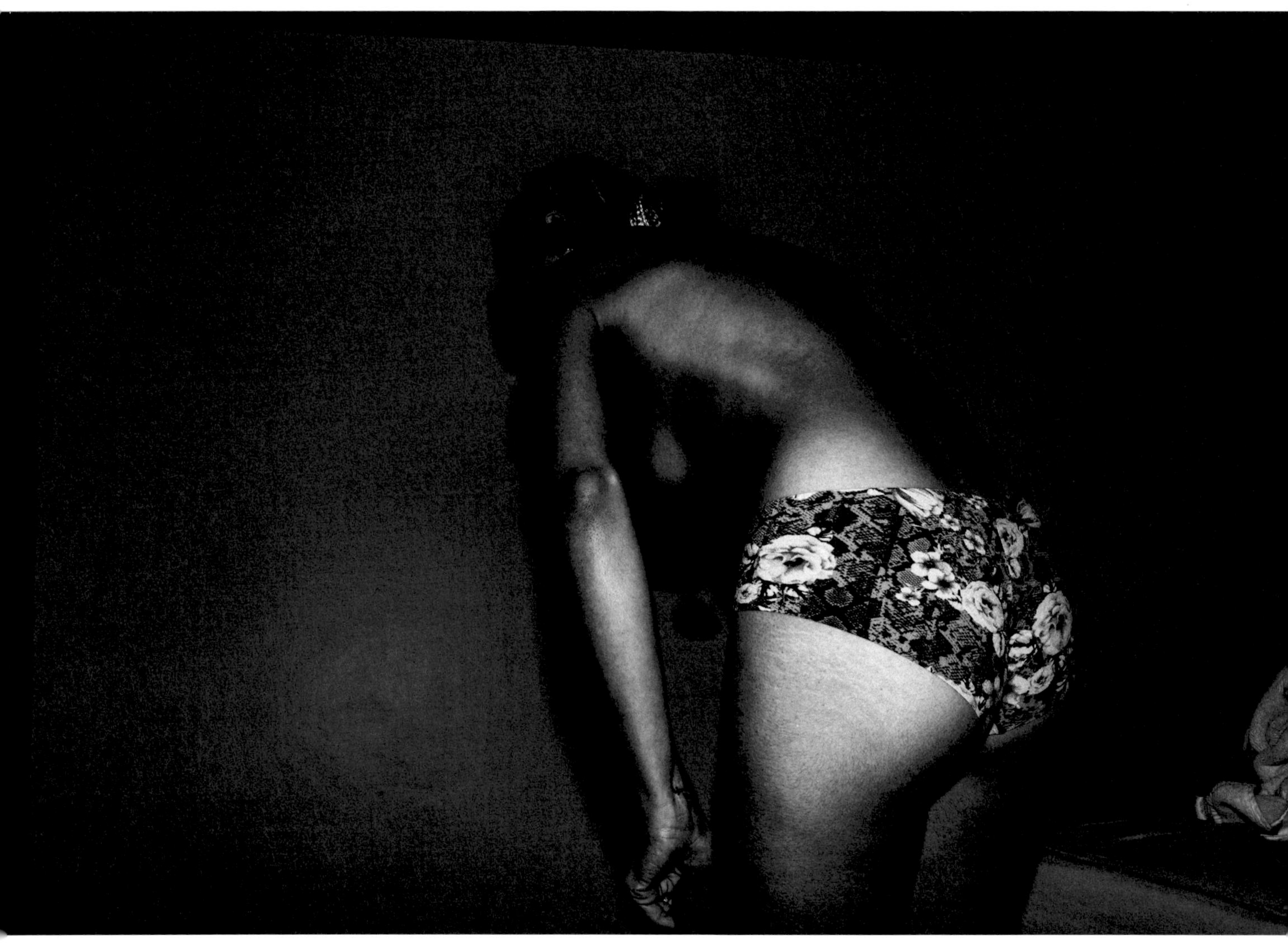

‡

I moved to where you lived in the middle of the night. You
handed me a glass of wine before I got inside. We talked
with our eyes around the kids and waited for them to sleep.
I cooked for us in your kitchen. You pretended like you
couldn't. I thought it had something to do with your mom.
She decided not to live and then died slowly for a week.

You wouldn't let the dirt in. You set things by the door that
lost their charm. I joined your gym and painted your rooms
and wore your clothes that didn't fit. We laughed and talked
forever but you only shared a little. Your sadness kept you
busy trying not to stop.

We made love make sense until it didn't. Until it lurked in
the pauses between breaths. The dents of time marking the
surface, drying like fruit. Curling around the soft and sweet
until completely unraveled. I want the time back just before
you left. You said you wouldn't be long. Your eye twitched
and you tried not to notice. I heard you moved back to the
city. I got married without you.

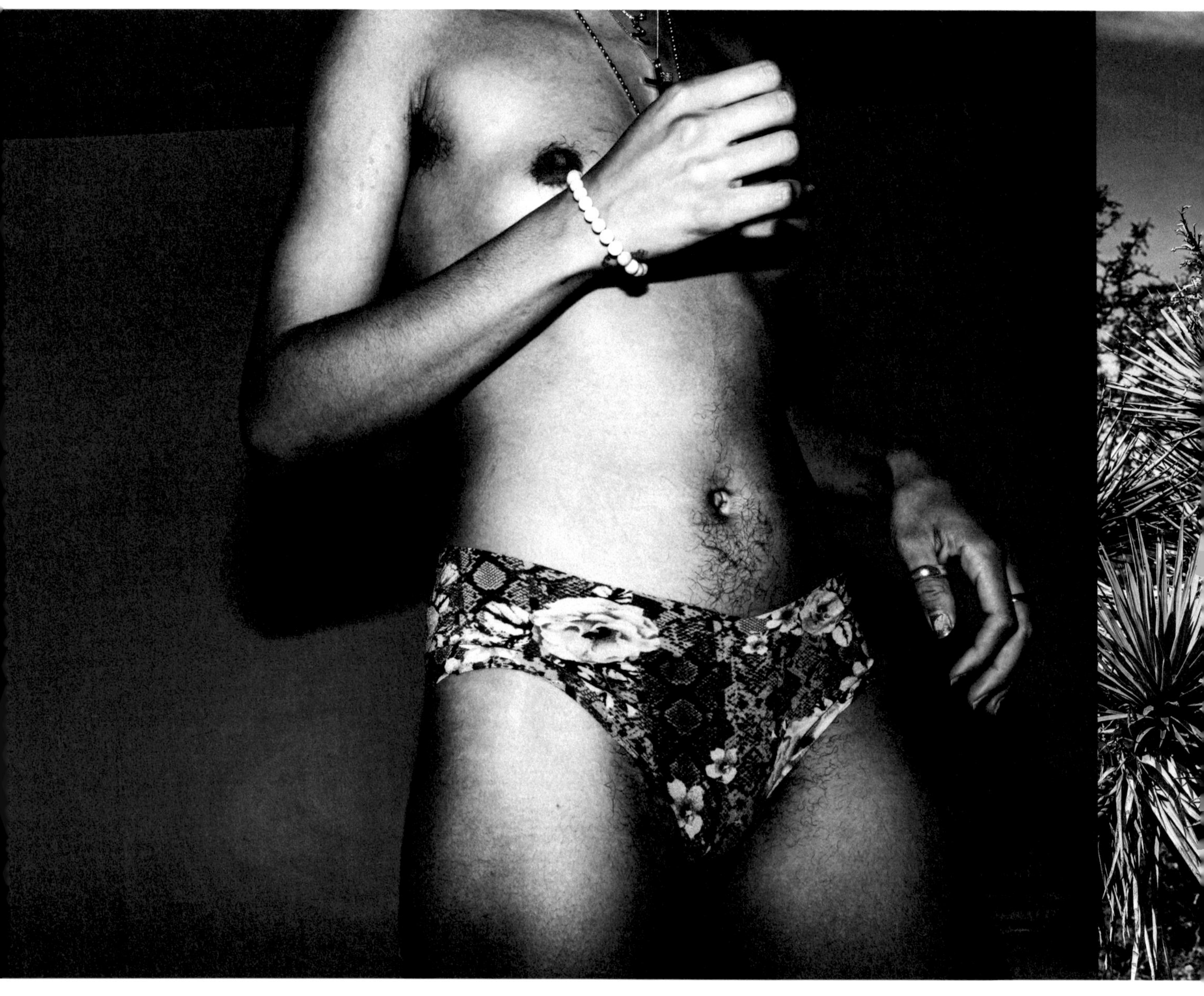

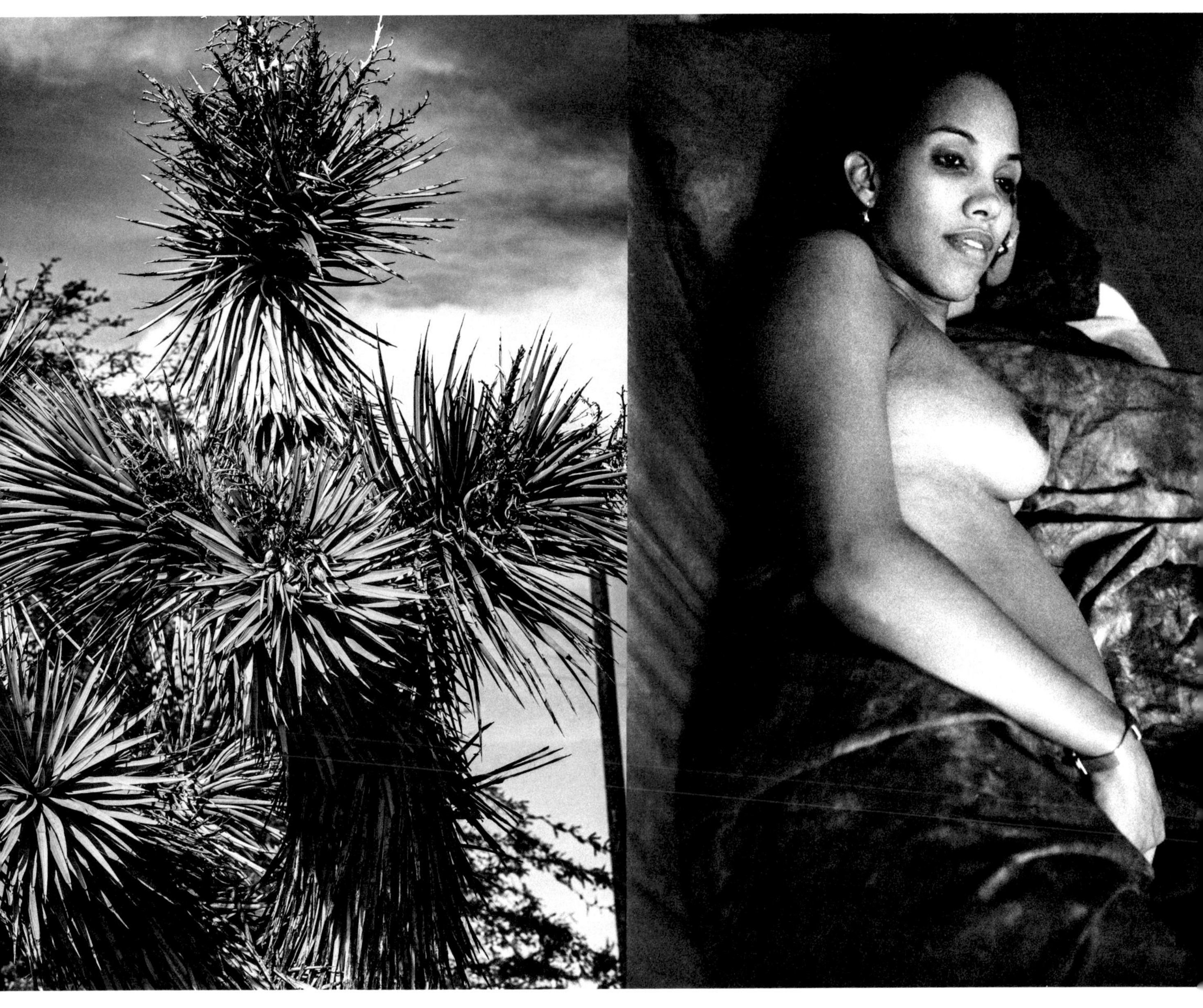

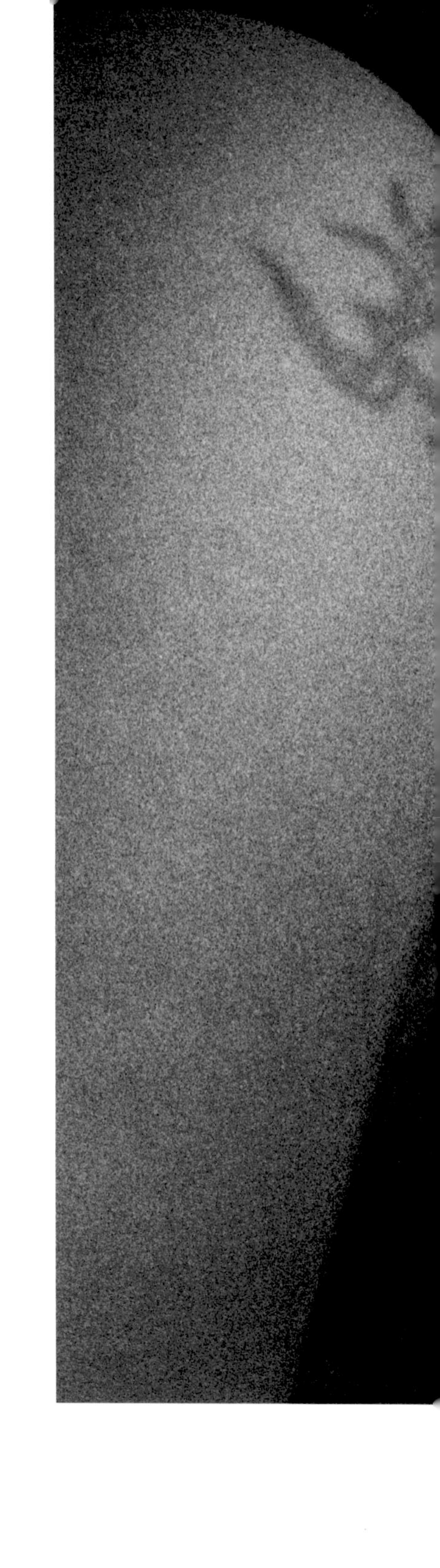

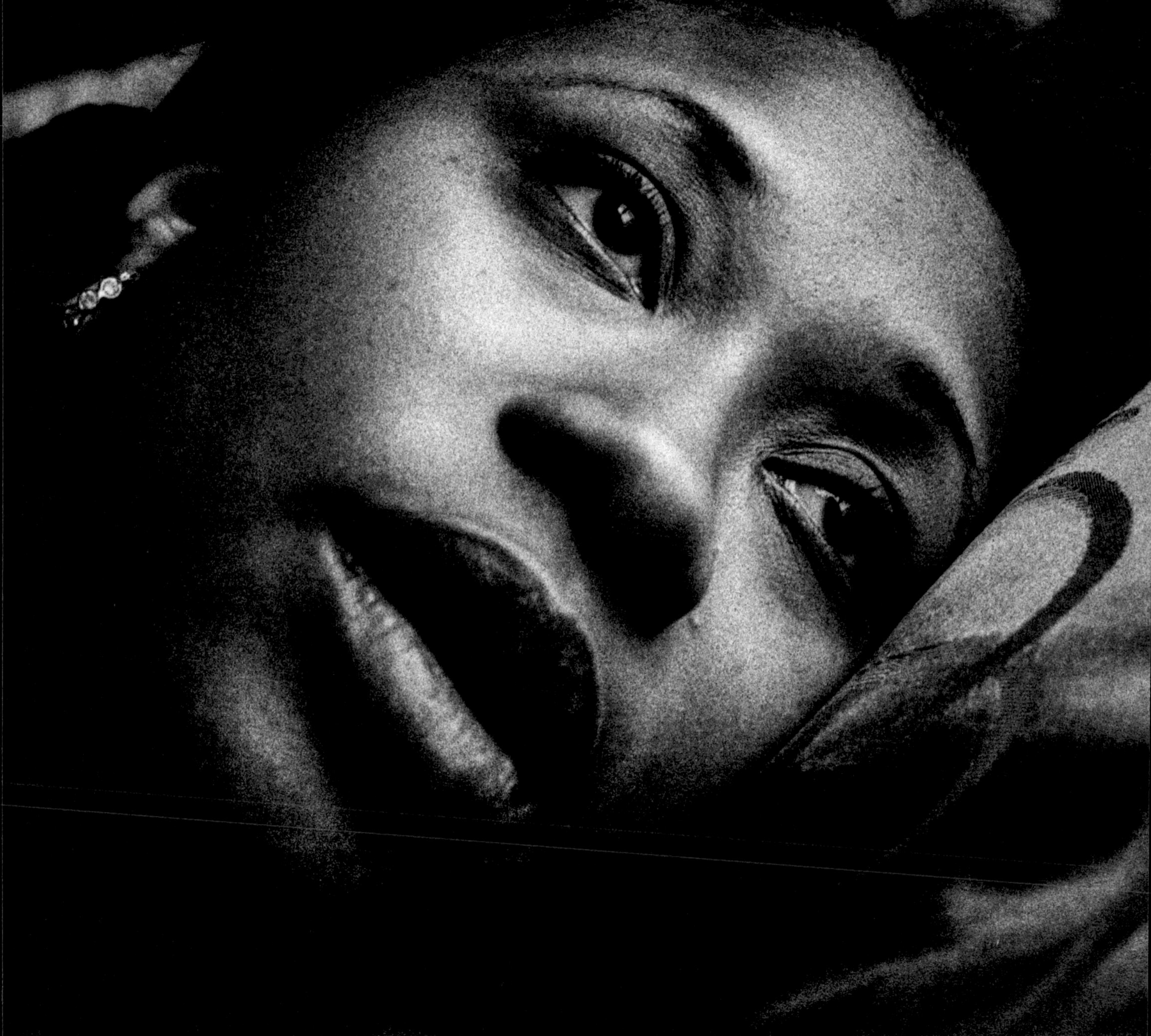

✛

We read your stories aloud as you lay still. Swaddled to avoid bedsores that were already winning. We passed the hope between us, careful not to let it fall. It was five weeks this time. Relentless moaning, beeping and clicking. Roaming dim hallways in the middle of the night. The smell of decay and sanitizer. "Take care of your mom for me," you said. I could feel the heat from your breath and the tickle of your mustache on my cheek. I said of course but wondered if I would.

I called your sister in Haiti and held the phone. You reminisced about the summer you crashed your boat on a lake in Maine. You managed a tiny hiccup of a laugh. The last one I remember. Some days I wasn't me at all. I was an actor that you liked. I played along because he seemed to make you happy. Whenever the nurses said I had to go, I hid my relief in case you saw my face. Mostly your eyes were closed or staring through me. I kissed your forehead and convinced myself I had done enough.

We had a meeting without you. The doctors minced their words. We listened intently bound to the grief that was coming to take us. They said, "It's time to consider a systematic withdrawal of treatment." The weight of this challenged our grip. We sat in the emptiness long after the doctors filed out nodding their goodbyes. The vending machine buzzed noisily. The pale gray linoleum floor tiles stared back. The hard edge of the metal chair dug into my hip as we perched forward holding each other bobbing gently as we wept. The sounds from the hallway of nurses directing orders that no longer mattered.

We shuffled slowly back to your room. Your body flinched while a nurse checked all your connections and tapped the machine's alarm, pulled his purple gloves off with a snap and bounced out of the room.

Mom rode in the ambulance and we waited in your apartment on the twelfth floor. The woman from hospice gave us paperwork and new words. She said you were "actively dying." I hoped you knew we were close. Days without names. Cheyne-Stoking, rapid and breathless, we waited with you until the rattle stopped.

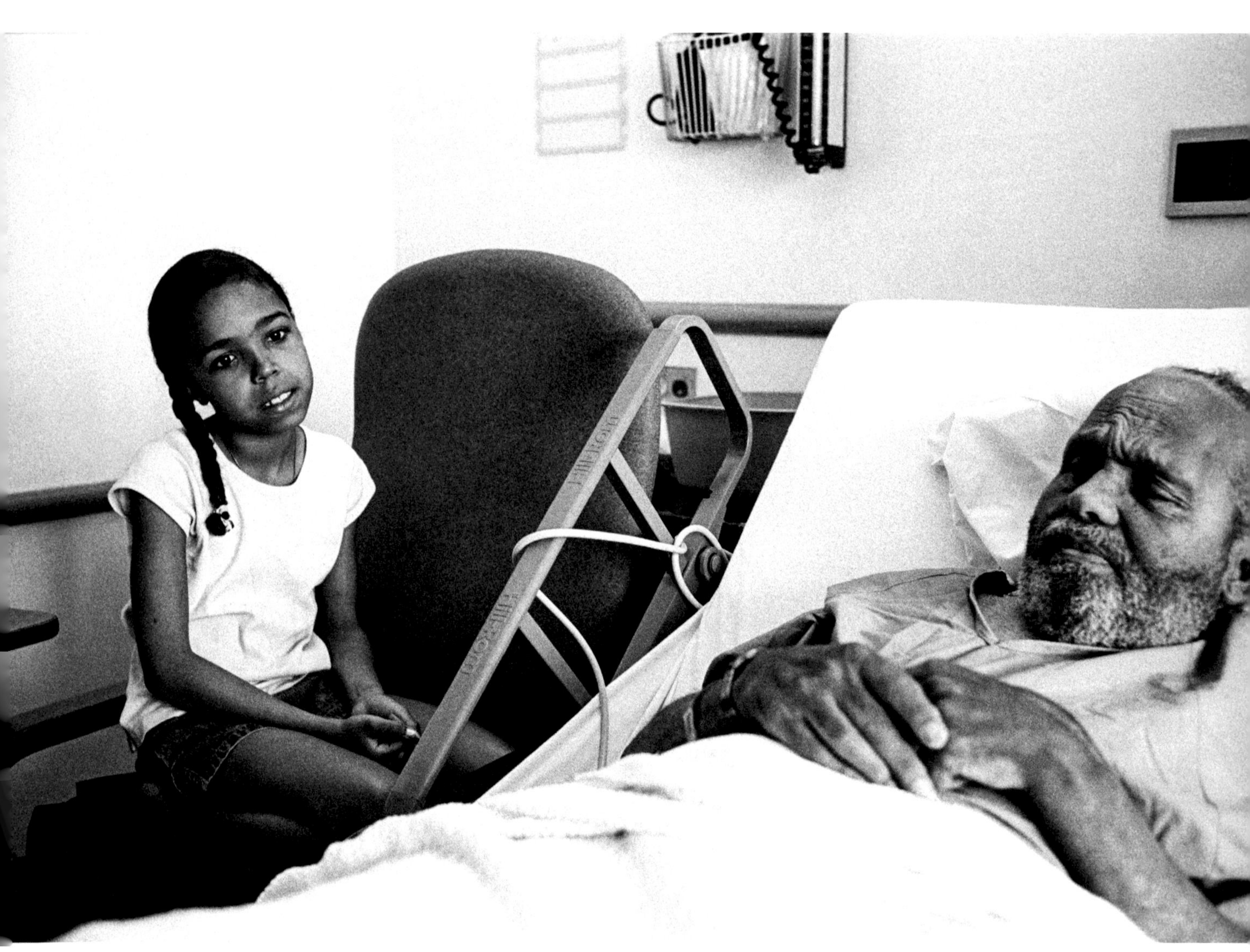

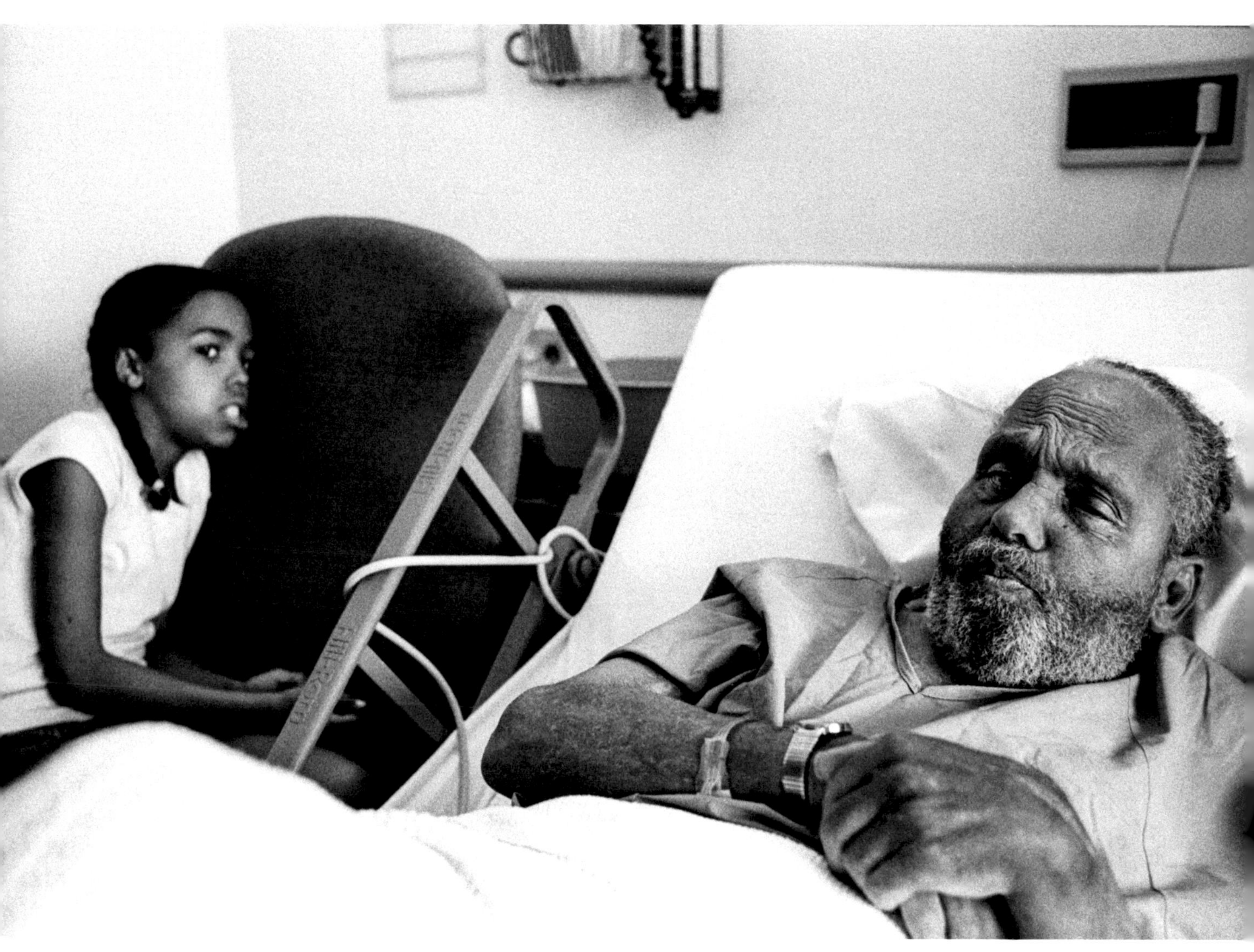

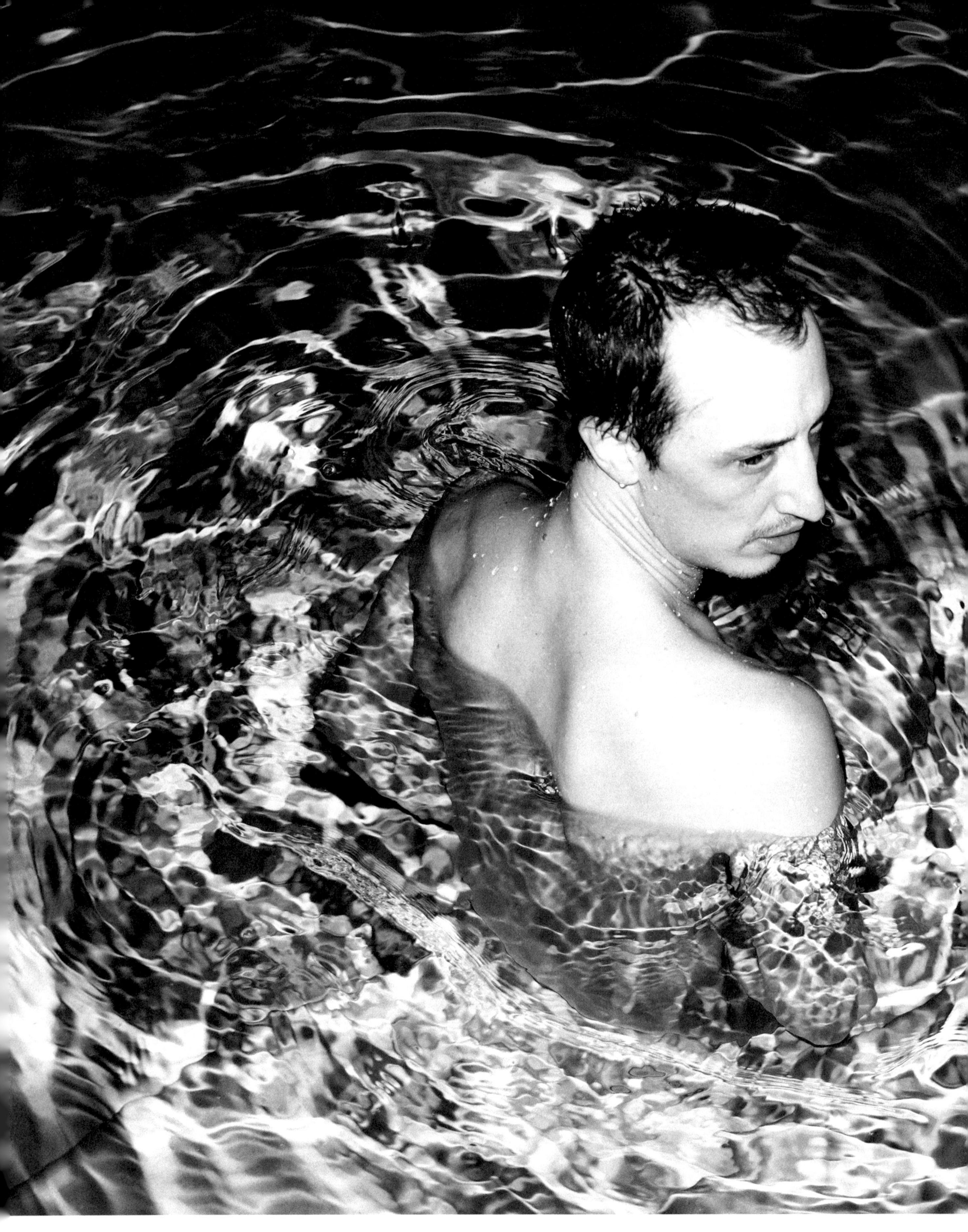

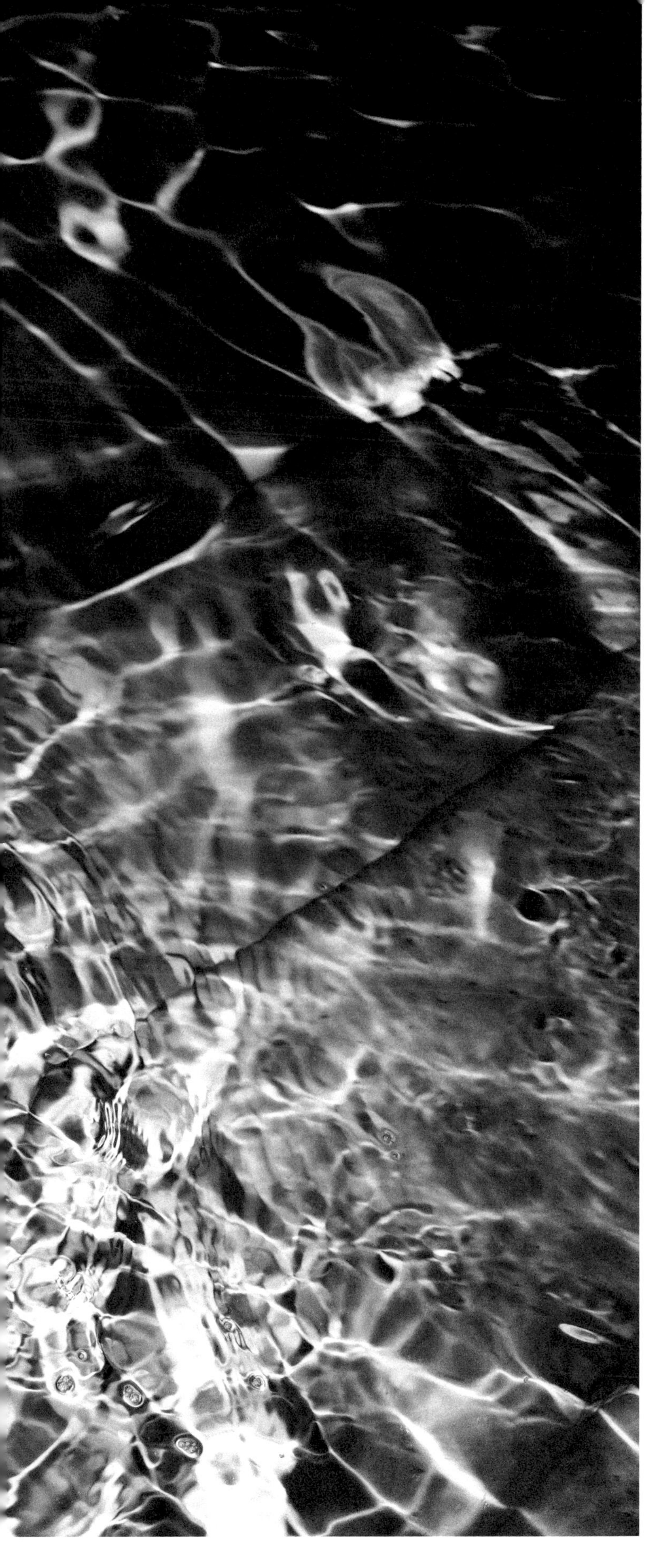

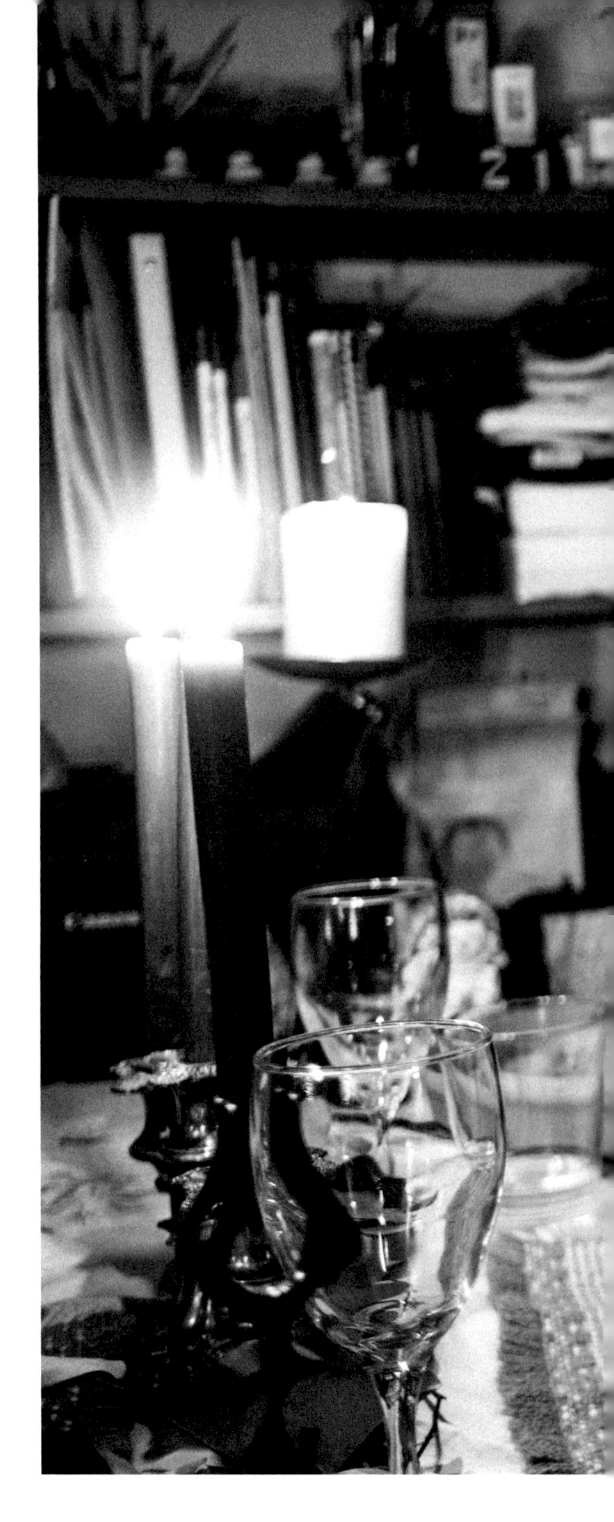

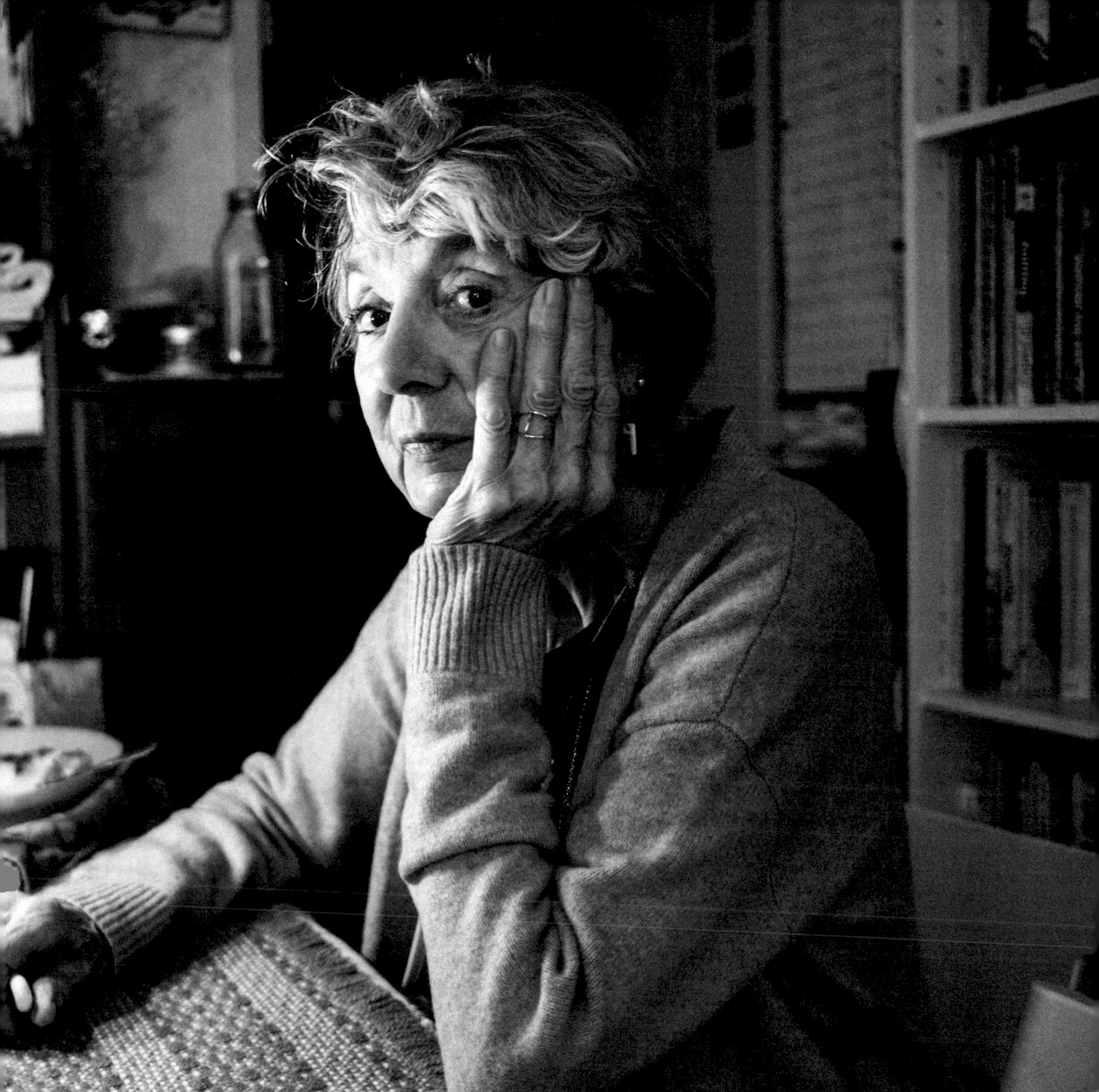

Fierce and complicated. Wretched and worn down to the bones and skin. I tuck you in. I help you breathe. You call me crying. I tell you to take deep breaths and suck the air loudly and exhale slowly and you follow. I say the things you would say when I was little standing at your bedside with my fears and bad dreams. Ducks on the pond. You laugh. I tell you I'm getting a flight in a few hours, not to worry, that I'll be there soon.

You've lost weight. Bound to a bed—linked to IVs, pumps and monitors tracking your rhythms, trying to break your racing heart. You acquiesce one day and not the next. The ride is bumpy, and I usually get off abruptly, but this time is different. No one had ever spoken a timeline into the room. Even with Dad, they never said until the very end. But now, two years. Like blinking. Lymphoma, Chemo. Leukemia, Chemo. The doctors are younger than I remember and sometimes I have to remind them to address you too. You get annoyed easily and your mood winds around the information like ivy growing over the windows. I later repeat most of what they say and sometimes you don't believe me.

Puttering and muttering, my sister says, when I ask how you are. I can hear you narrating while sorting and adding to your collections of lids, tops and bottoms that will never match or be used again. Saved and stacked, filling the cupboards. Time feels elusive and fleeting as though it doesn't belong to me anymore. Let it crack. Maybe the sound will wake me up. The lighting is harsh and the knives are dull. The silverware is stored in old tennis ball containers with the labels peeled off, arranged neatly in a glass cabinet. The sayings about hope and fortitude in colored pencil tacked above doorways gently mock us. There are notes and poems and embarrassing art projects framed and pinned anywhere there is space.

You asked me if it was your last Christmas and I said no, emphatically, unable to consider it myself. I watched my daughter as she watched me take care of you and wondered what she saw. In my expression. In how she knows me. Does she see the future. Like the flat rocks that skim the surface, it goes fast until we sink. The hurt and confusion of outgrowing one another is the syrup left at the bottom. Sticky and dark. Too thick to pour out.

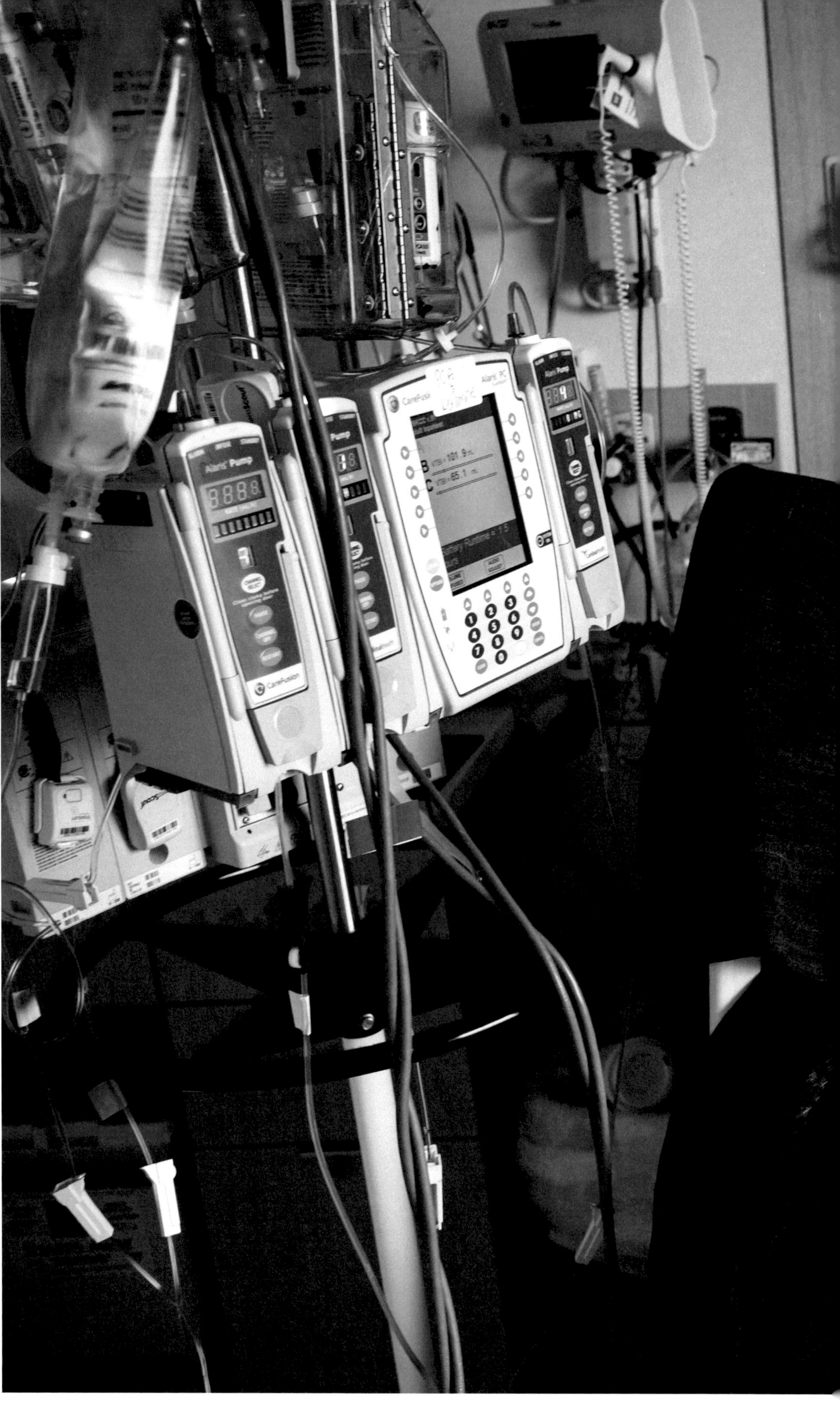

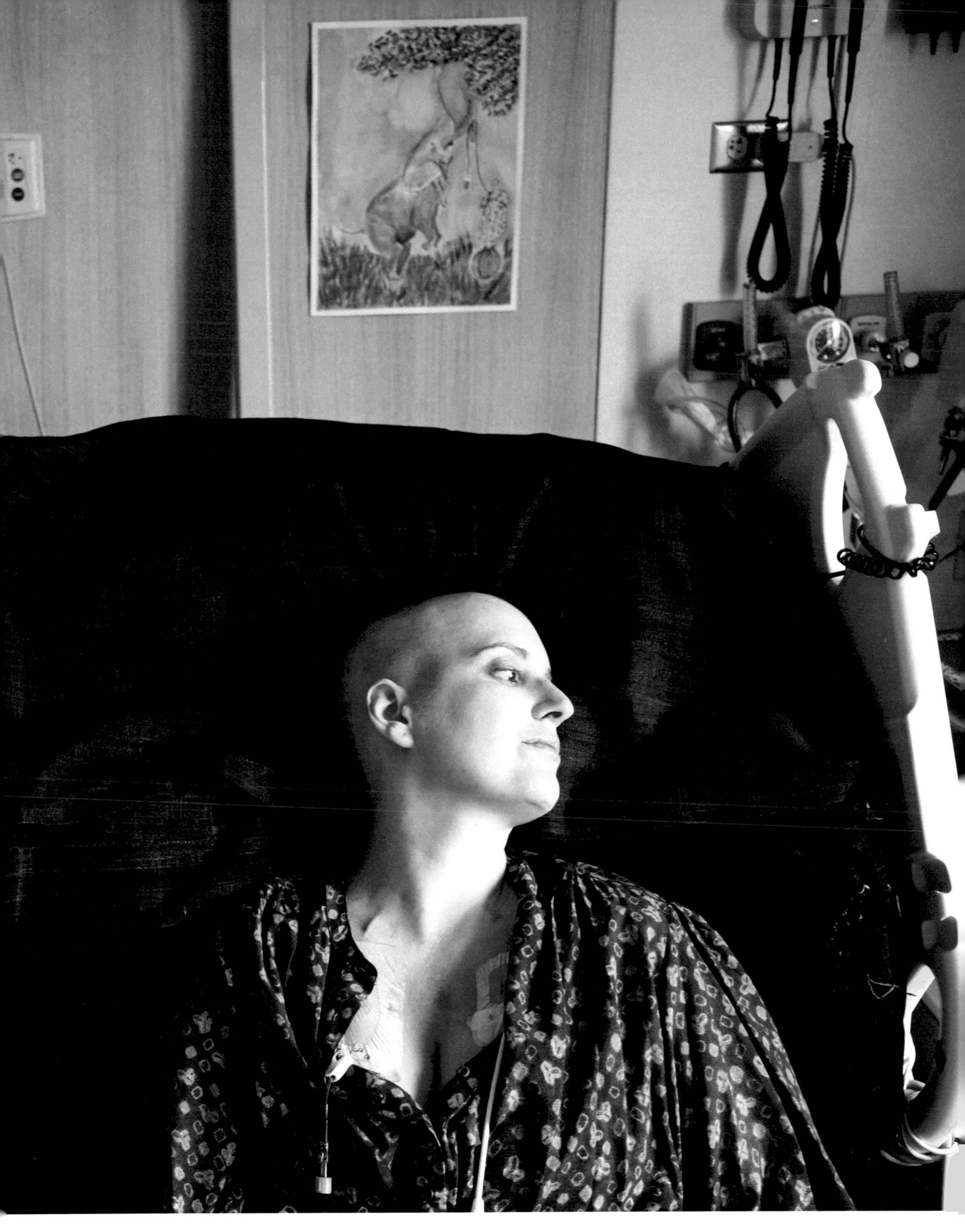

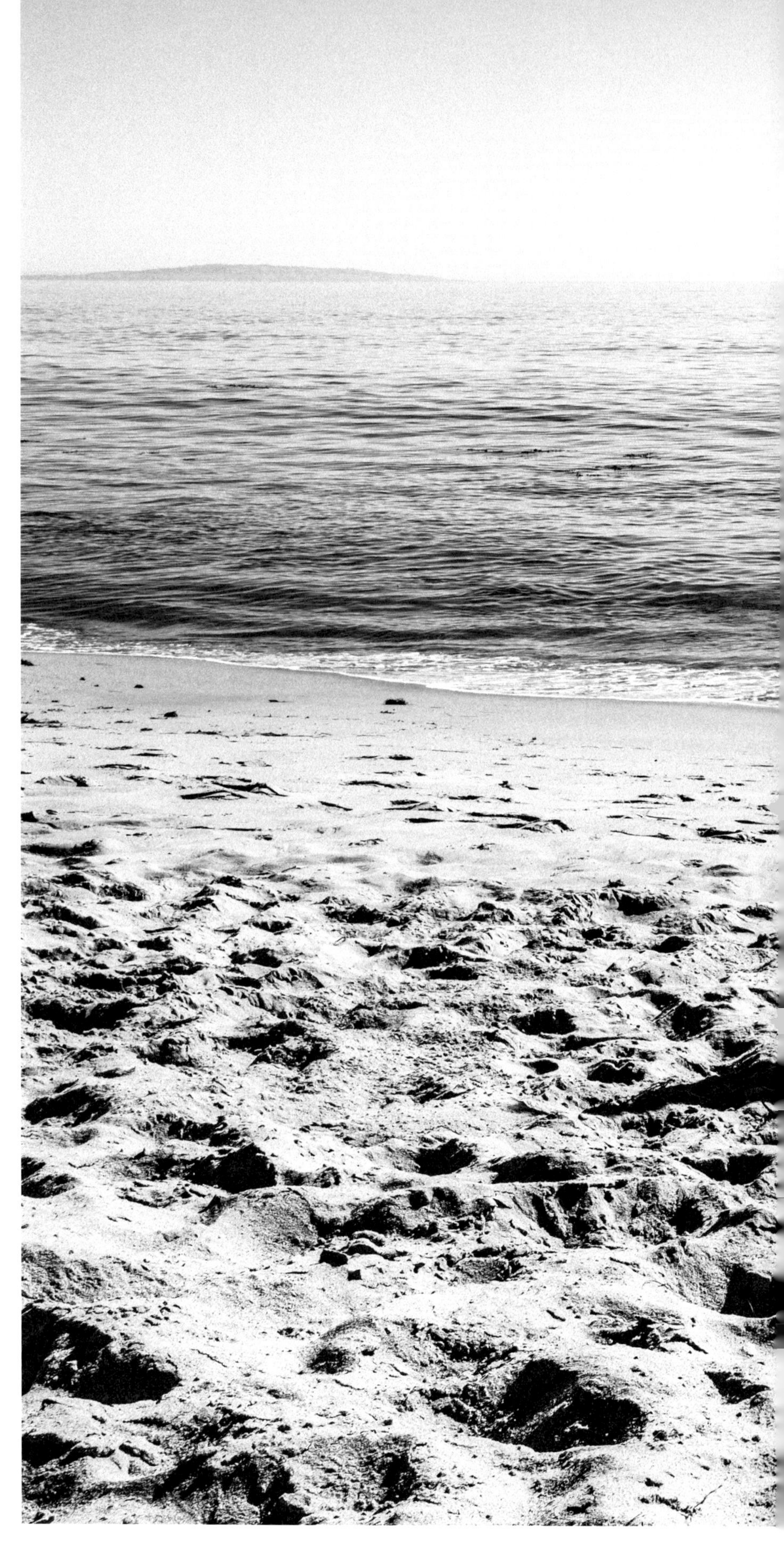

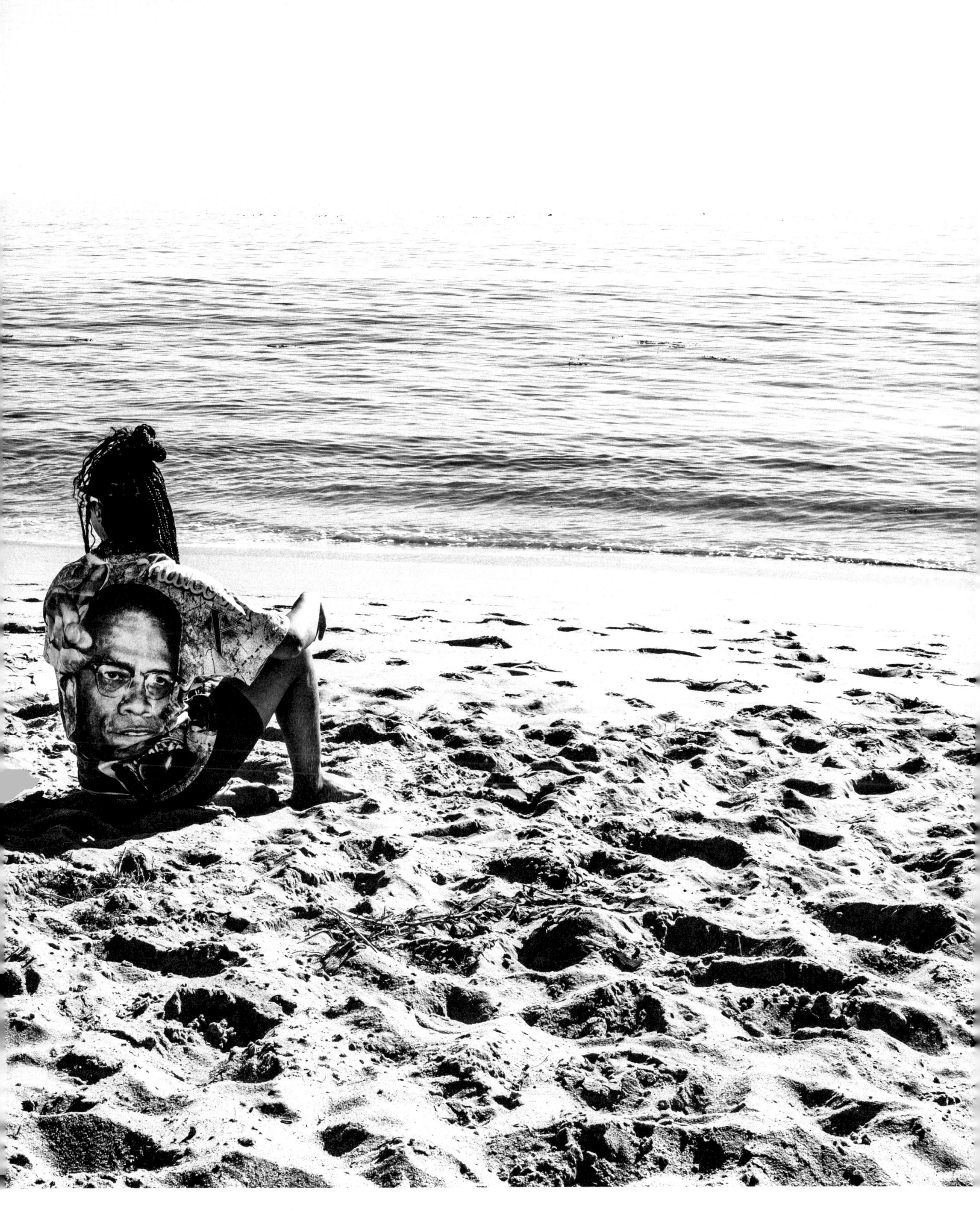

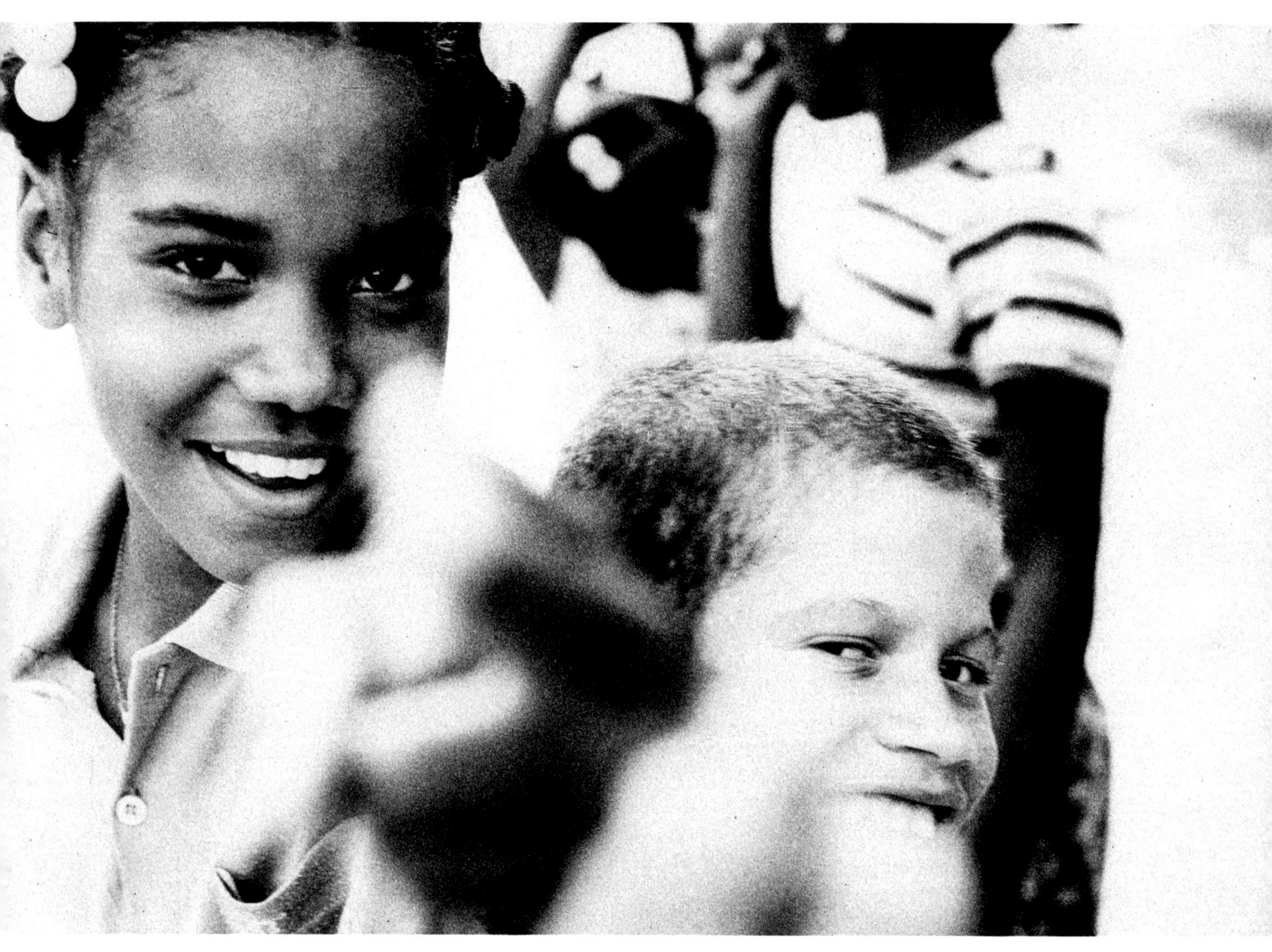

✜

I was the nanny at sixteen. She drank a lot. We ate cheese fondue
together after the kids were asleep and smoked cigarettes out
the back door. She was erratic and beautiful and light skinned like
me. Her shirts were always unbuttoned enough to see everything.
Two daughters, no dads. One was a cousin of mine somehow but
he was sick somewhere. She spit his name. She would come and go
but didn't seem to have a job. Frantic and yelling and laughing.
Her favorite daughter, the youngest, was pale and blonde.
The older one had dark brown skin and tired eyes. Some days I
thought I was there to love her because her mother couldn't. I read
them stories in the top bunk. Everything felt unsteady and
unreasonable. I remember it in pieces, like right before you wake
up. I left before she wanted me to. I found out years later that she
died of AIDS.

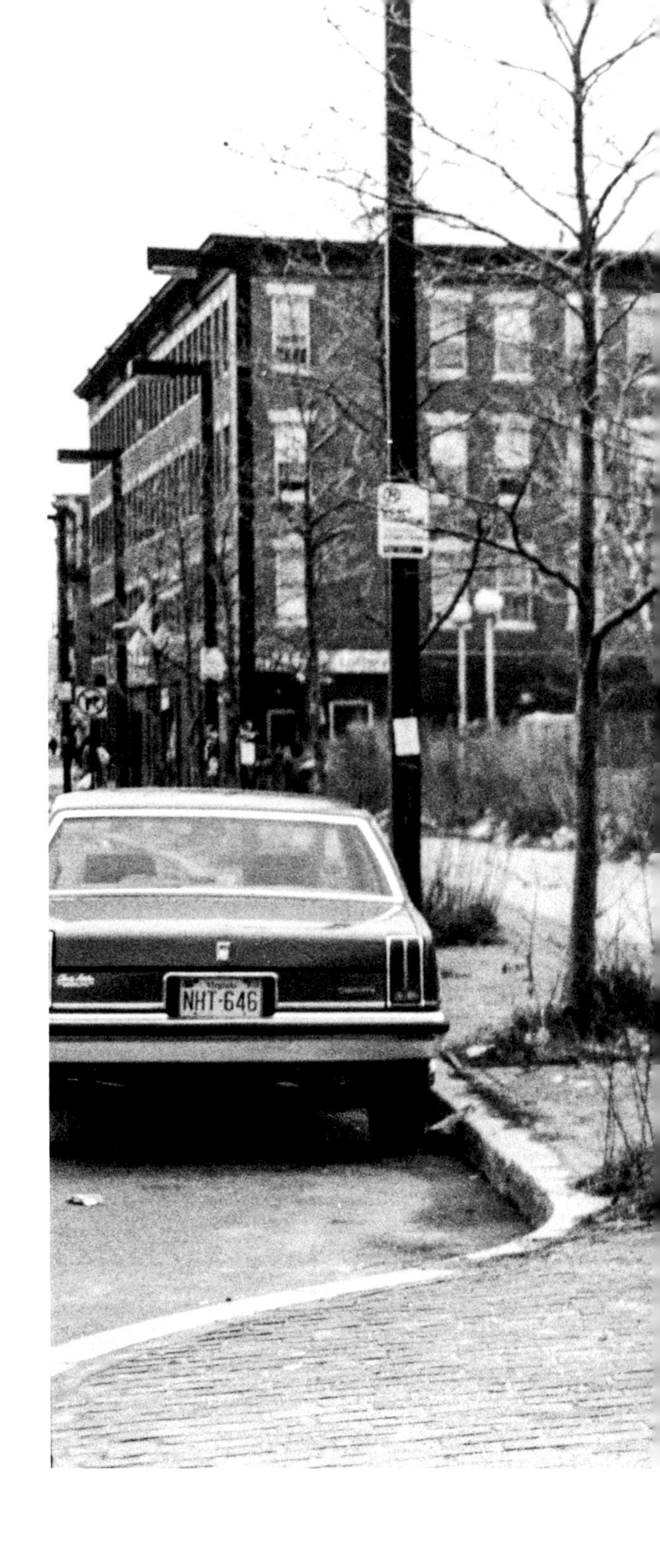

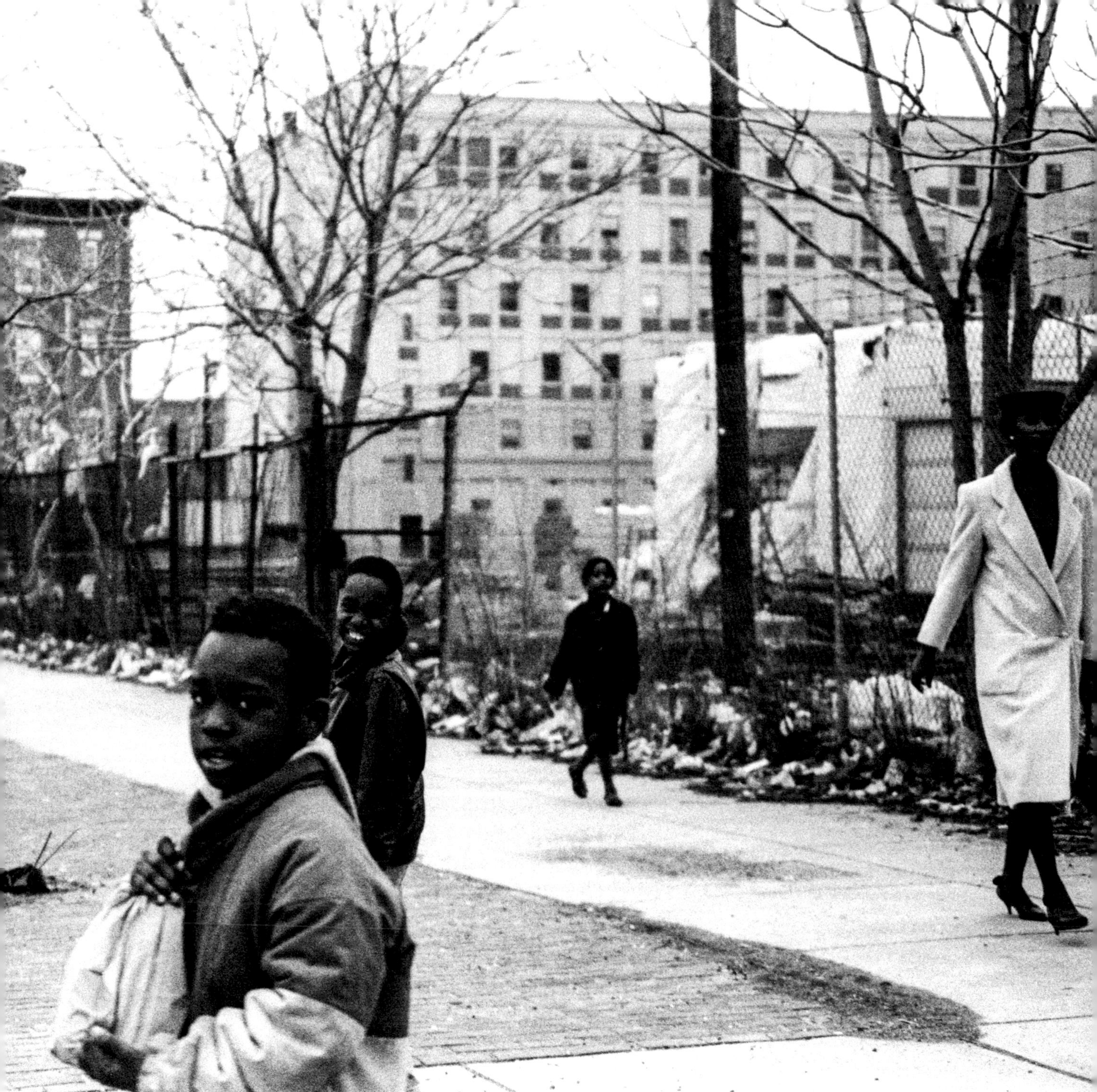

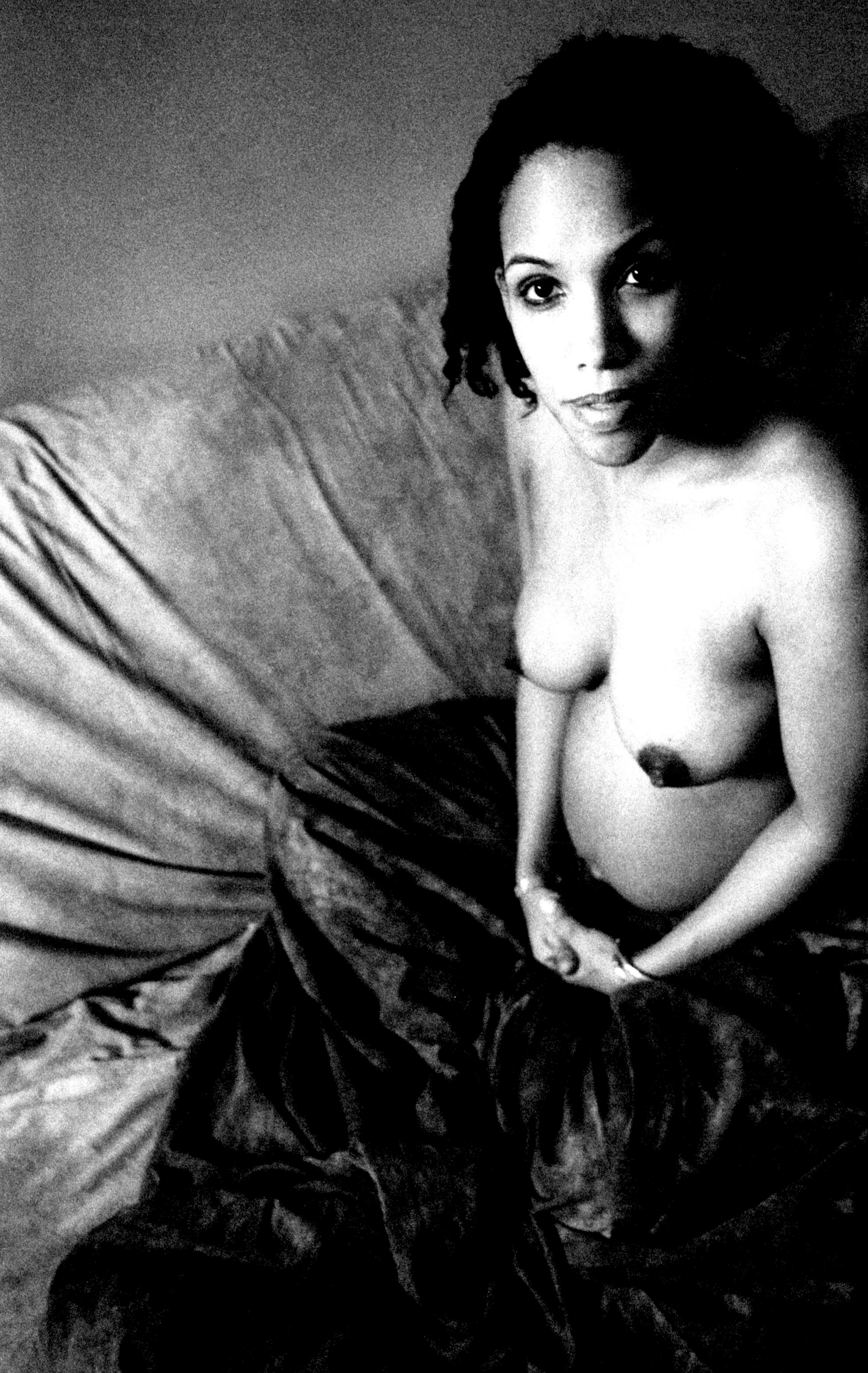

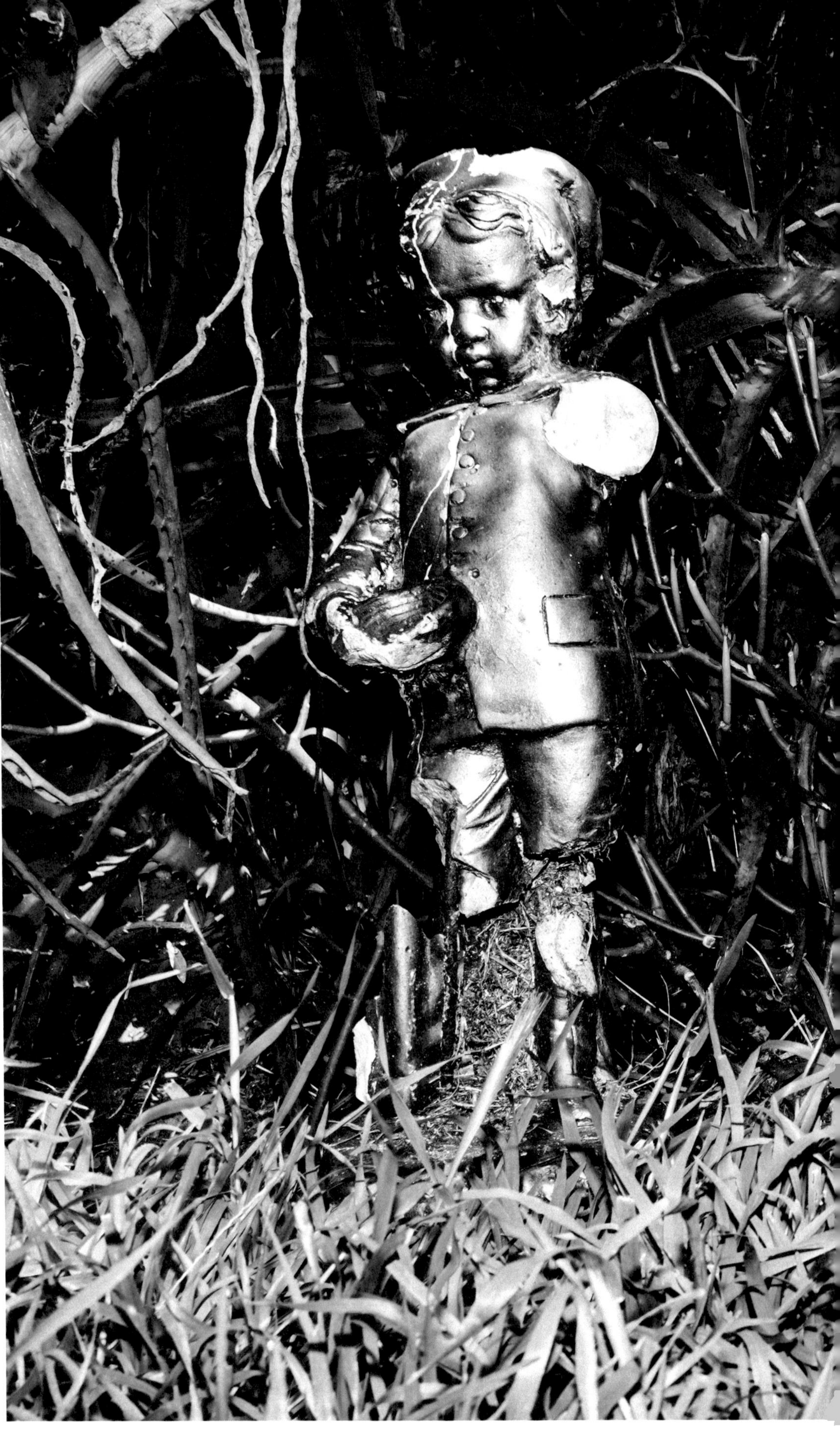

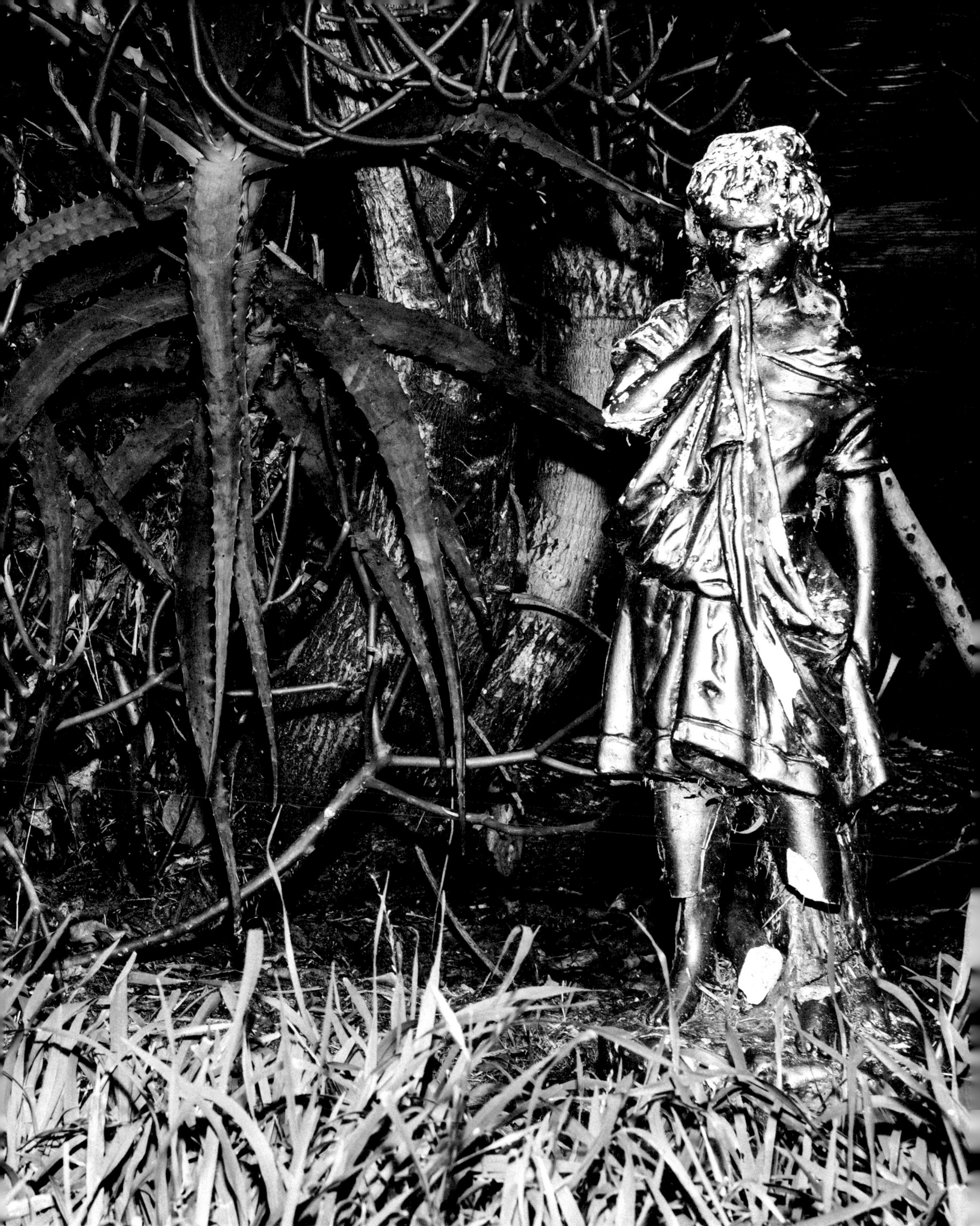

You were older but not by much; soon they had to ask. You loved me and hated me and I could feel both. The redness of anger in your cheeks, burning lines into mine from your eight-year-old nails. Lashing out like a cat who's had enough. You had plans and schemes and told me as much as you wanted to. It took so many years of asking to know you would never let me in. I had taken something from you that I couldn't give back.

I told you I loved him. You tried anyway. Letting your shirt fall off your shoulder and laughing at nothing. He was greedy and liked secrets more than he loved me. Your lies were strong — melting only a little under the heat. It happened in my mind before it actually did. You used your magic to smile and told me you weren't coming home. It swallowed me whole until I couldn't see. I followed him to New Orleans and tried to stitch back a dream that I couldn't remember. You visited me and said I should leave him. I packed in the middle of the night. He used his fists instead.

Our closeness is a burden that neither can lift. Our pretending has found us again. Your grin drips down one side outlined in a jagged red stain of last night's lipstick. Our memories are tangled and choke the truth. Tightly wound in a stubborn trap. We seem to be getting younger and going back for more.

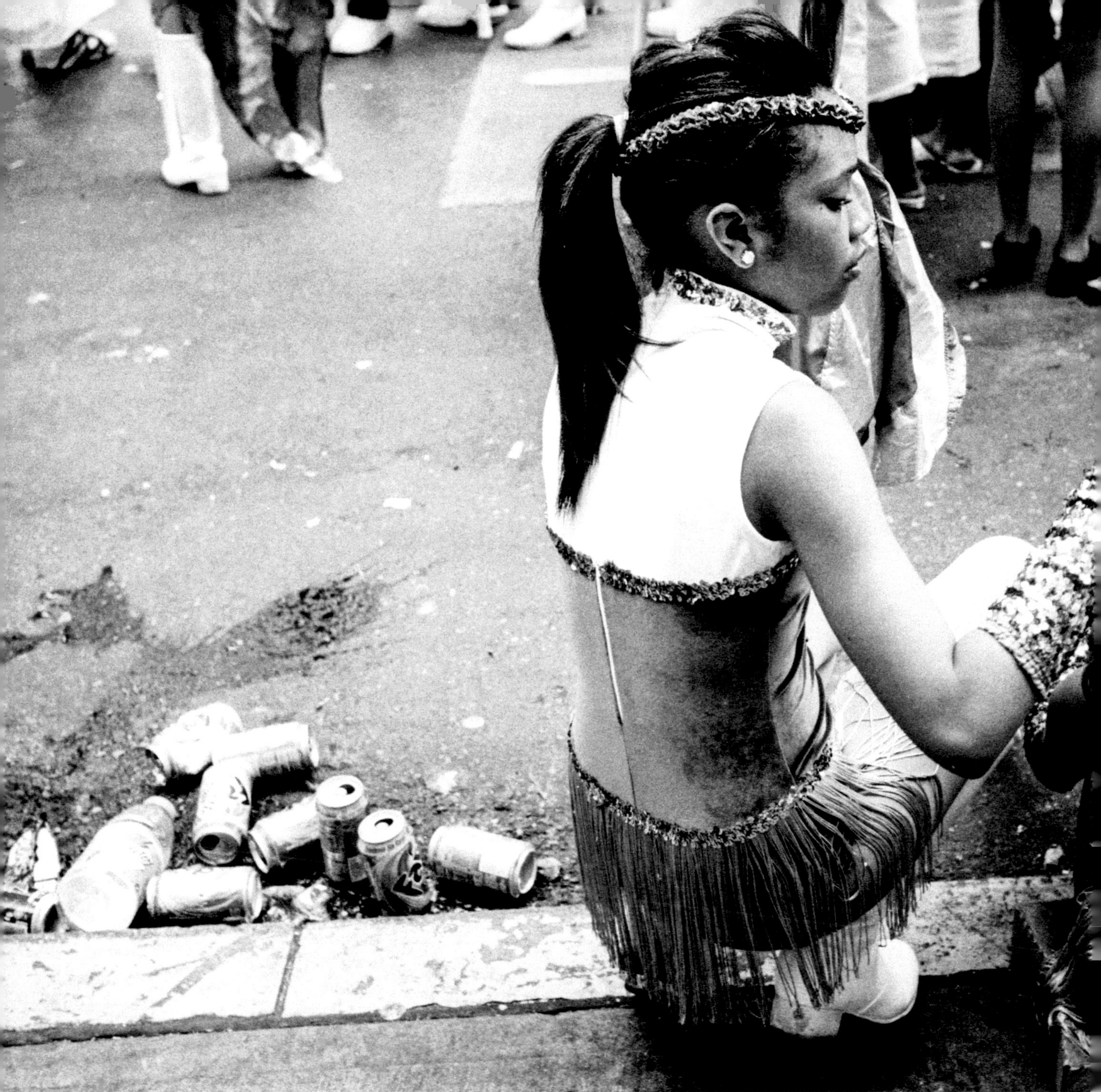

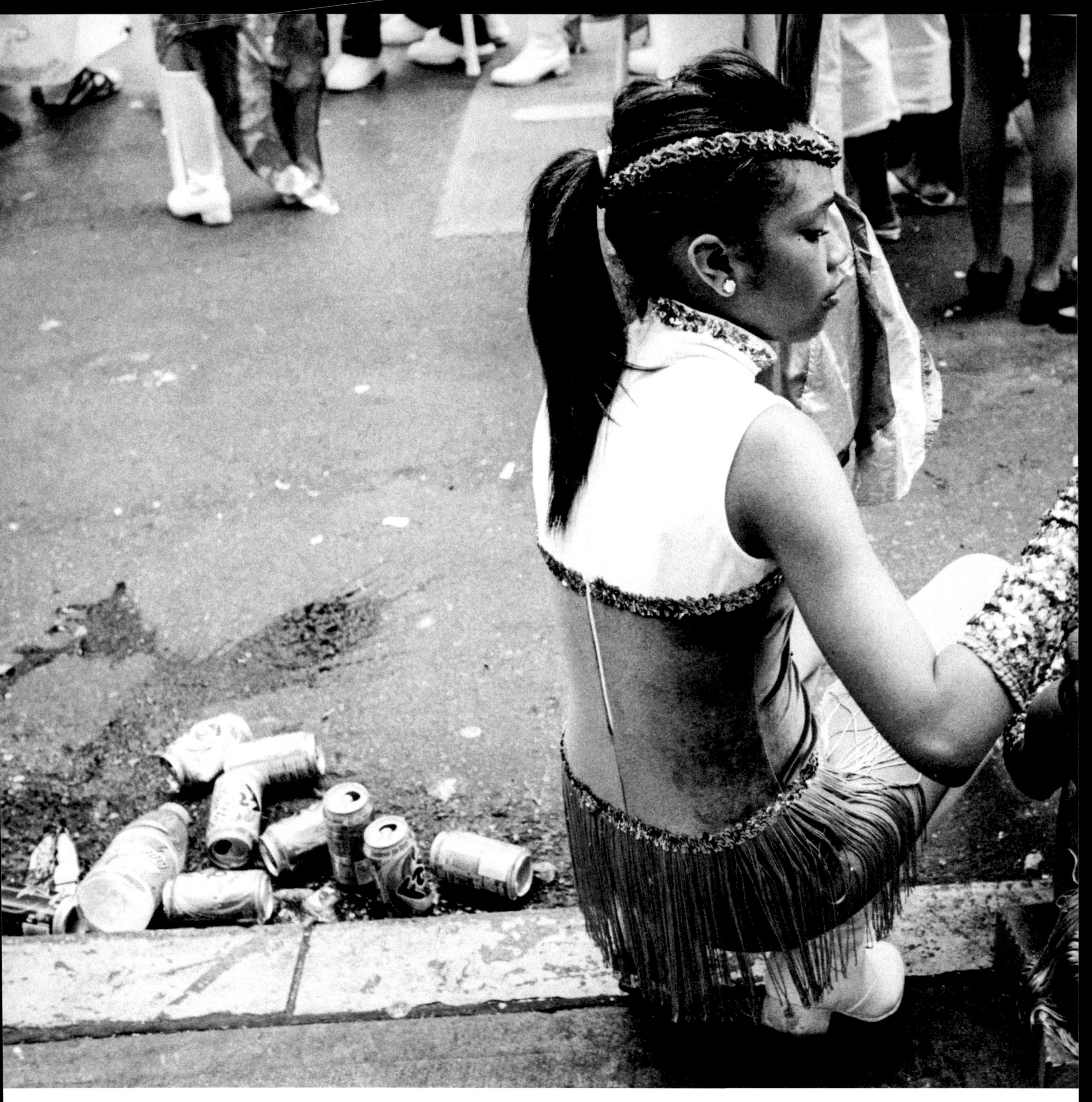

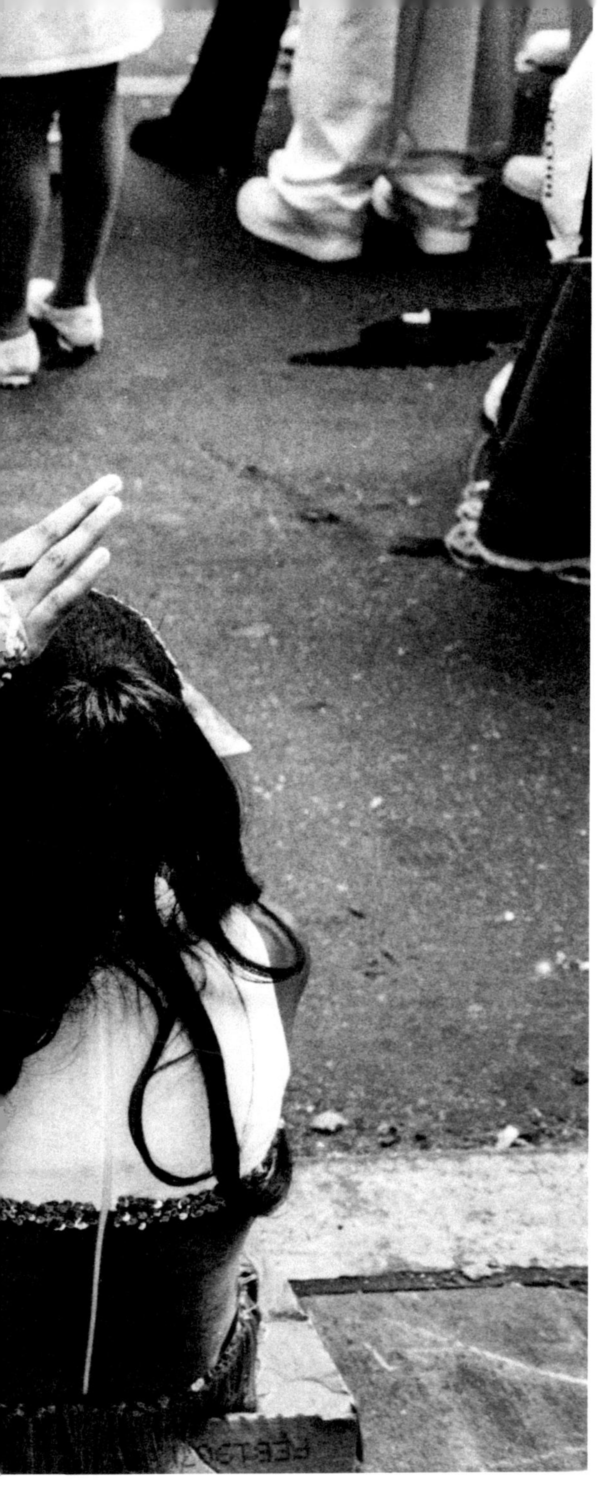

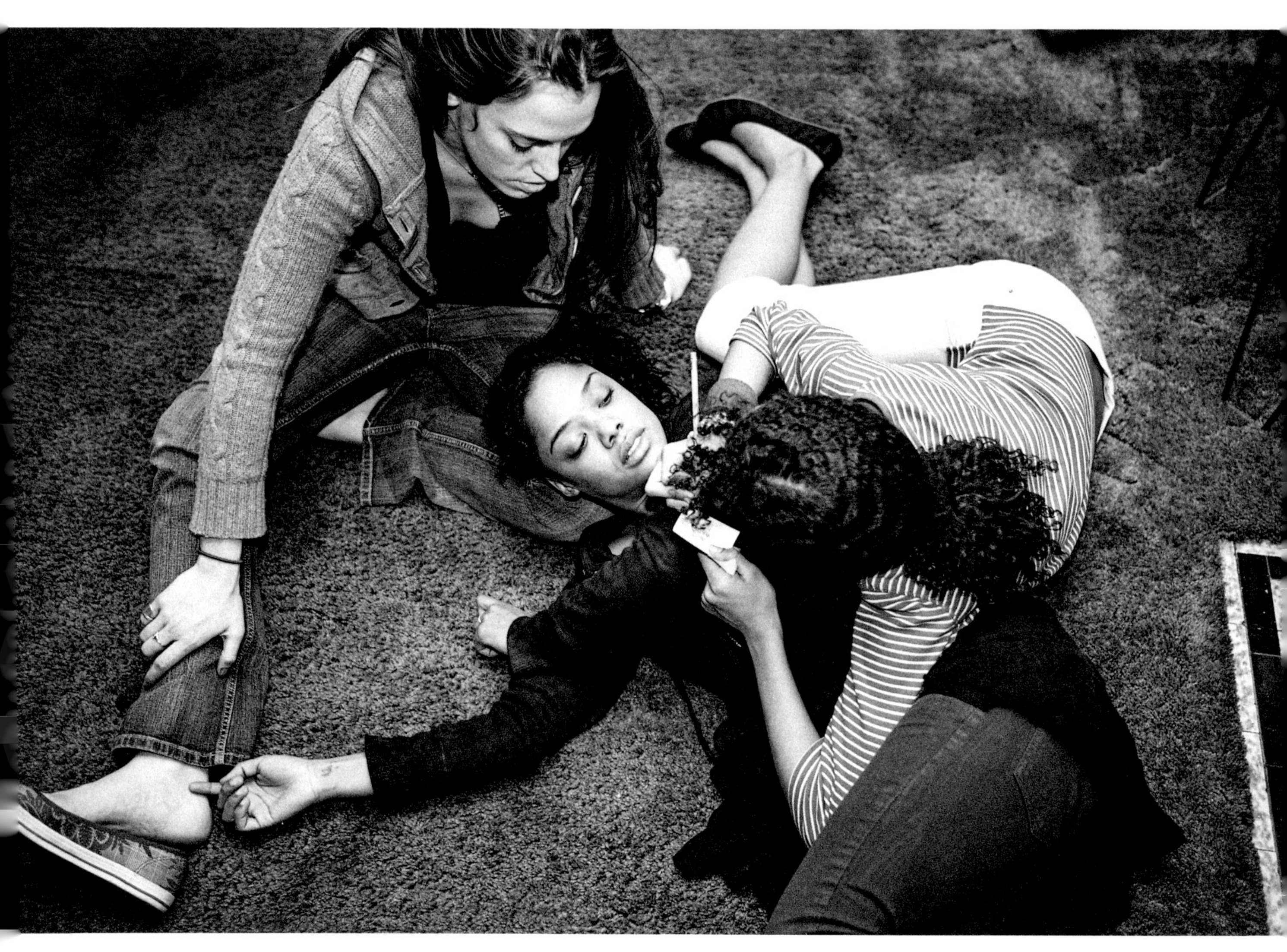

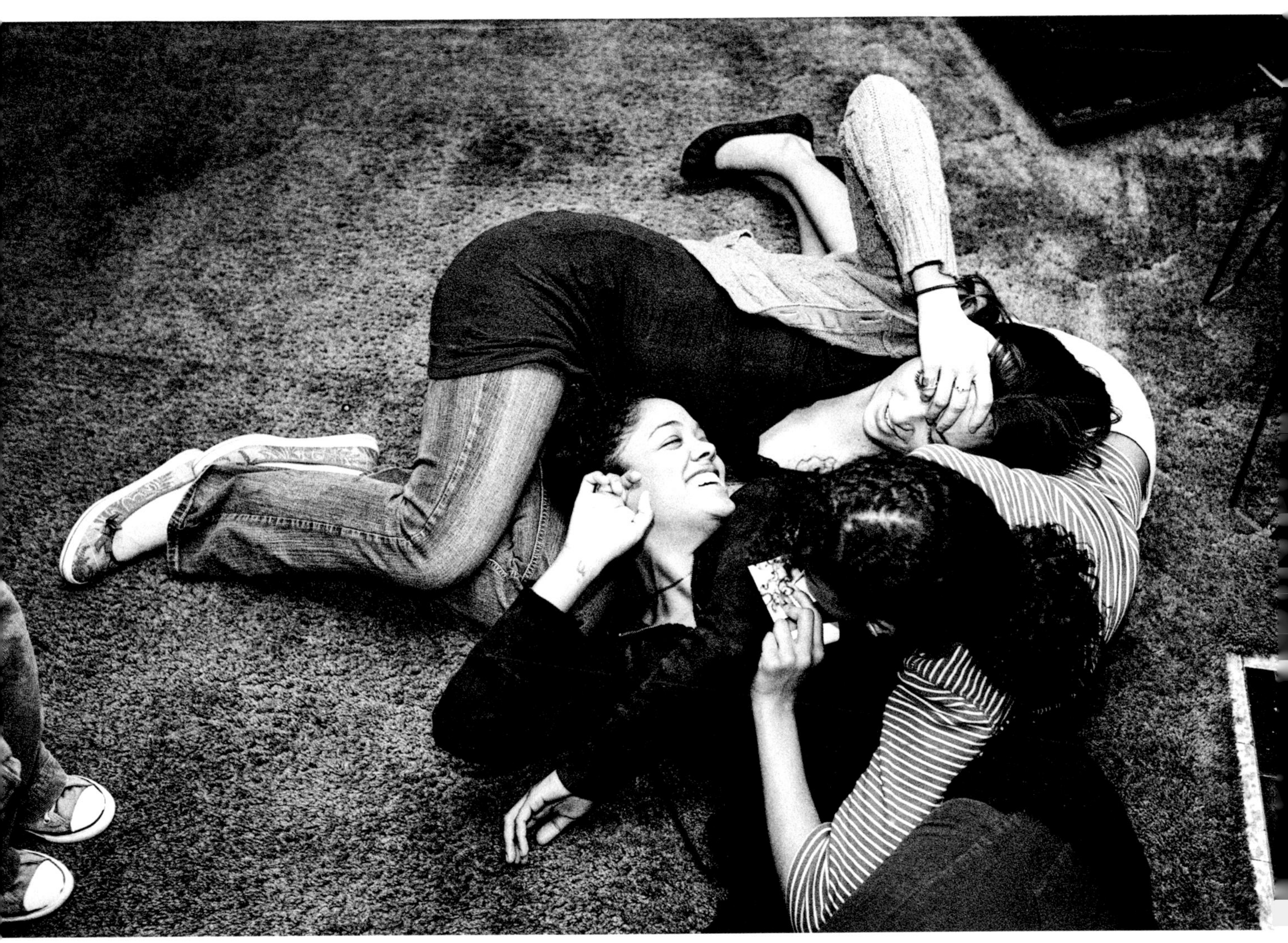

Time oozes slowly like old glass, rippled and sagging at the sill.
The light is sharp like it wants to fight, searing everything
beneath. I wanted to find you but you left and forgot to tell me.
I looked everywhere and only found your clothes. Write from
your scars, not your wounds, they say. What if they never heal?

We talked in circles and you watched me weep. My body knew.
It shook, draining the sadness. My mind tried to make sense
of the lies but there's too many, and it doesn't matter.

Let the light fade. Let the color of the leaves darken—black
edged, drooping in wait. Let the sky molt from crimson to lilac.
Let all the vibrancy of day leave until nothing below is
distinguishable. Only the colorless glow holding the space above.

One of our dogs likes all the doors open when the fireworks
start. She shuffles from room to room looking for refuge. I wish
I could tell her it's just for fun.

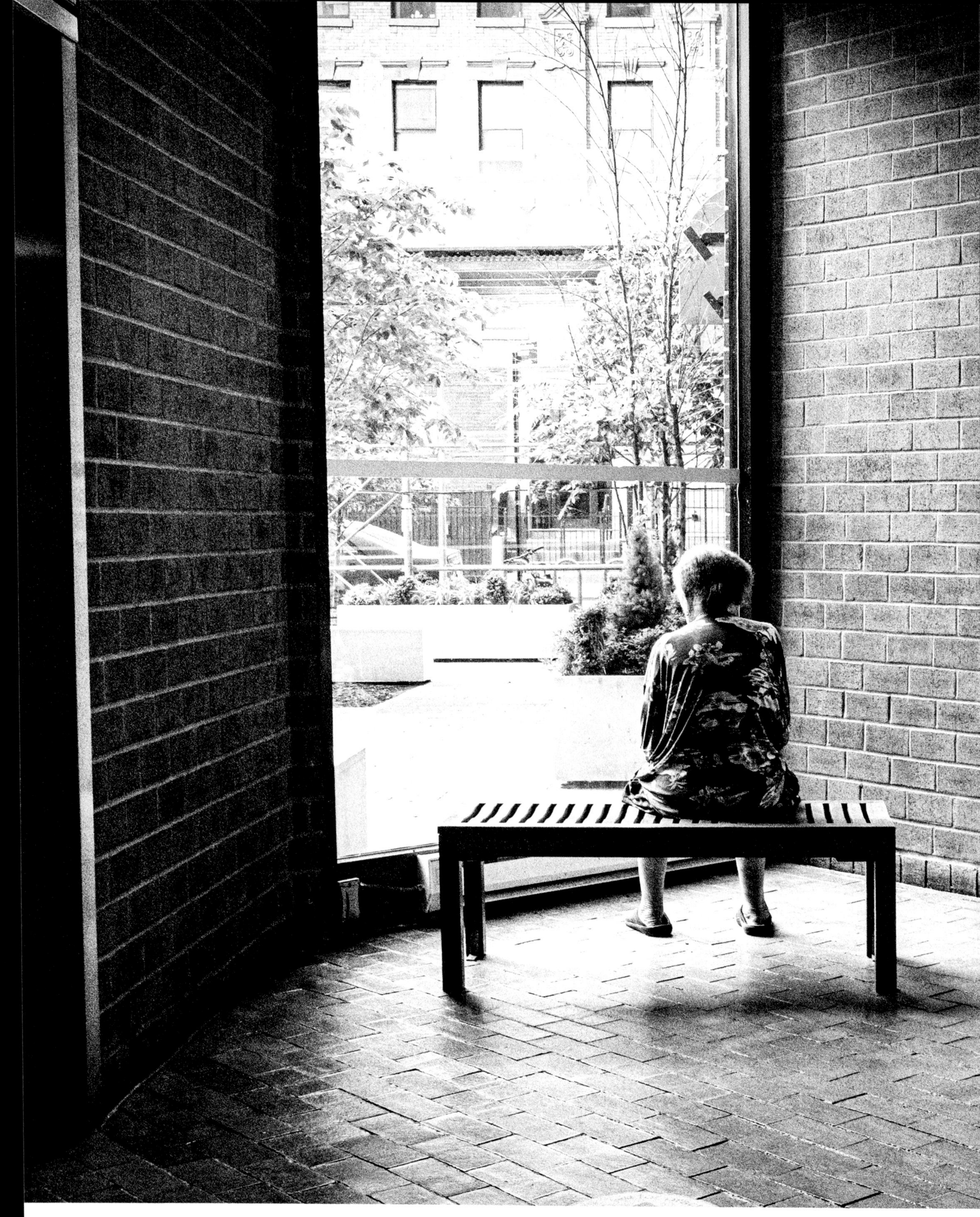

✝✝

I forgot to win. I placed my sword back in its case and reminded
myself of your age and why we were there. The infusion room
was cold. I pulled your cardigan around your shoulders. Thin pale
skin puddled over jagged bones and sharp rocks. You patted
my hand. I waited to withdraw and sat in the plastic bucket
chair and pretended to read. You repeated how the medicine will
make your pee orange. The nurse counted the drops in the IV
and locked the line. I nodded and tucked my disdain behind my
ear. Your knitted cap drooped down to the brim of your glasses.
Childlike and swimming in oversized clothes. I unpacked the
snacks we made the night before and handed you thin pieces of
sliced apple.

I felt my gaze from above with a steady hand. I motioned
through each task. Careful. Dutiful. Evaporating. From the space
in between, I crawled around looking for myself. Regret clinging
to my chest. Relief finding my breath.

I wheeled you outside and helped you sit on the concrete bench.
I worried the frozen cement would burn through your clothes.
I left you hunched and hailed a cab. My arm wrapped around your
back and the motion tipped your head to rest on my shoulder.

Your eyes seemed even larger without lashes or brows. Frameless
and smooth. I tried to dig out my softness but it was stuck under
something heavy. So I focused on making the right foods taste
good and tidying the clutter.

The curtains gave up and pooled at the hem. Faded and brittle,
ready to melt. The sofa wrinkled from memory. A sticky crust
baked on every surface. The paint flaking off like giant ash.
A discarded rind peeling back to good bones. Back to a beginning.
The scarred veins of an addict crawling up the walls. The keloid
bumps of repair starting to lift. The beauty of decay held us close.

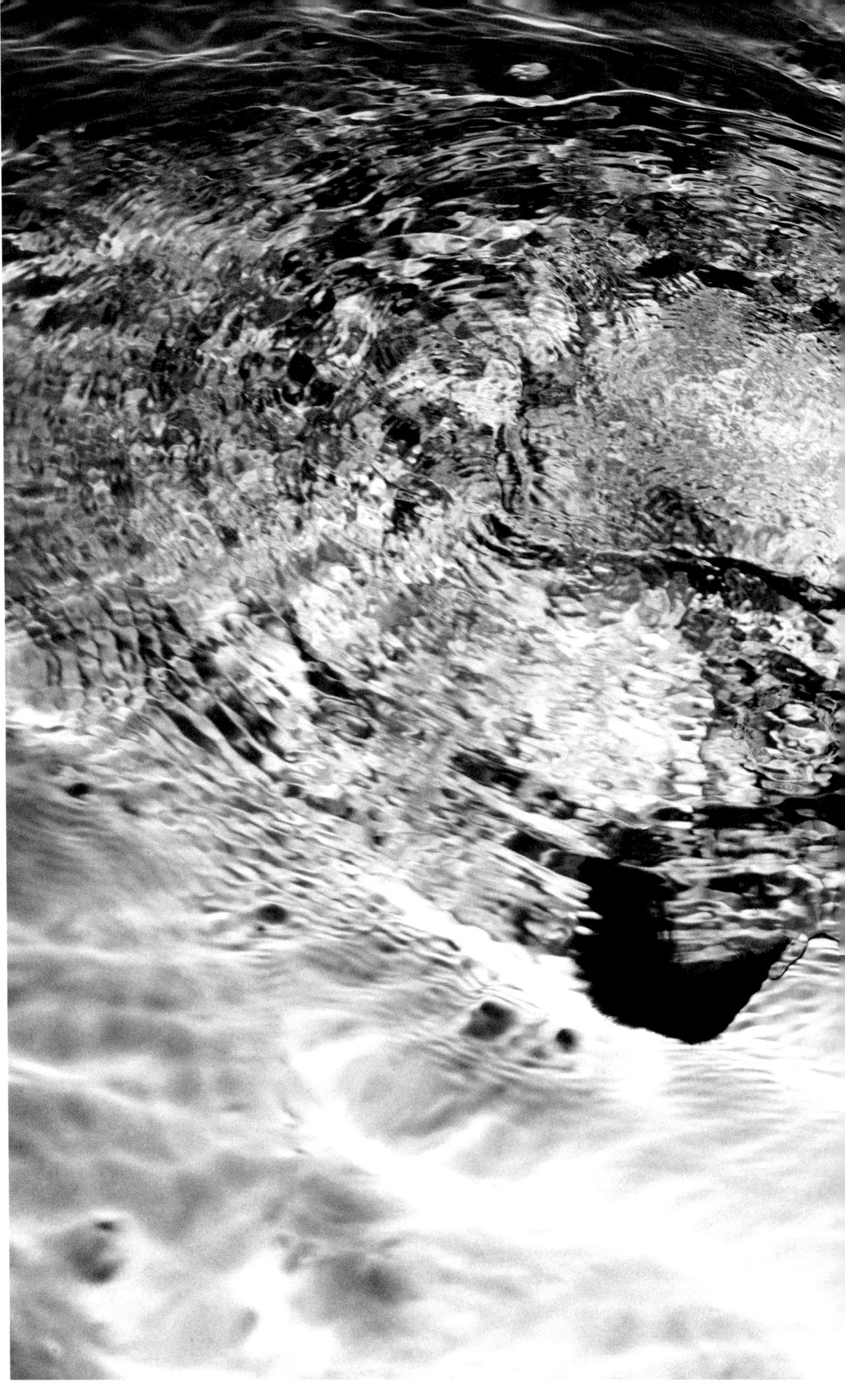

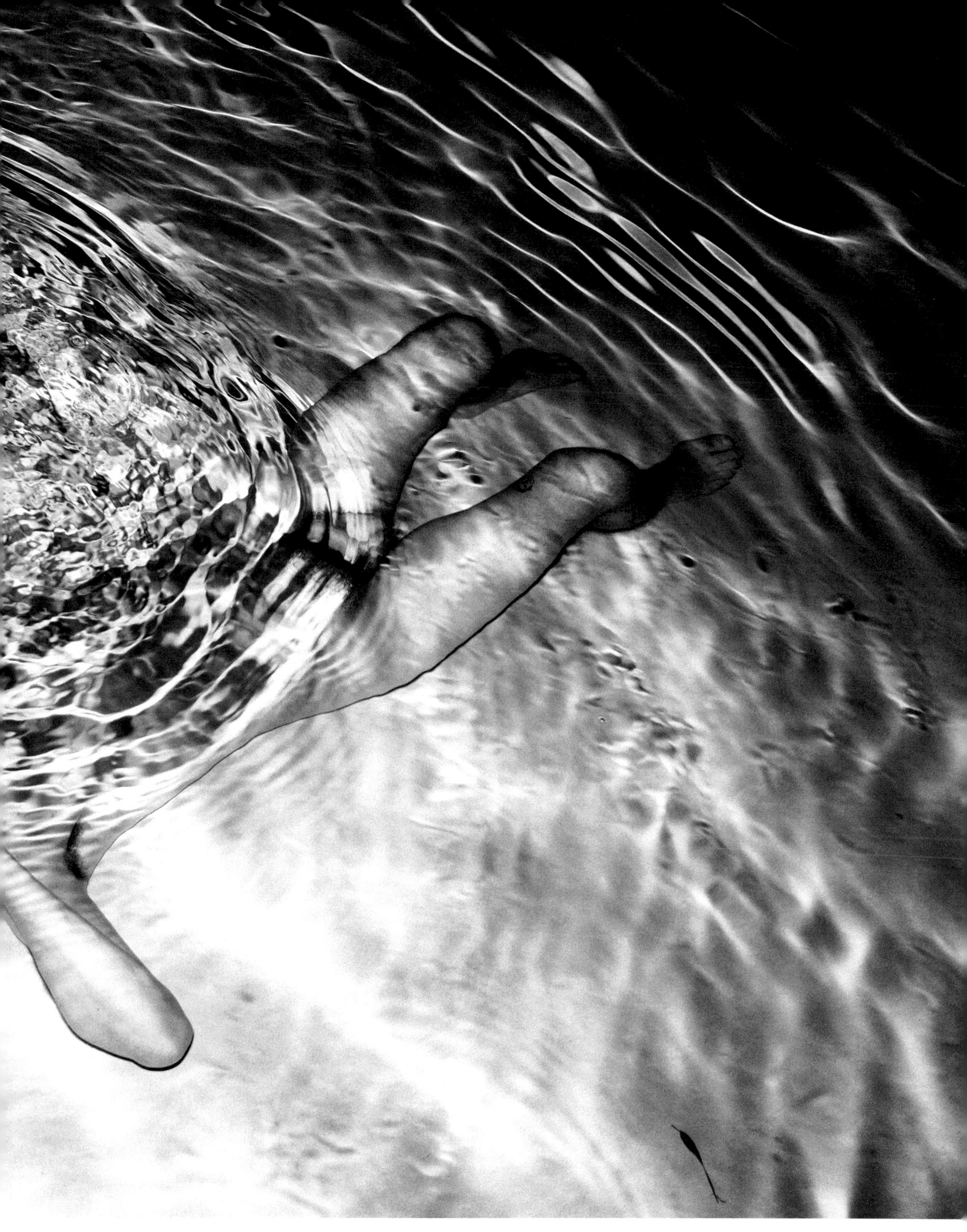

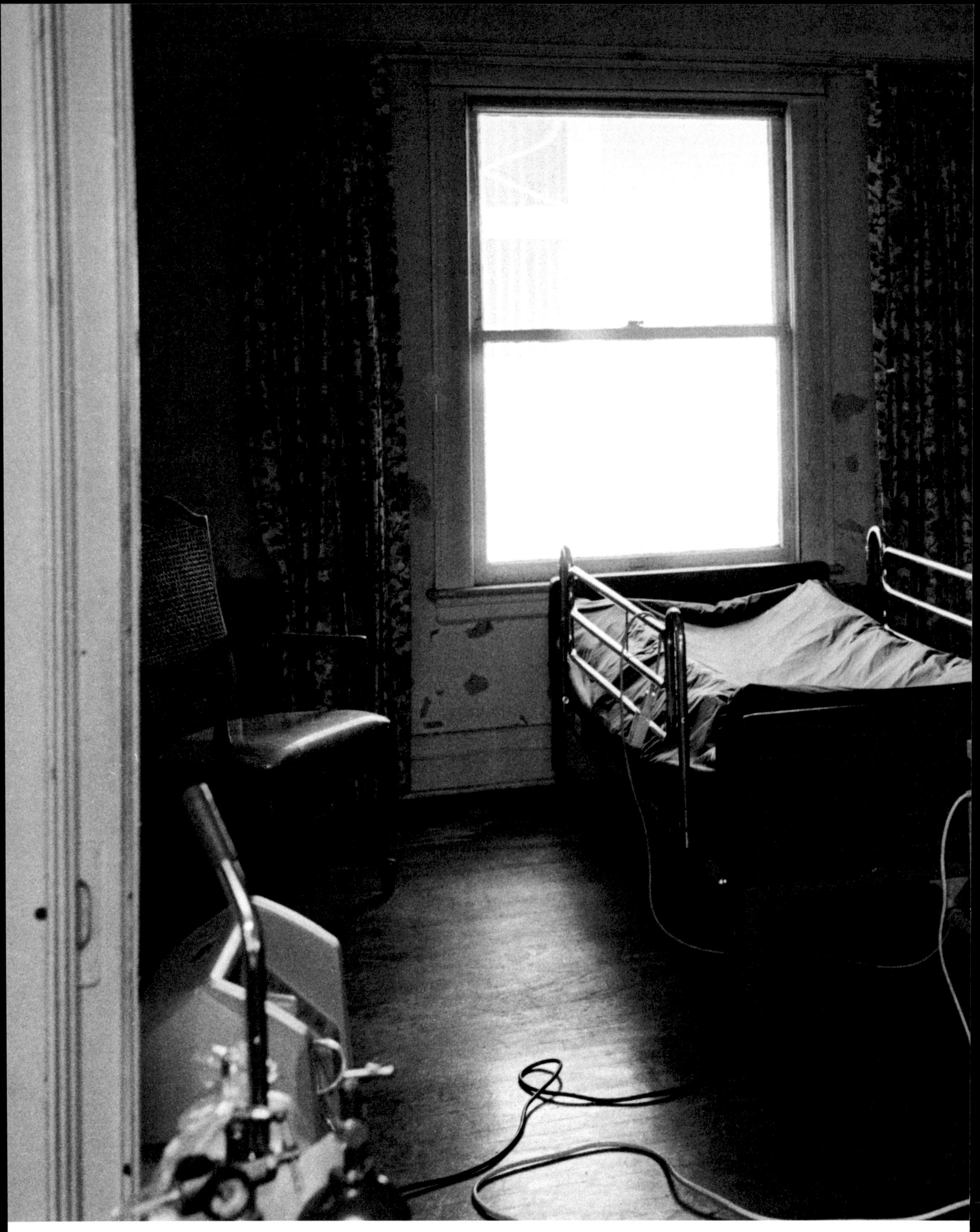

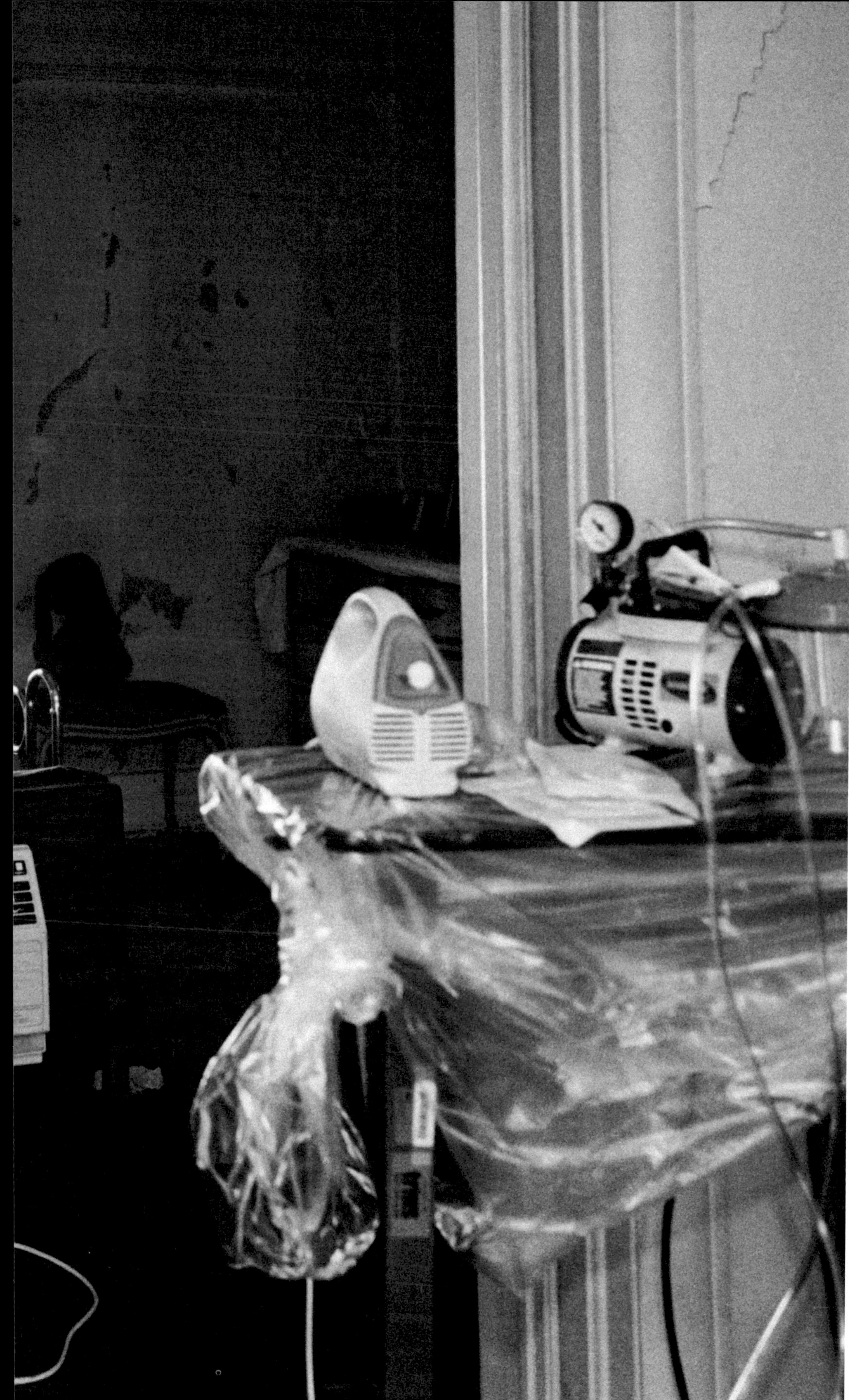

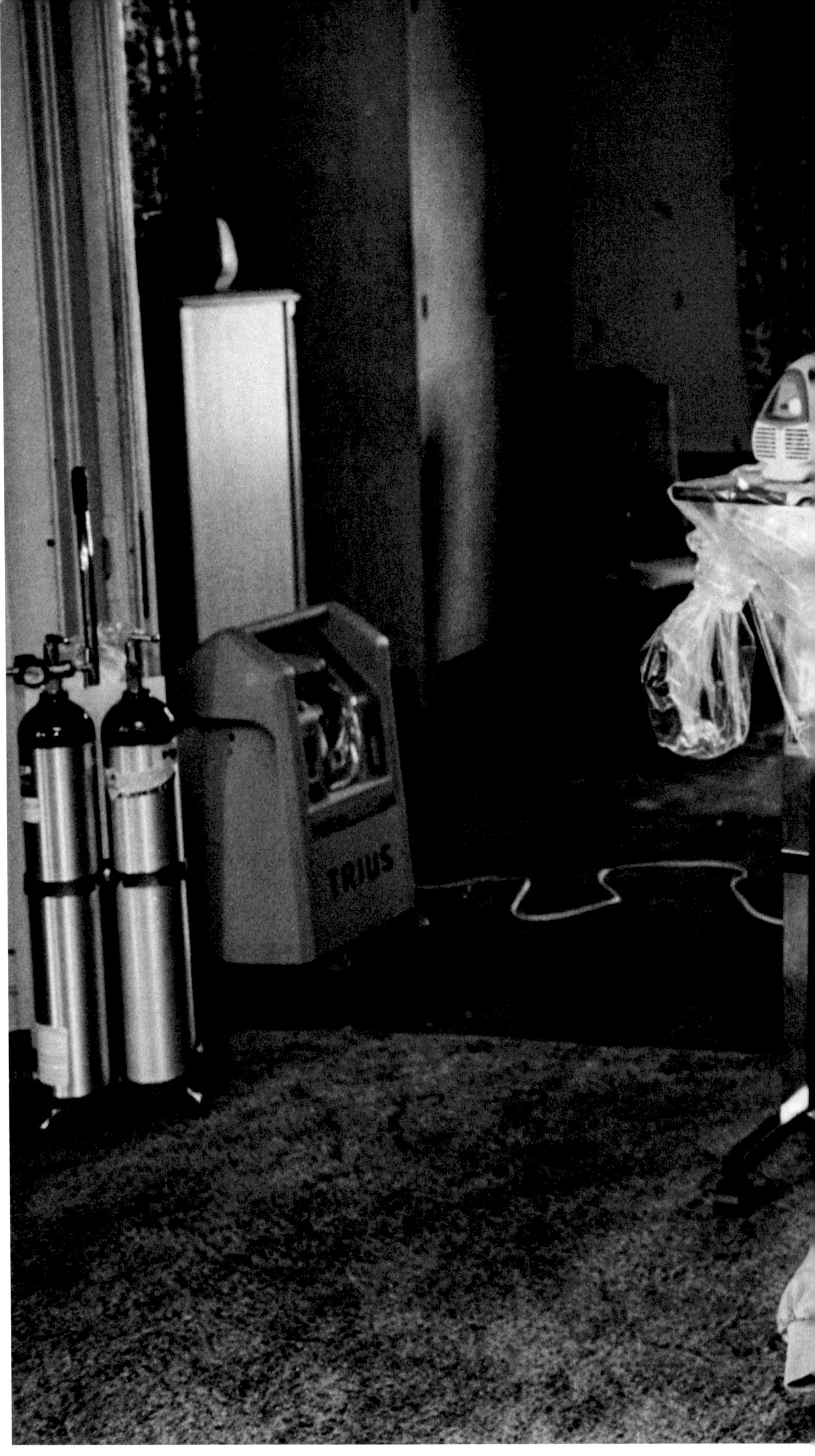
TRIUS

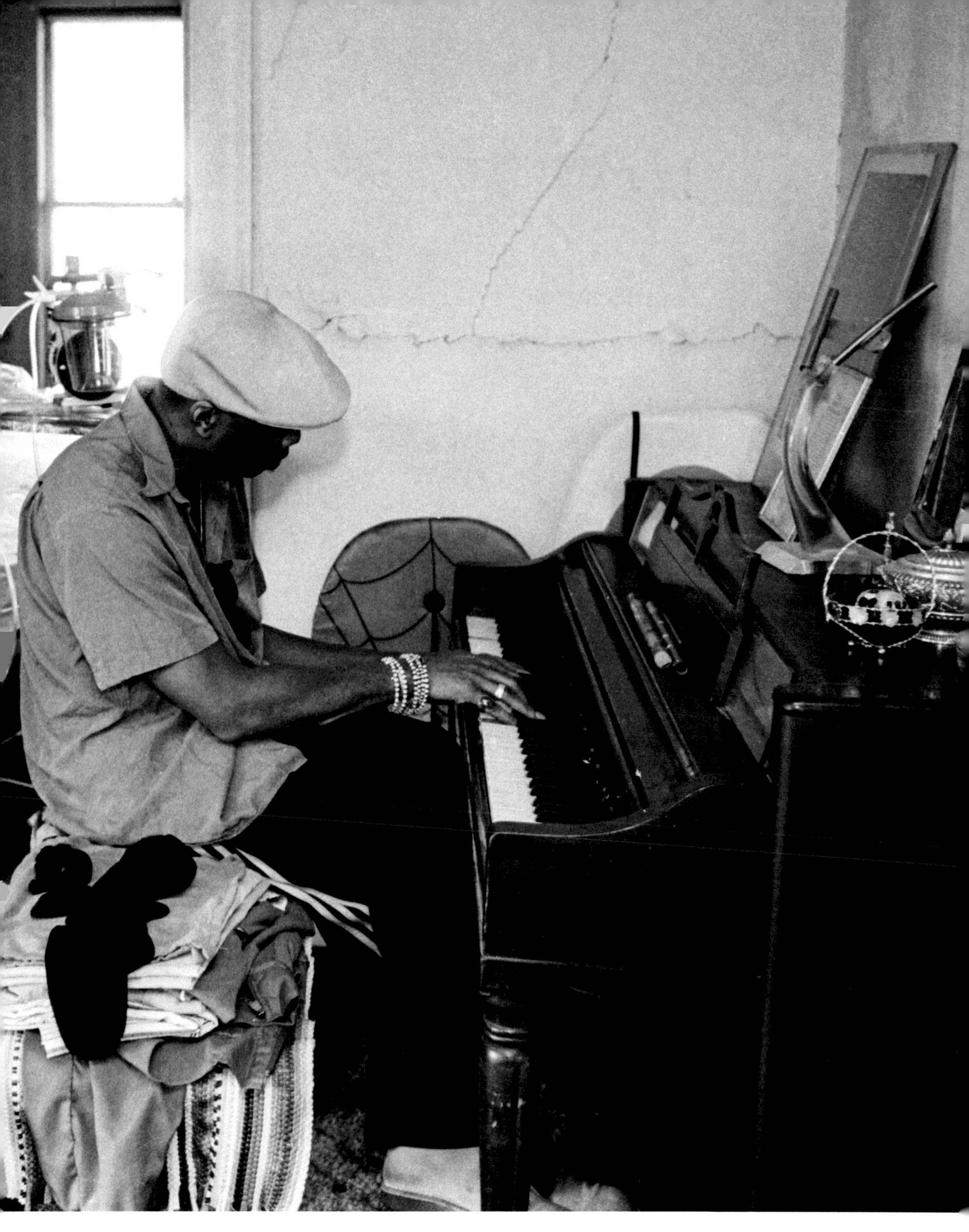

The bowl of soggy spaghetti sat next to her on a beige tray
until it was taken away untouched—replaced by more neatly
packaged saltless food. The week before, she wanted tacos.
She wanted beef. She wanted snacks. She wanted to walk. She
wanted to know when she could leave. She wanted her purse.
To please find her purse. She wanted to know why we hadn't
visited in three whole days. She wanted to know if we loved her.

At the time I met her, ten years earlier, she had no front teeth,
not much hair, a crack pipe and sticky change on her dresser.
She sat chain-smoking cigarettes in her messy room watching
daytime talk shows. Her relationships were strained and taut
like an old rubber band. Her body misshapen and sagging
with little use for real clothes. Her stories were old lies that
didn't matter.

Today she was sleeping, so I let her. I took a deep breath with
my eyes by closing them and telling myself it was only for
an hour. I pressed my mouth into a flat smile as I walked past
the other lifeless woman who moaned and stared at the
television. It dangled on the wall with no sound. I took my seat
near the window in the stale stench of shit and artificial lemon.
We watched *Guiding Light* and the local news. She woke a
few times and mumbled. I dipped the tiny corrugated green
sponge on a stick into a cup of ice chips and wet her lips.

The cancer found its way to her brain. Curled around the drain
in the stillness. Shrinking with each visit. We're almost there.
Soon she will be a phone call, a pause in conversation, a drift in
attention, a permanent absence and the guilt of relief.

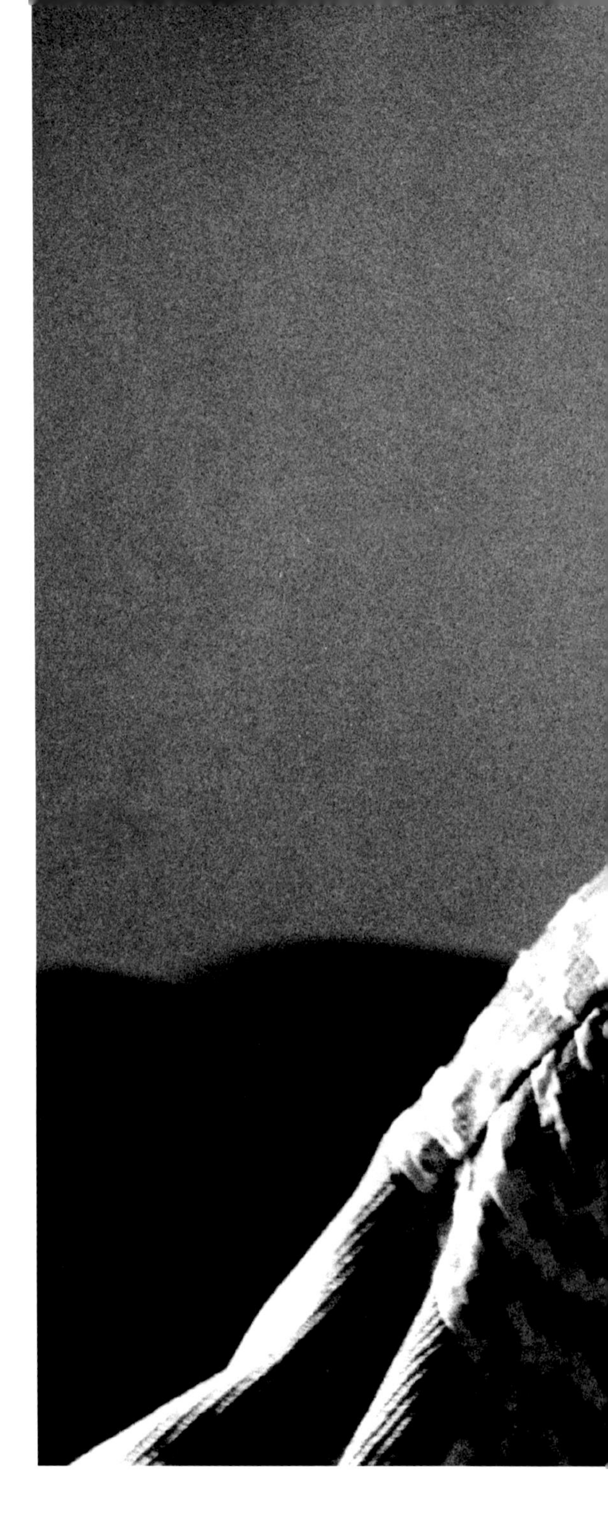

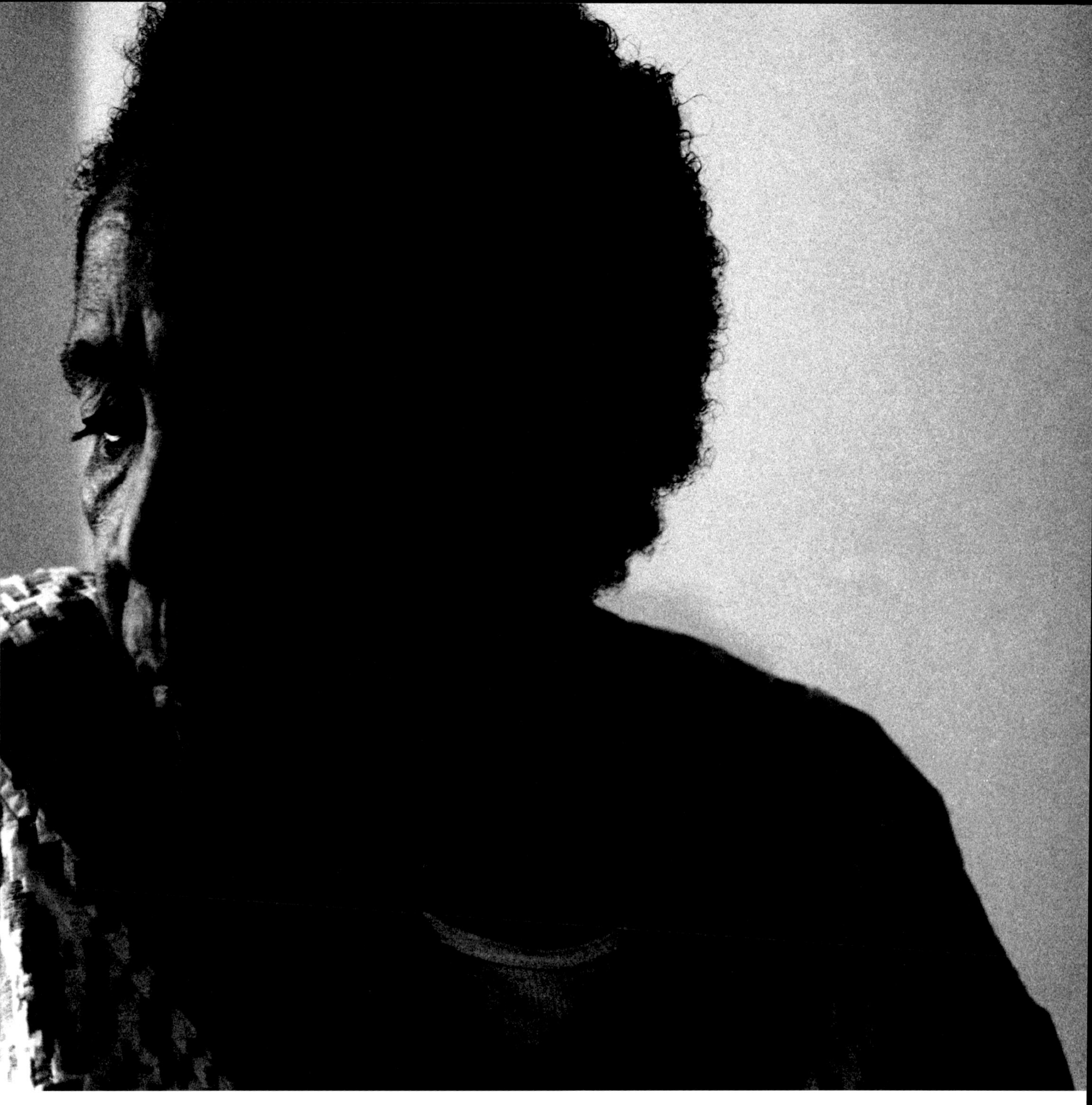

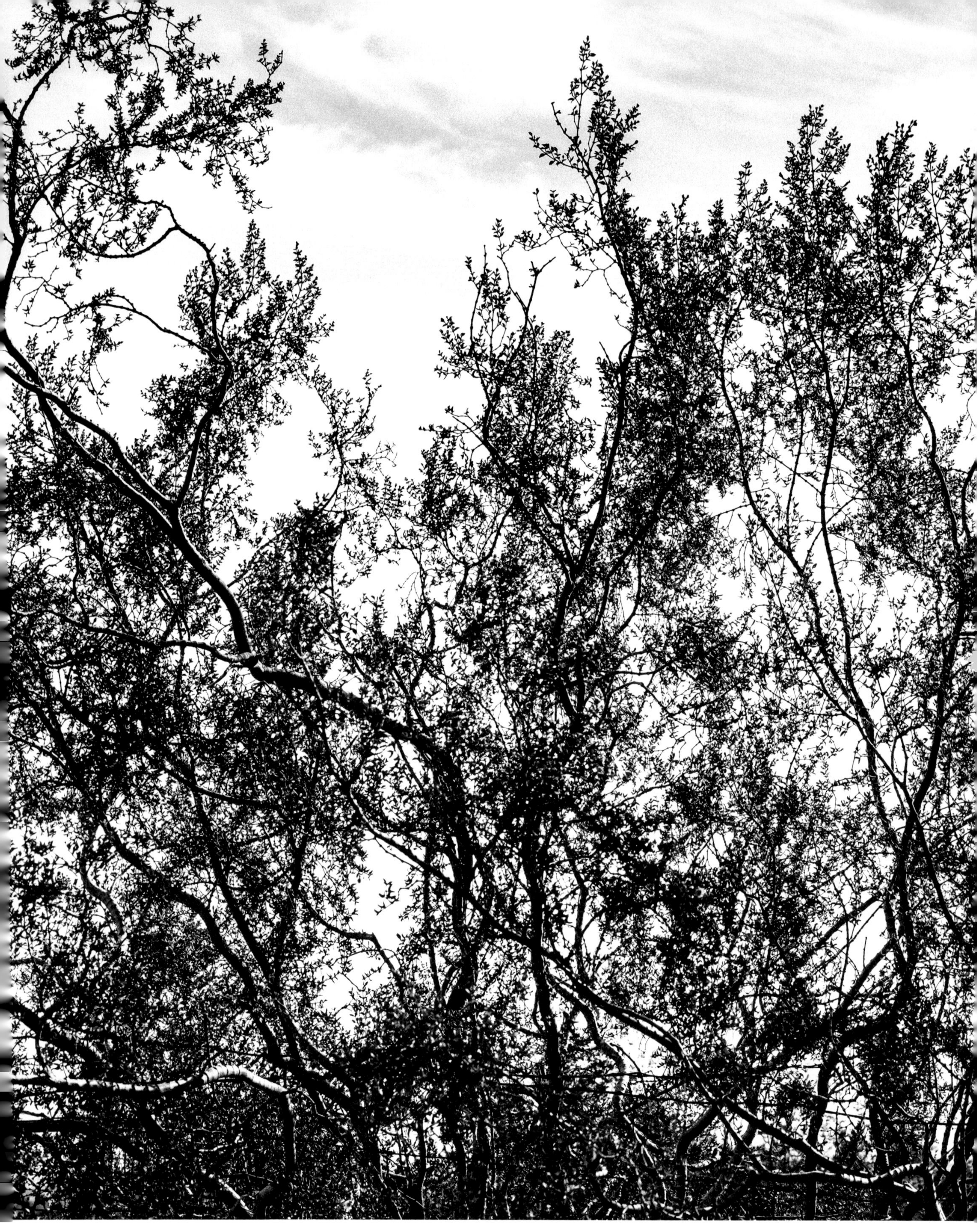

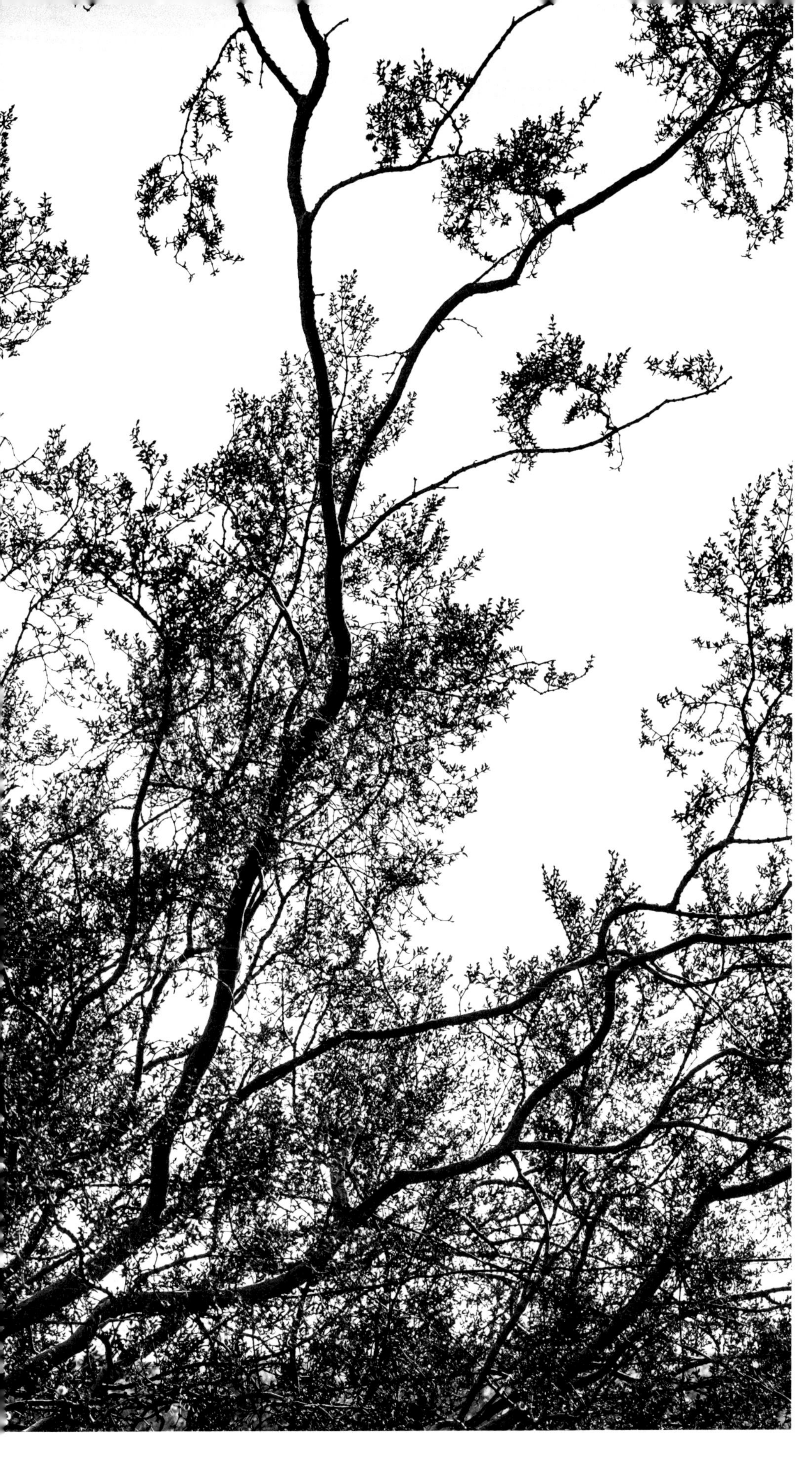

I already drowned once when I couldn't find the beginning. The mountains were small enough to crush between your fingers and the air was thick enough to eat. The heat was always winning until the rain filled the city like a bathtub and the boats came out.

Your legs wrapped around the pole, floating above the stale gaze sweating below. Pink feathers covered the rest of you but only lasted the night. Some drifted down with dollar bills that you had to collect at the end. I never liked watching that part.

You were older with a sadness we couldn't talk about. I can't remember your name but it felt temporary anyway. I steadied my hand holding your spoon as you drew out the hot brown liquid anxious to leave. Your sometime boyfriend helped me move out while mine sulked in his beer at the Whites Only bar across the street. They sold cigarettes at a window so they could take everyone's money. My heart thumped in my ears and my cheeks stung from the night before. We worked quickly bagging up what we could and left quietly. I joined you sitting on the floor sewing sequins into stockings. Soaked in sorrow with envy spilling out staining your mouth. Your skin, sun bleached like it was left in a window to fade.

In the offing, the tropes of age sneak in. Forget the regrets you diligently saved. There's plenty to feast, scales and all. Maybe I can write you out of my thoughts. The words can carry the pain of you and ink it to a page for someone else to read. I want to start this before you go. Maybe I will avoid the sharp cuts ready to claw through my strongest days. The loss will find its way to my face and change the way I see. Looking ahead at the shorter forever.

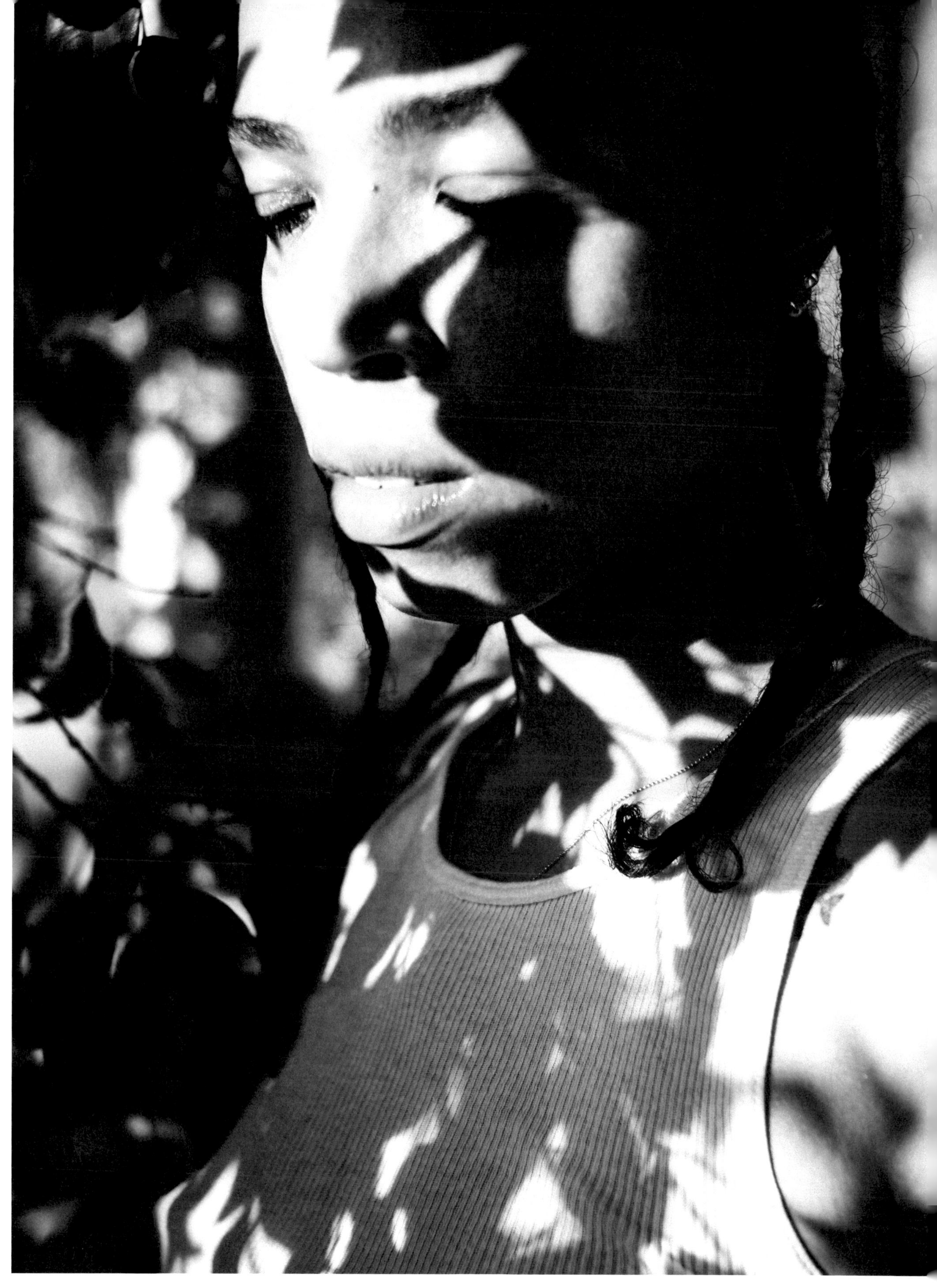

I used to sit in a tiny room and write. Now, I can see through the walls and I'm older. Looking for the thread to crawl in and remember. Baby birds still fall from the eaves. I find them on the ground below. Some brittle with death and some heaving slowly, featherless and pink. You held one in your hand until it seemed cruel to try and keep it. I climbed up to place it back in its nest and then watched for it to drop.

I am your parts and pieces always shifting not to get stuck long enough to resemble you. The age that no one dreams to be, here in the fading flesh. I have the ones as close to me as skin. Pulling as they should until I'm naked and nothing and ready for sleep. Challenging my word for what it tries to be. Steady in step, irrelevant like sheep.

There's a Korean word, *han*, that means generational sadness. Tearing at the skin like tiny wounds that grow and swallow us with a gulp. An assigned position to haul around the heft of grief. Always looking for the root or the rot. From a space in between the freed and the free, I feel the generational disappointment nipping at my heels and confusion leading everyone into a corner disoriented with loss.

My mother is seventy-six and lives in New York City, alone with a cat in a high rise in Hell's Kitchen. When I call her, she tells me about her doctor's visits and the people that she doesn't like. She called nine months ago and said she was having trouble breathing when she laid down. Six months before she thought she had bird mites from the pigeons she fed and loved that nested on her balcony. She scratched her legs and arms until they bled but it wasn't bird mites, it was cancer.

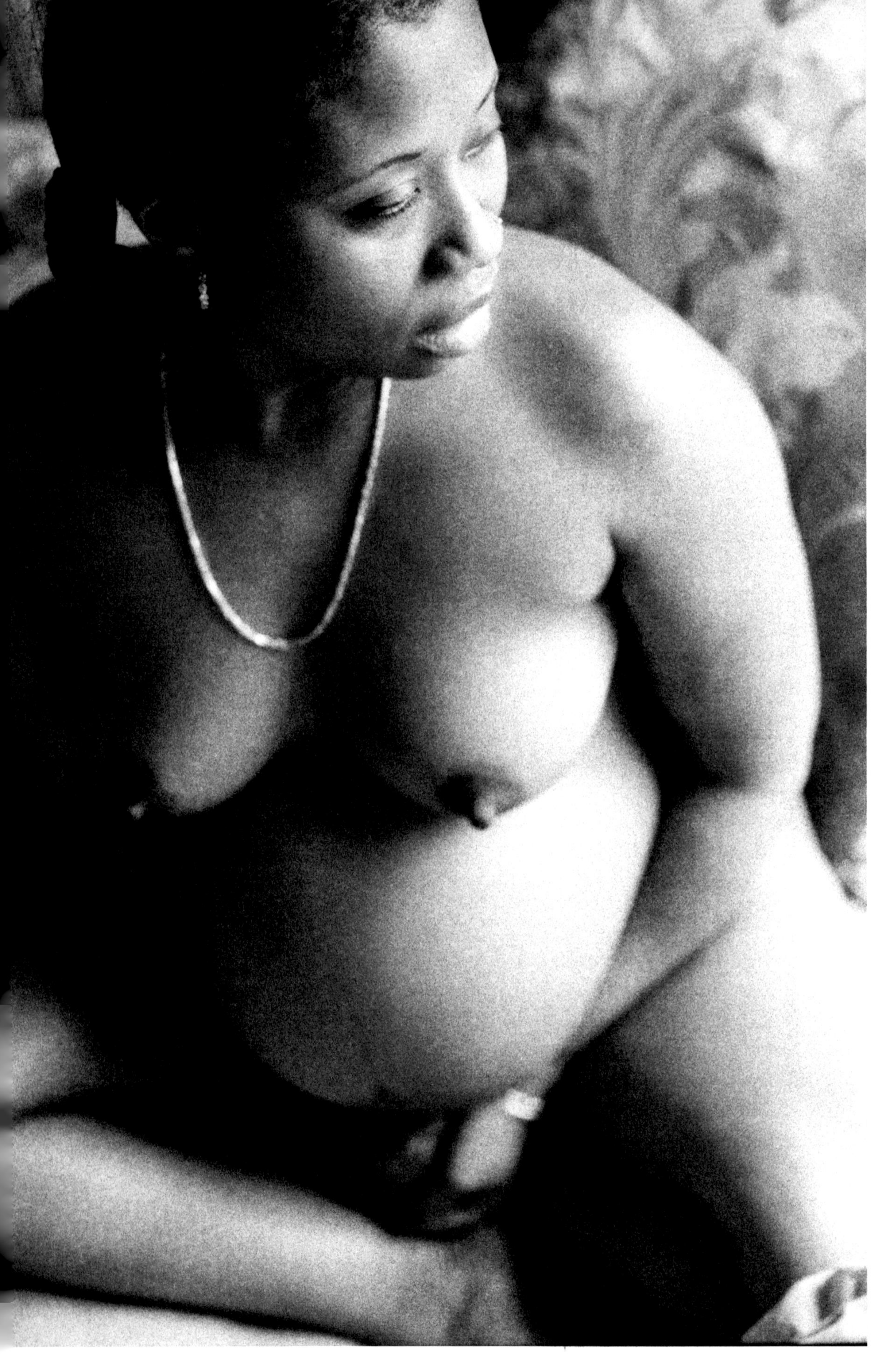

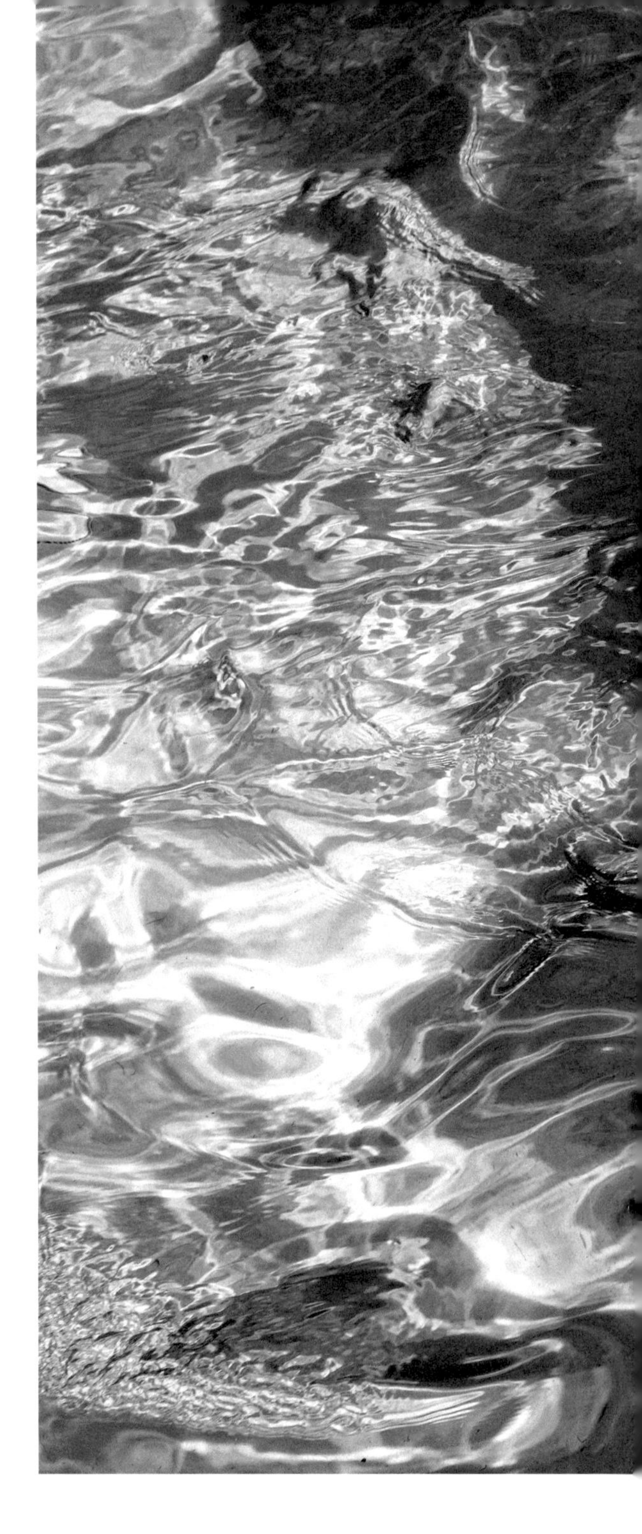

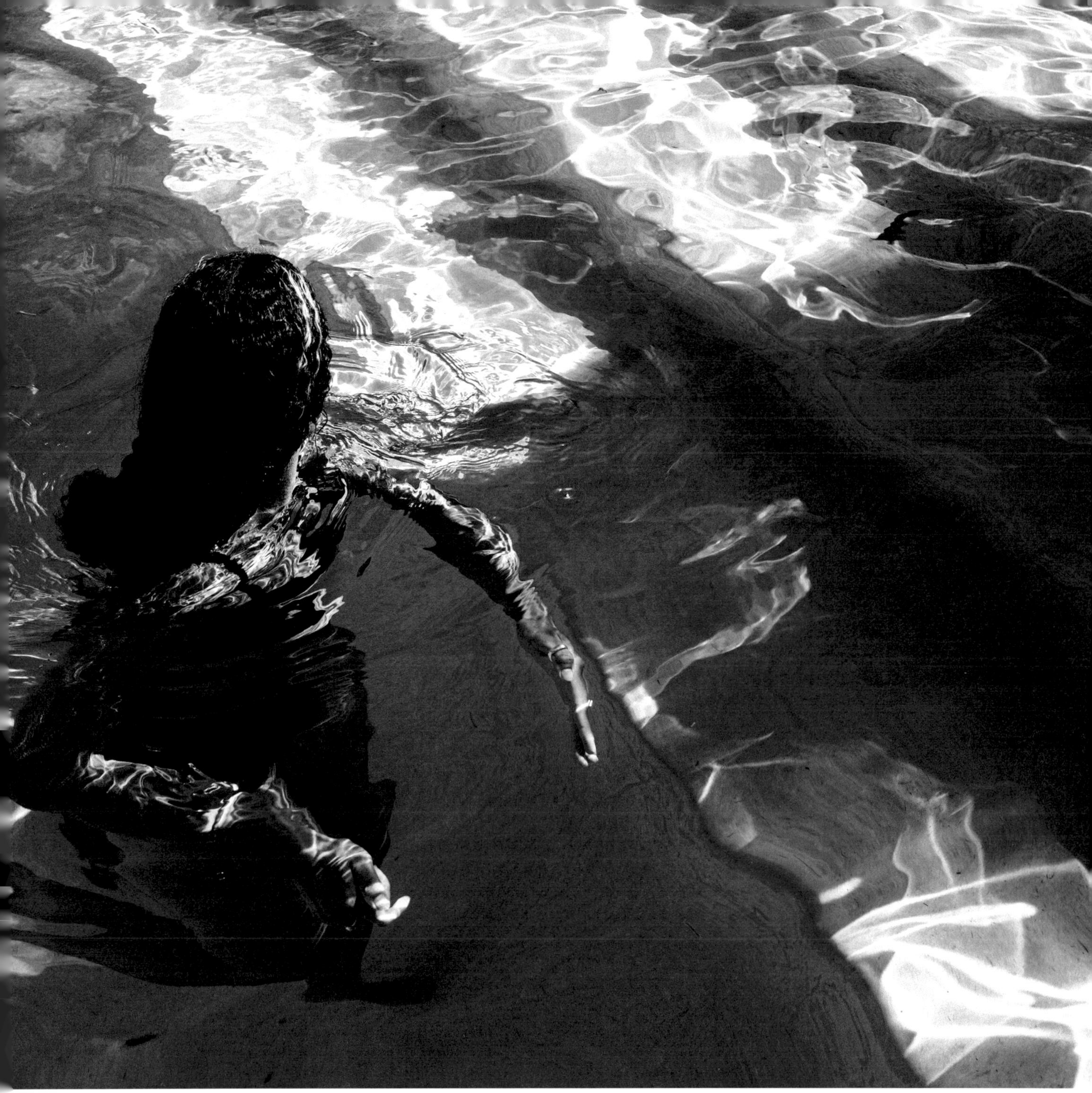

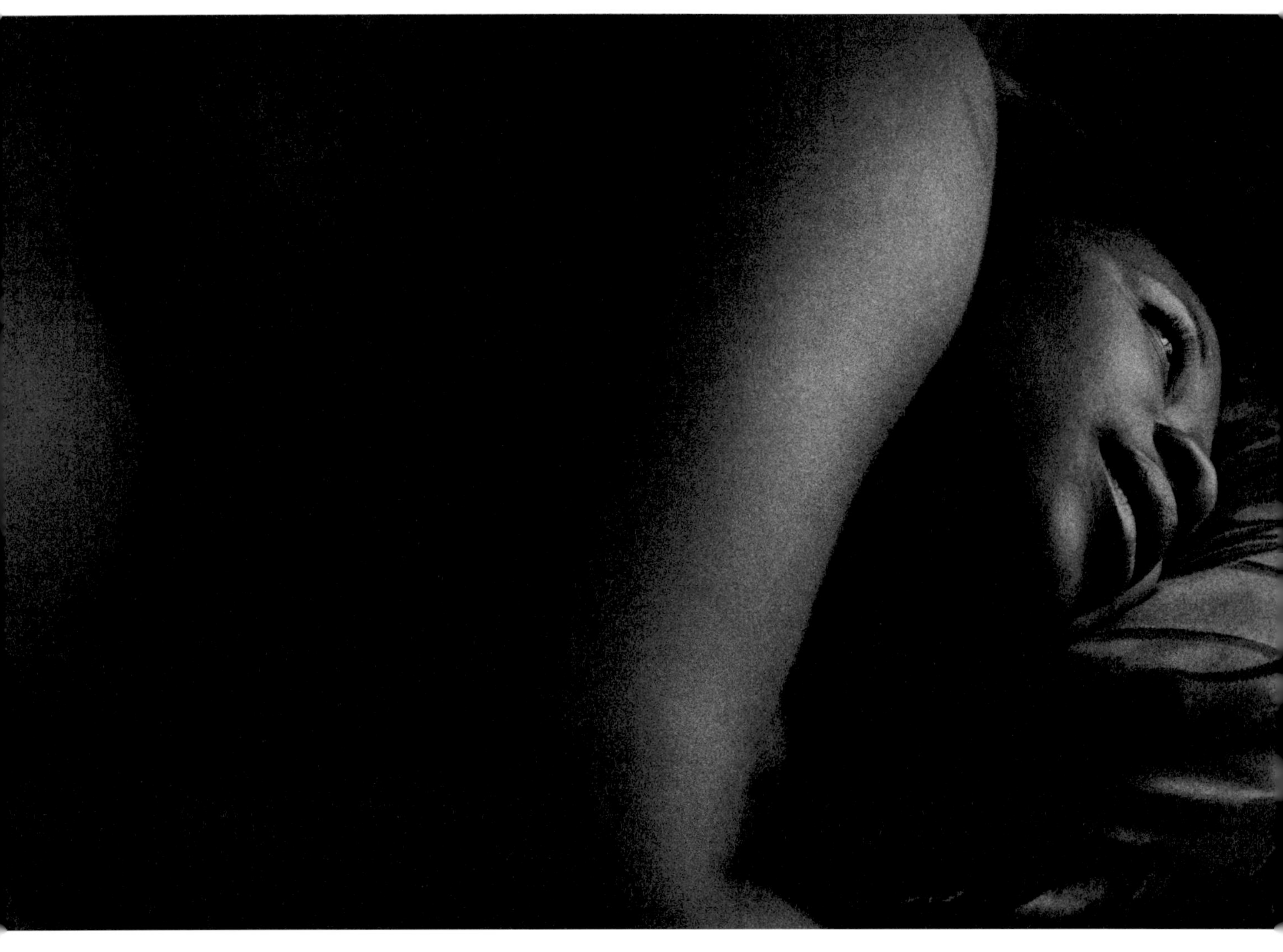

I tiled the kitchen wall after staring at it for a year and saying
I would. My fingertips pruned from the mortar. I thought
I would feel better as though I accomplished something finite.
Instead, the floors and other walls now look dingy and need
paint. The wind ripped branches off the trees in the backyard
while we slept. Young limbs wrapped in bright green leaves
grinning with spring. Lying on the bricks motionless with
the air whipping above.

My mind feels tender as though it might leak. With any
pressure, tiny parts could collapse. Maybe I would forget
my life until this moment. Perhaps my legs and arms would
lay down next to the branches or the sound of the whipping
would drown completely—replaced by a thudding pulse.

My thoughts stack up on both sides like stiff lining holding
my crown. Remembering words like clues. The shadows of
leaves dancing on the curtains that I can still see when I
close my eyes. The light's warm glow right before it goes and
the slow afternoon chirps of one bird. One by one. The day
is finished, ready or not. Without a plan or exhaustion I feel
lost in the void of the leaving light. Wait for me, I say to no
one. I'm not ready to fall or break again.

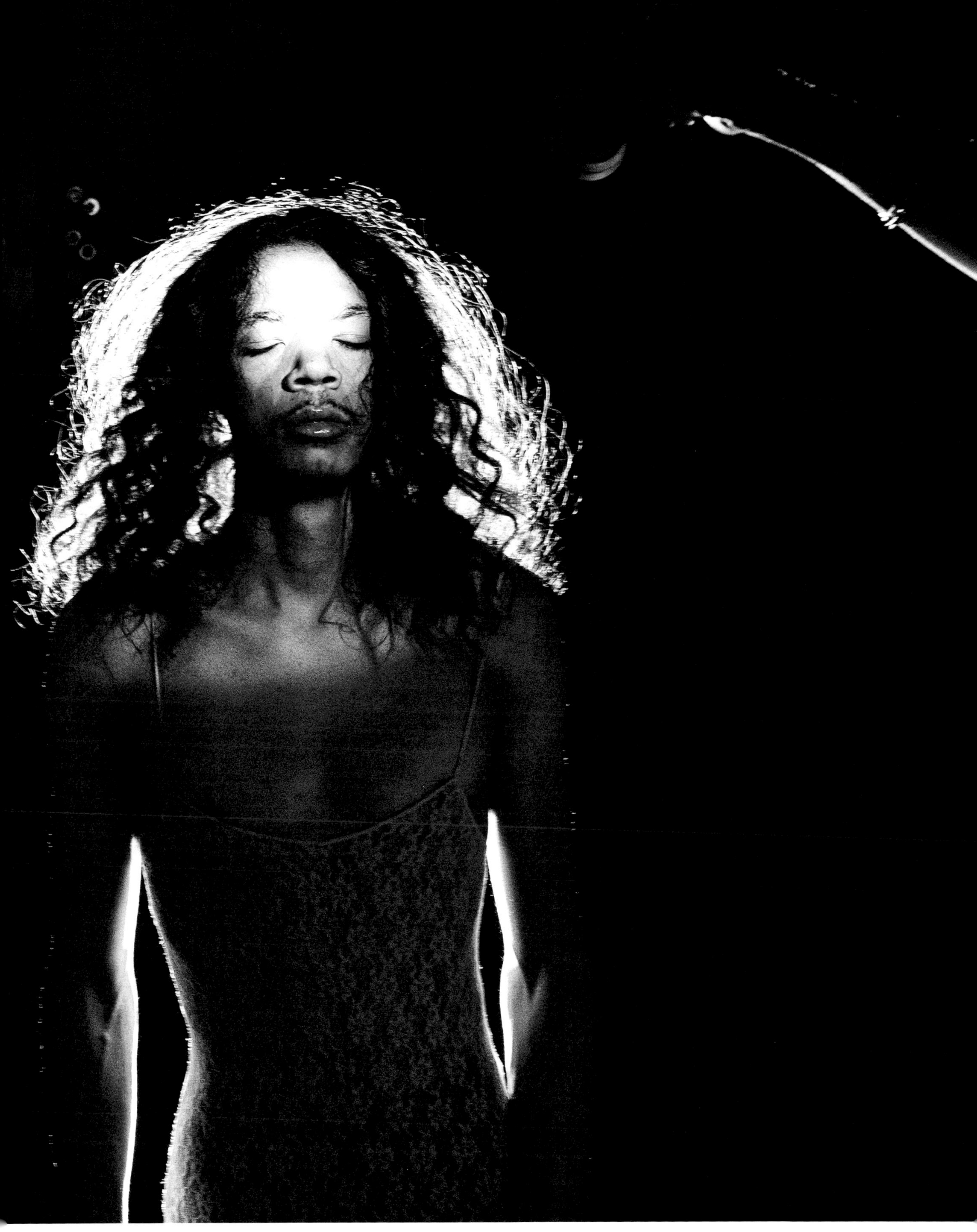

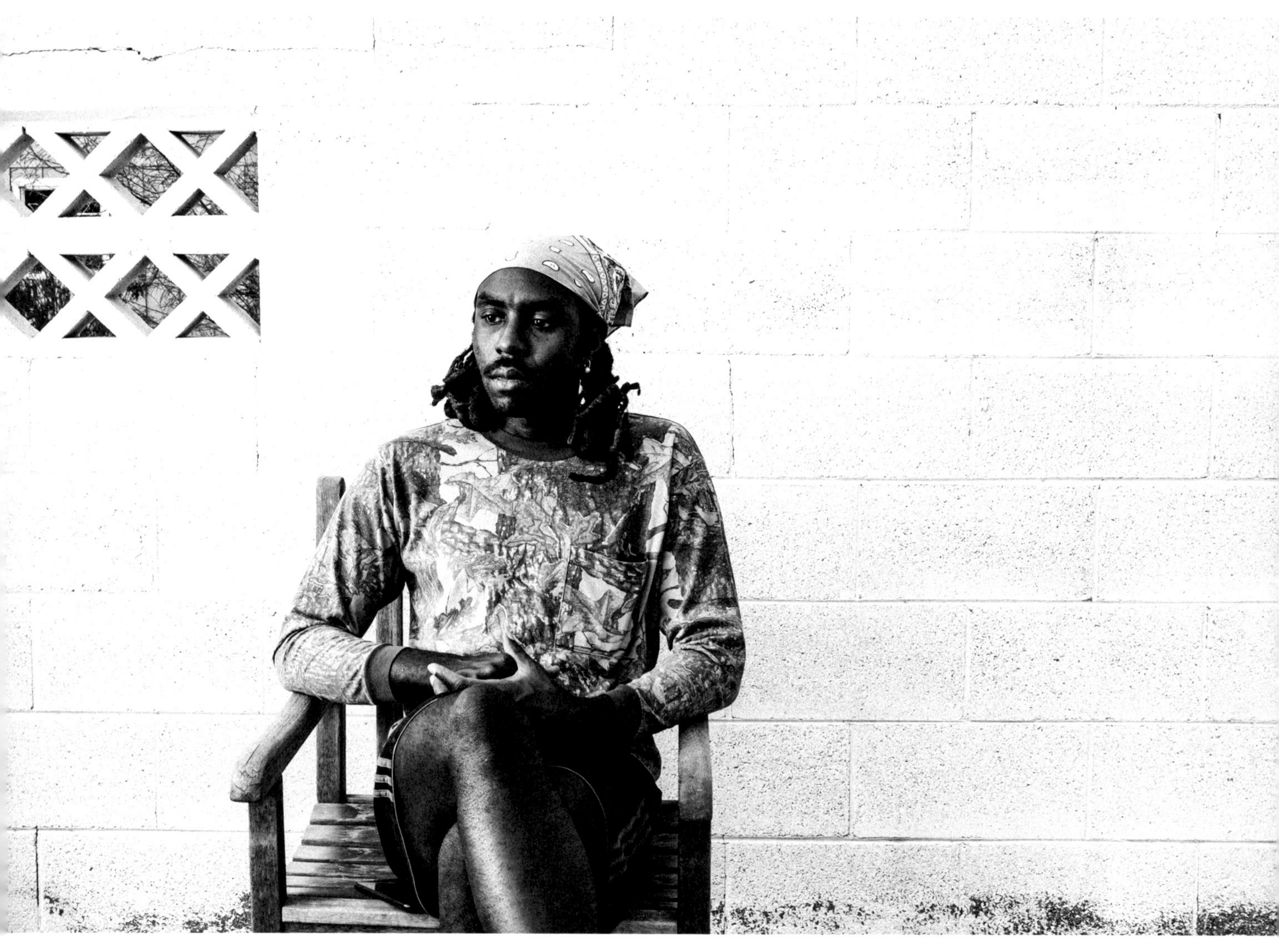

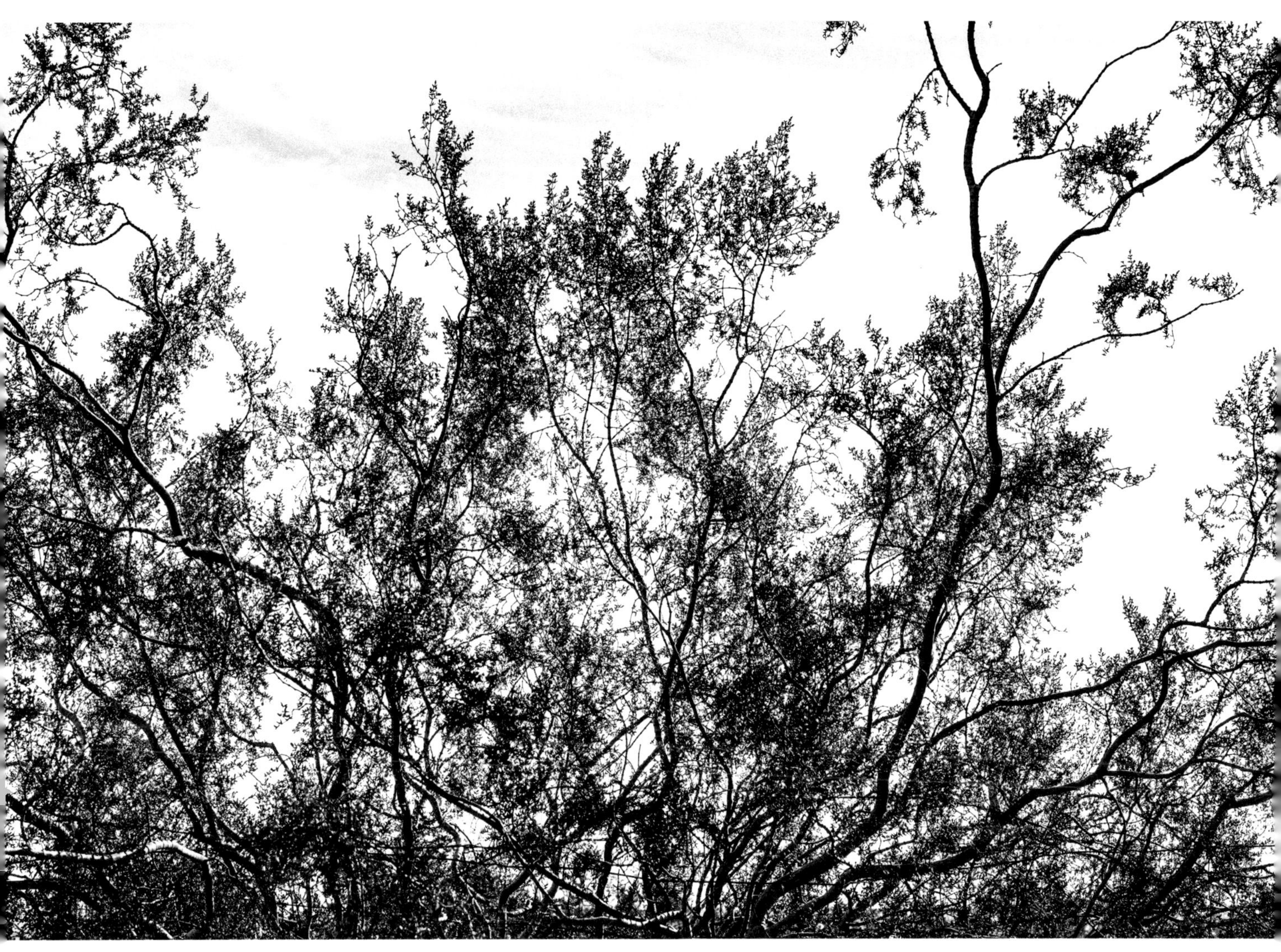

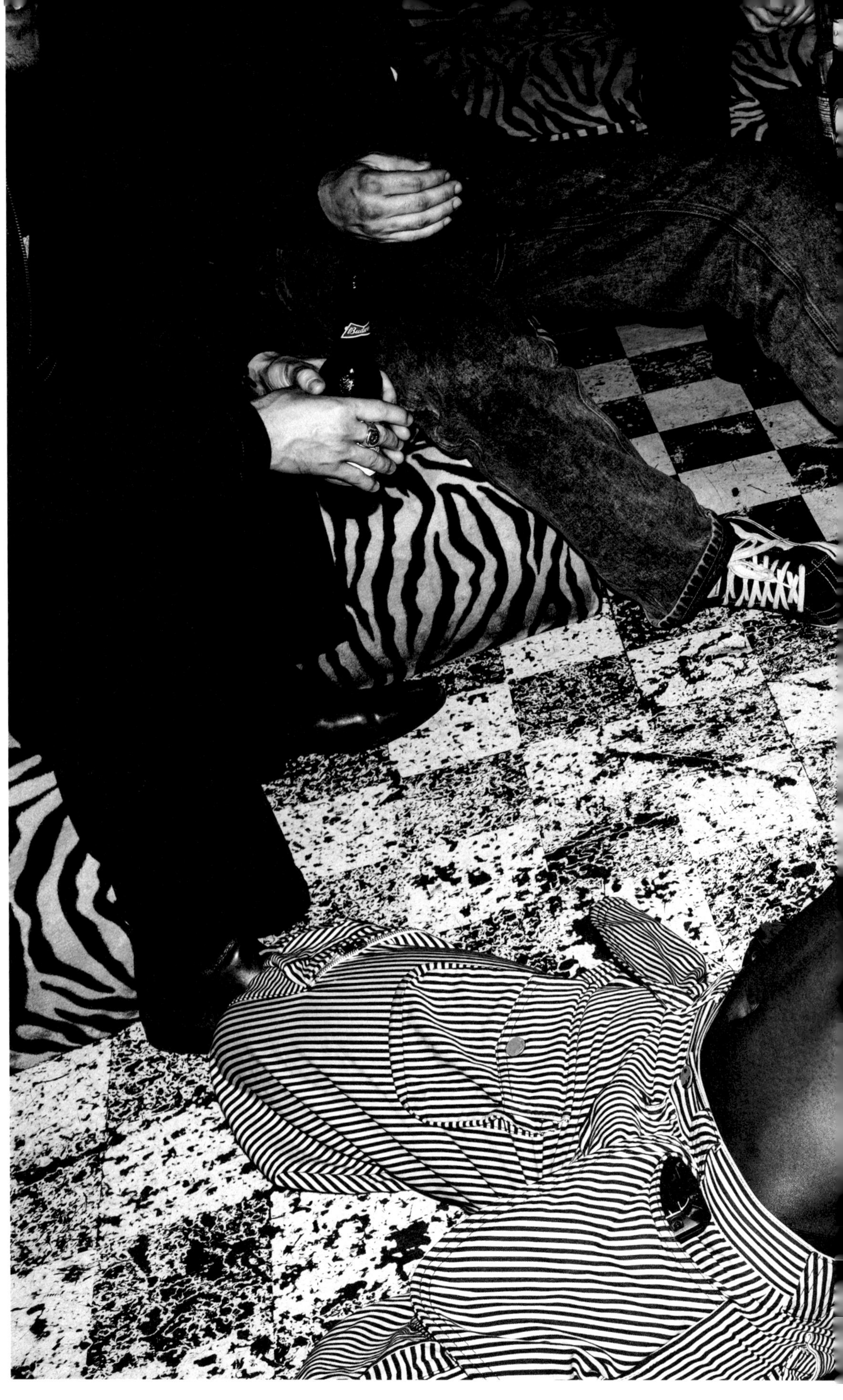

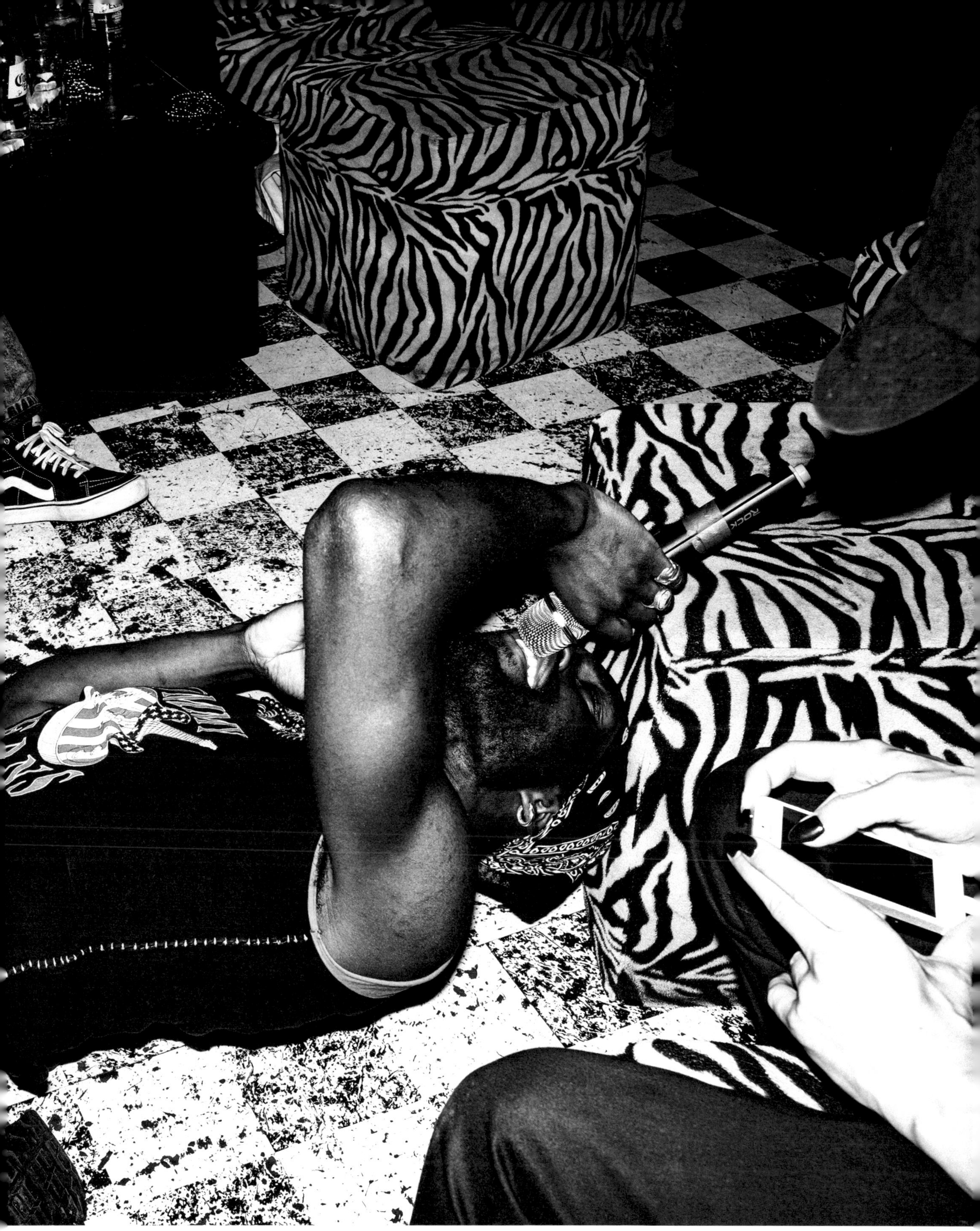

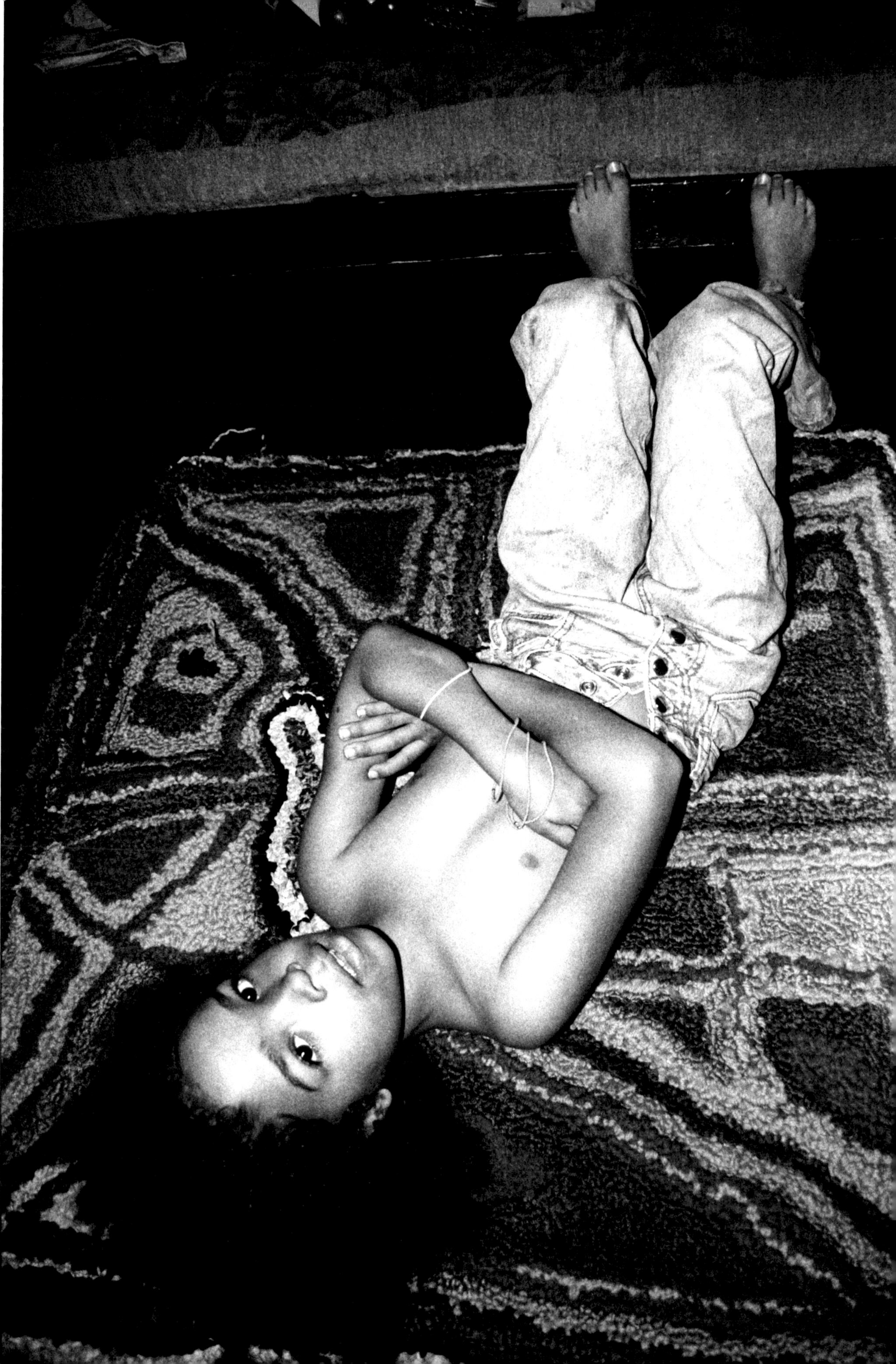

‐‐‐

You cried and screamed until the police came. The neighbor
called. She didn't like us. We just moved in. You were three.
You were a tornado. Nothing worked. We just had to wait. I
sent them away after seeing you writhing on the floor. Short
rapid breaths. The television loomed in silence, unplugged.
That night, I threw it out.

I can't get far enough away to see the shape of you. Holding
on biting down wordless. Tender-headed, small and
frameless. Sometimes, I would wake up and watch you breathe.
Years later, I looked through your room for clues. Once when
you called from school my knees buckled and I let them.
Bent on the floor, I listened carefully through the words. It
was what you never told me that wouldn't let me sleep. The
air stopped just before you spoke and when you said you were
ok, I knew you weren't. You buried what you could no longer
make up, hiding the stitches and the truth until both fell out.

I went out with you and your friends. Some were my age. You
had to sneak in. Everyone did too much of everything. I thought
we died together in a cab on the way back from the city. The
realness of morning wasn't convincing and all the details were
missing. I let the story unwind itself. Storing it safe from
memory to dissolve. Now I try to move in a way that won't annoy
you. I limit my questions and bury my smile. We live across
a city neither of us like. You're too busy and I call too much.
There are tiny invisible strings attached to what we remember
and mostly they remain tangled.

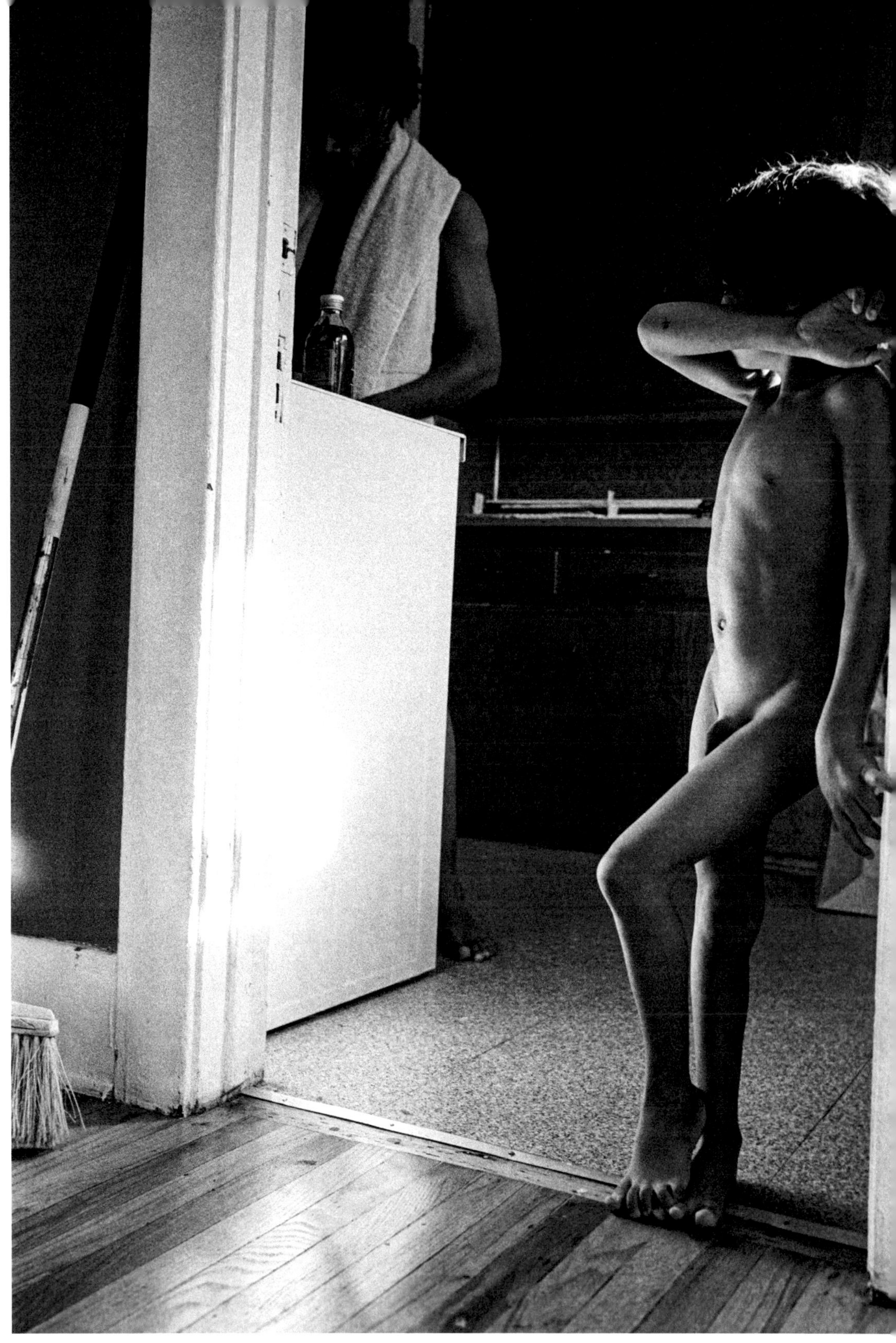

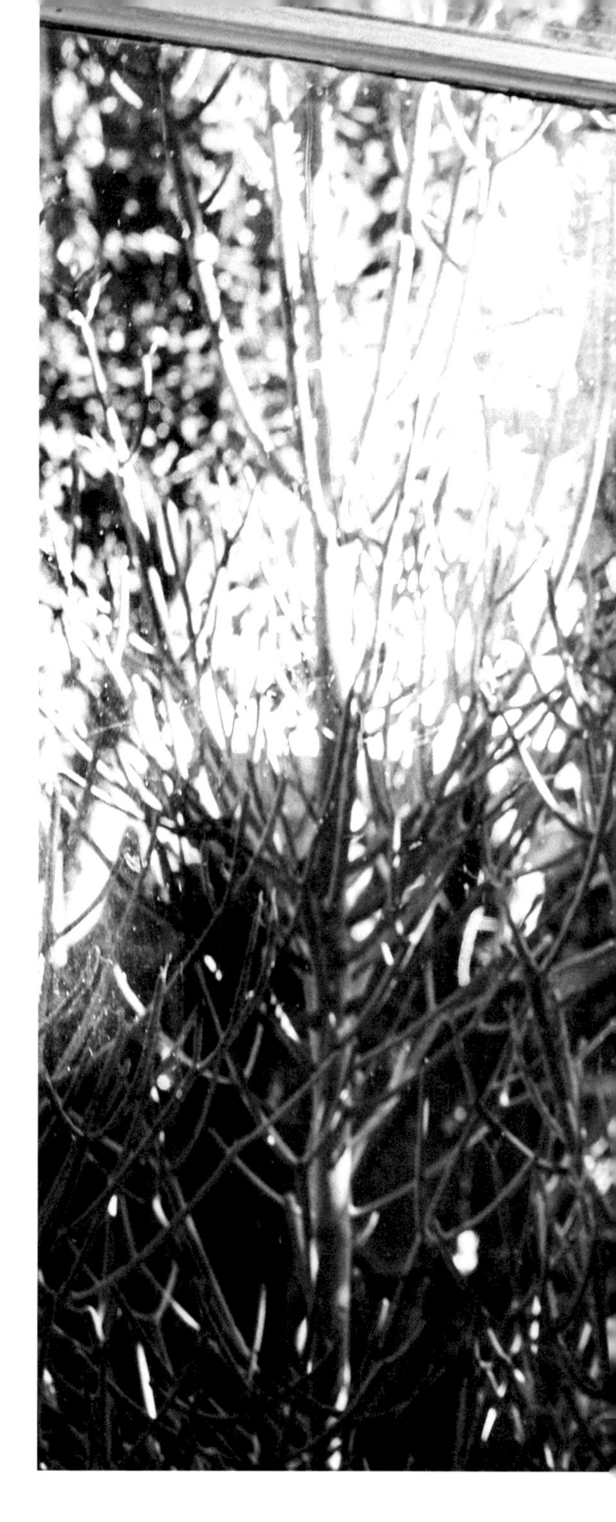

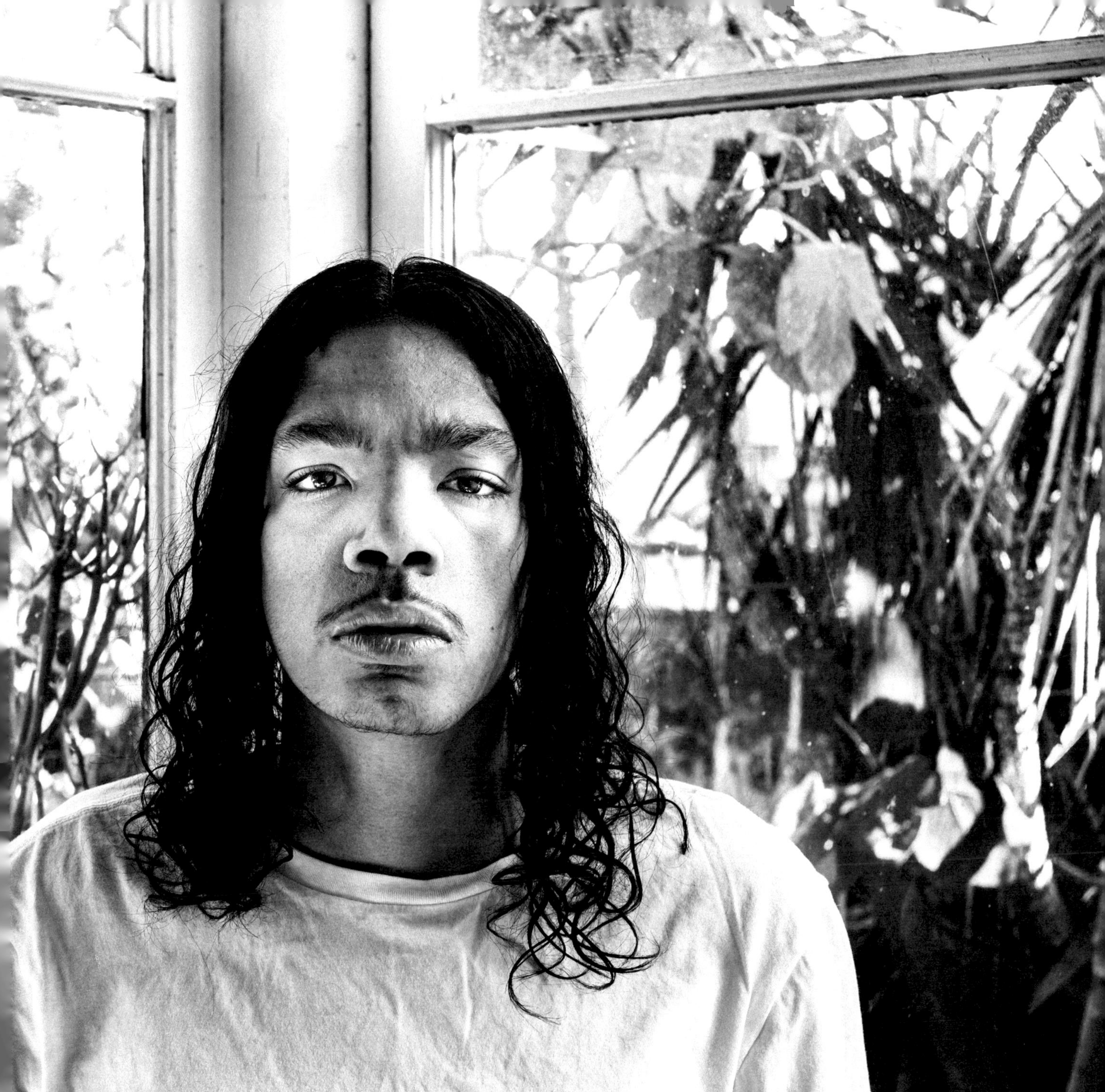

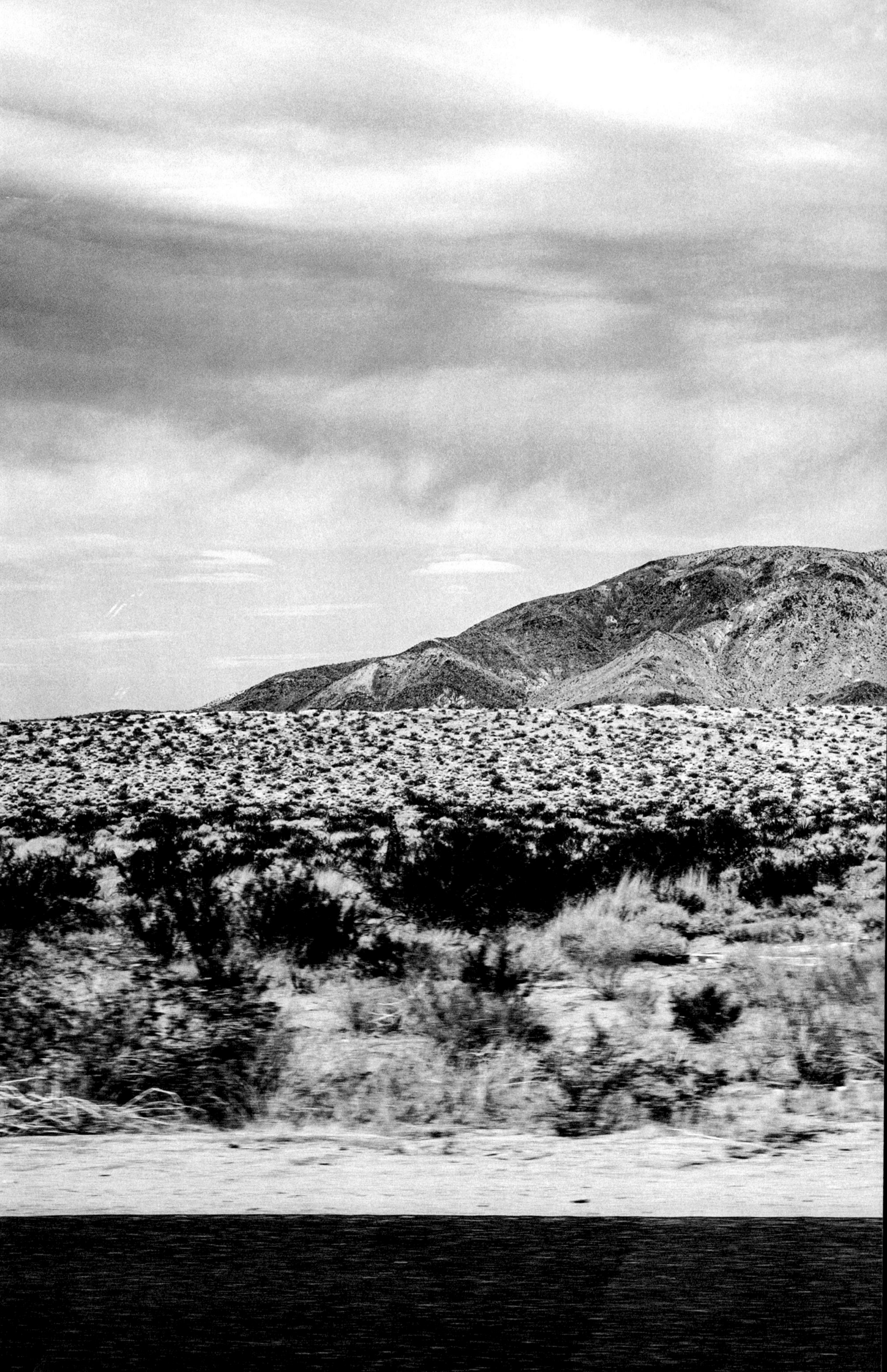

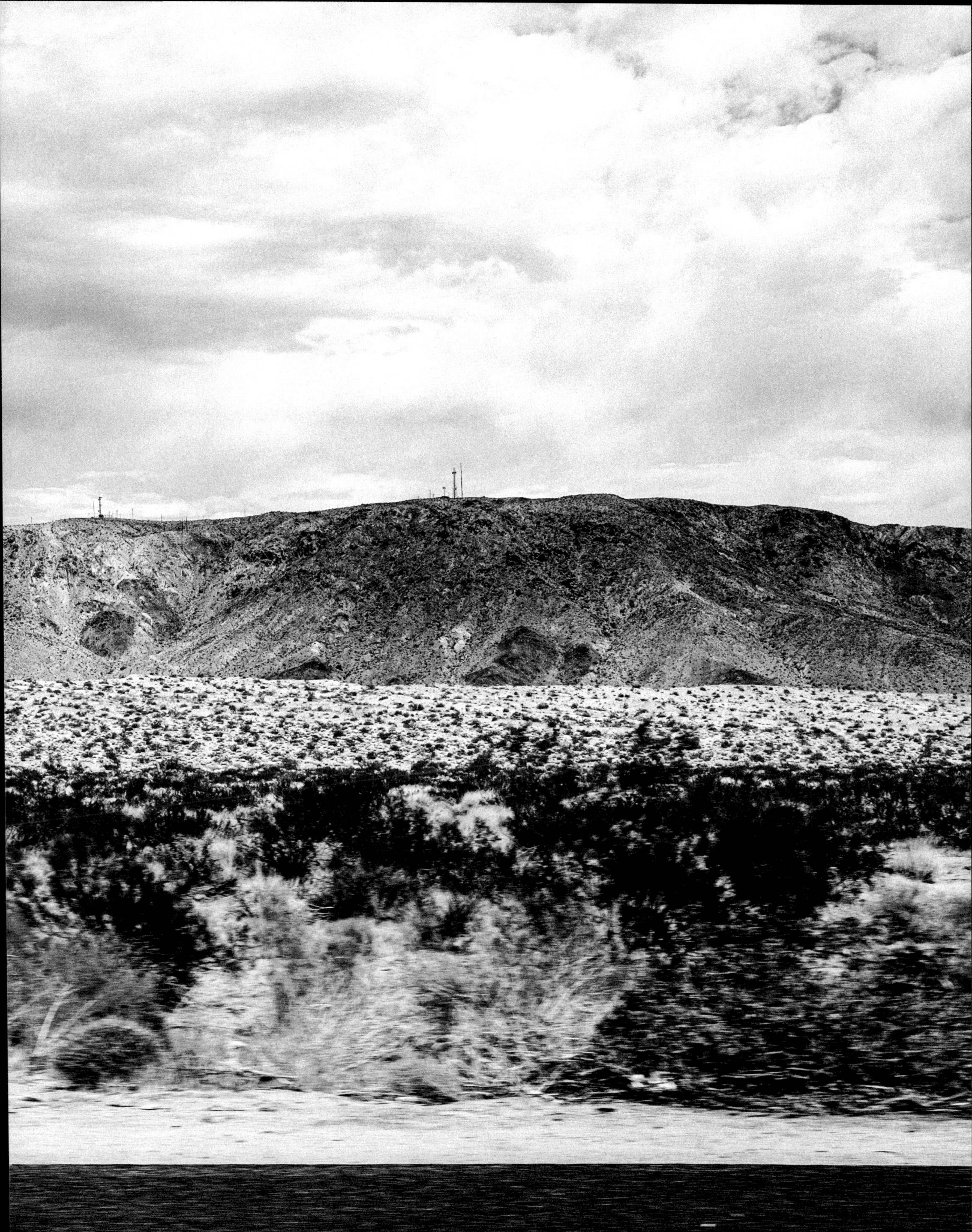

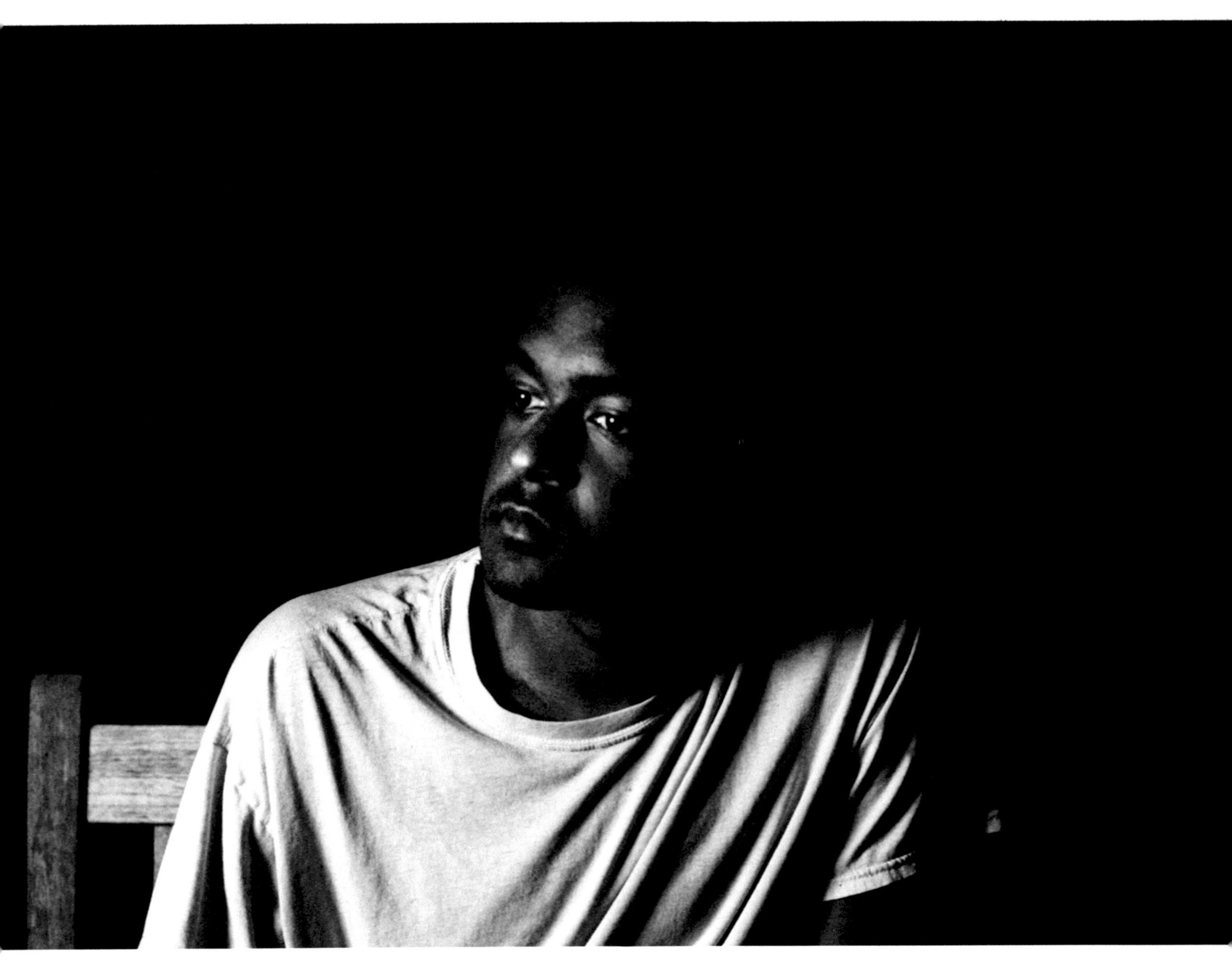

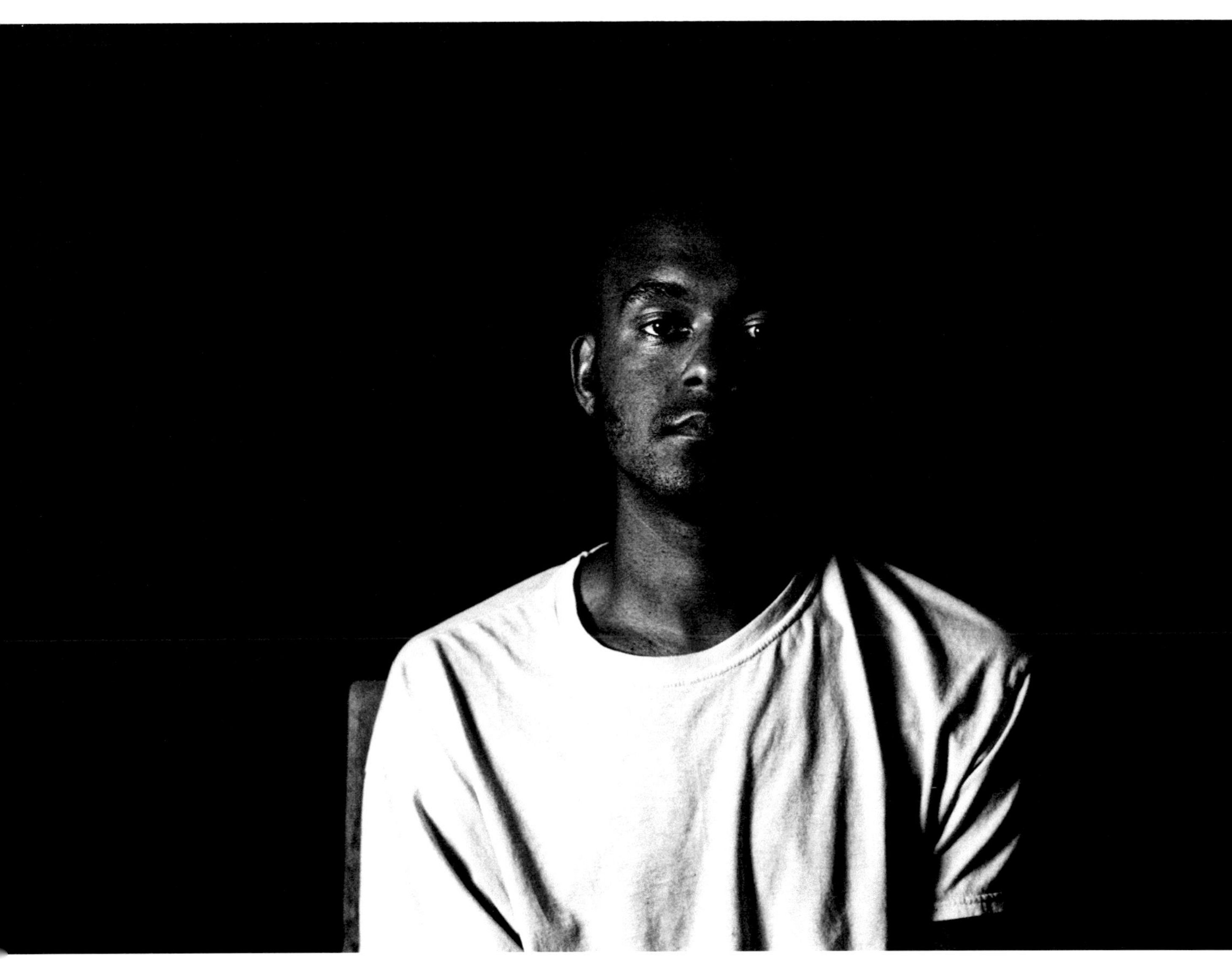

♰

You visited me in a dream. It felt real, even though you had no
skin below your mouth, just bones and blood. Mom was melting
in the background seated at a table. You had been attacked
and beaten years before outside your apartment in Hell's Kitchen.
Your lower jaw was the only part of your face unbroken. The
doctors needed a photograph to see what you looked like.
I gave them the one I had printed in my high school darkroom.
I thought it belonged inside a book jacket for a novel you had
written. You agreed.

I got a call in the middle of the night. I told my livery driver that
I was going to identify my father. My voice cracked, and he told
me he was sorry. We sat quietly speeding up the FDR in the
almost morning.

I couldn't see you through the blood. The doctor said the body
swells to protect itself. I thought of the movie *Mask* about Rocky
Dennis who had lionitis. I recognized your hands and confirmed
your name, before my knees gave out and I woke up with a nurse
patting my shoulder in the hallway.

Your teeth were wired shut so you scribbled out messages on a
notepad. You said, "Make me look like Alec Baldwin." The white
doctor chuckled, and I felt empty under my own laugh.

I was flying home from burying you in fresh dirt and I didn't
care if the plane crashed. I decided that meant I wasn't afraid of
flying anymore and I was grateful, drinking tiny bottles of vodka.

I found an inscription in a Sylvia Plath book that you had given
me on my thirtieth birthday and wept uncontrollably, slumped
on the floor next to my bed.

The last time I saw you lucid, I had been at the hospital for long
drowning days. When time ticks but refuses to move. I was bone
tired and you wanted me to stay but I left anyway. The sharp
edge of that choice never dulls. Made of seagrass and bamboo,
wrapped in muslin for the final peace no one wants, except
maybe Sylvia.

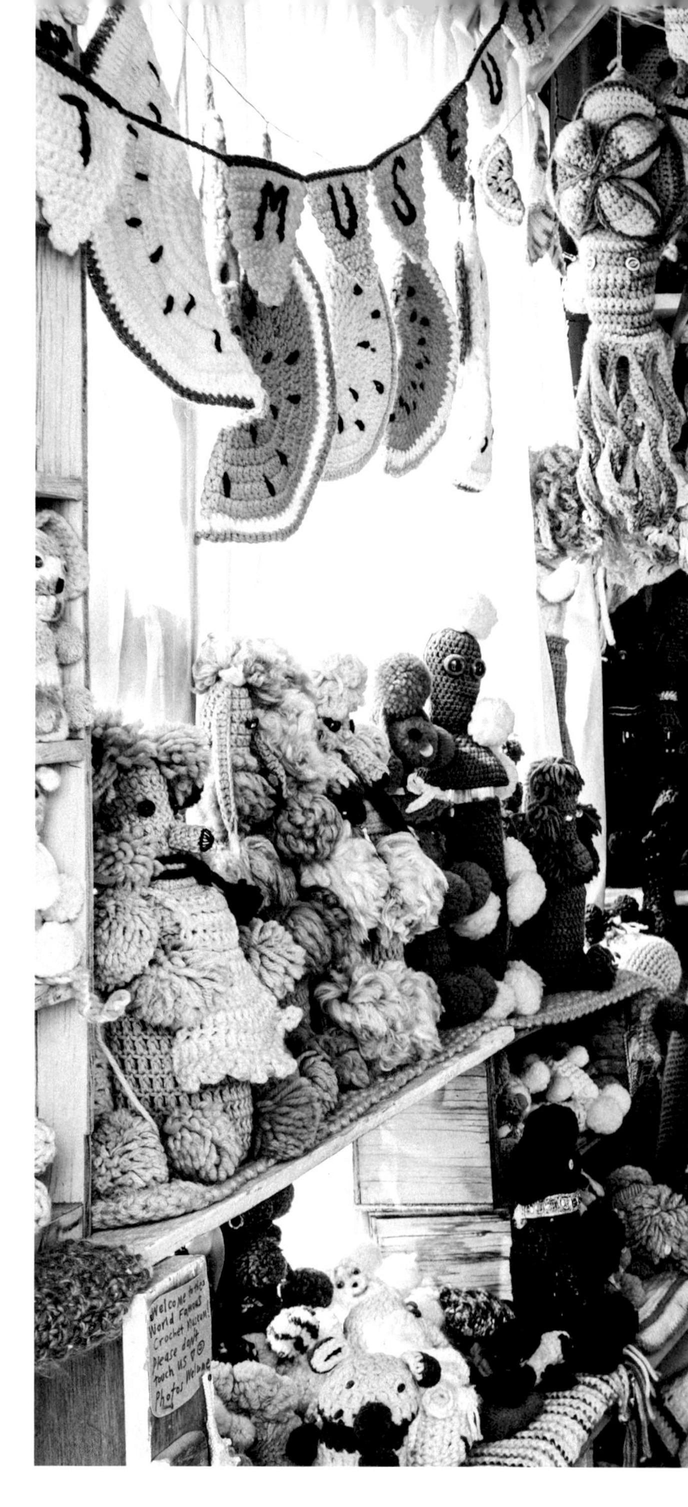
MUSEUM
Welcome to the
World Famous
Crochet Museum!
Please don't
touch us !
Photos Welcome

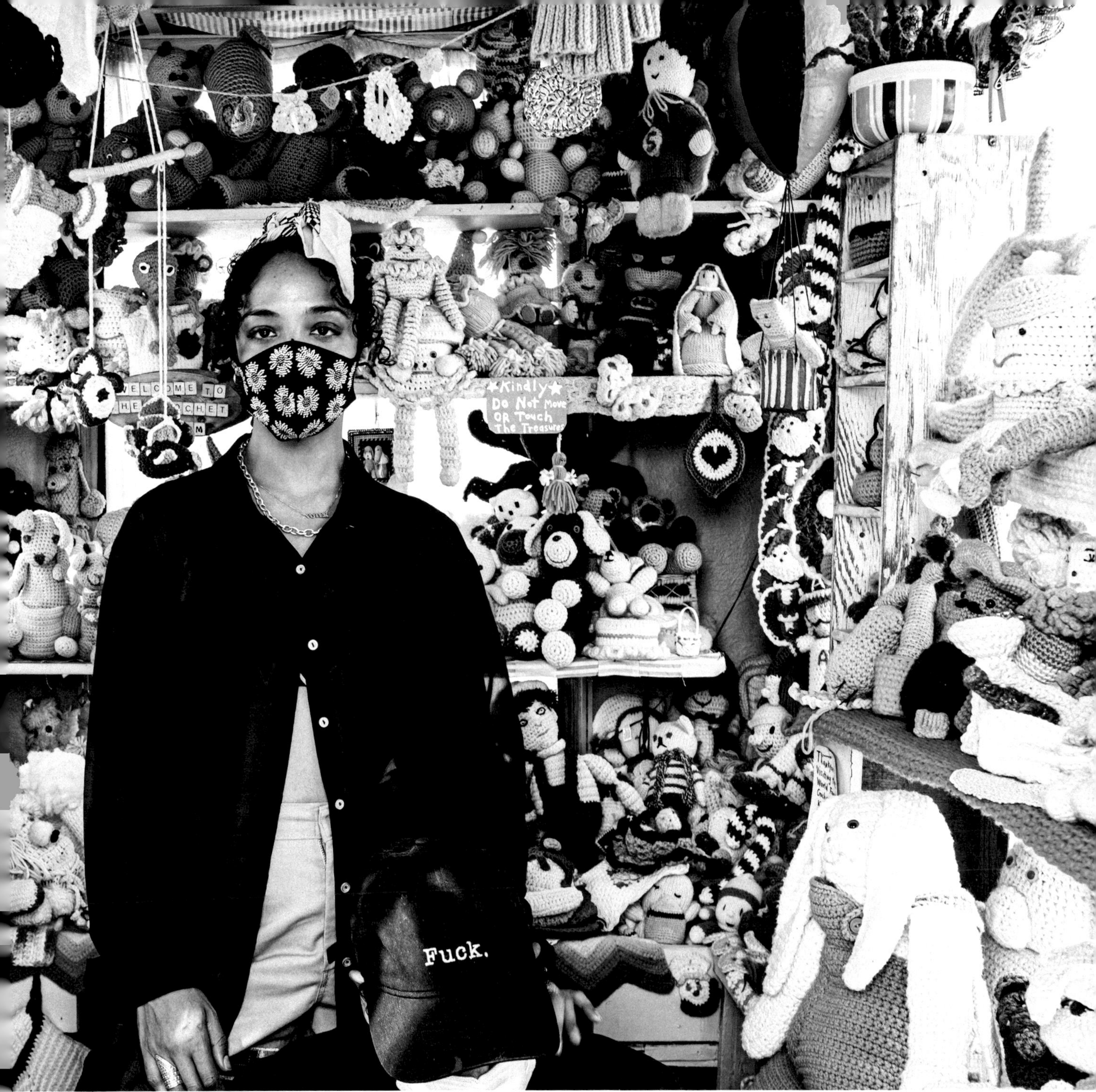

WELCOME TO THE CROCHET
Kindly
Do Not Move
OR Touch
The Treasures
Fuck.

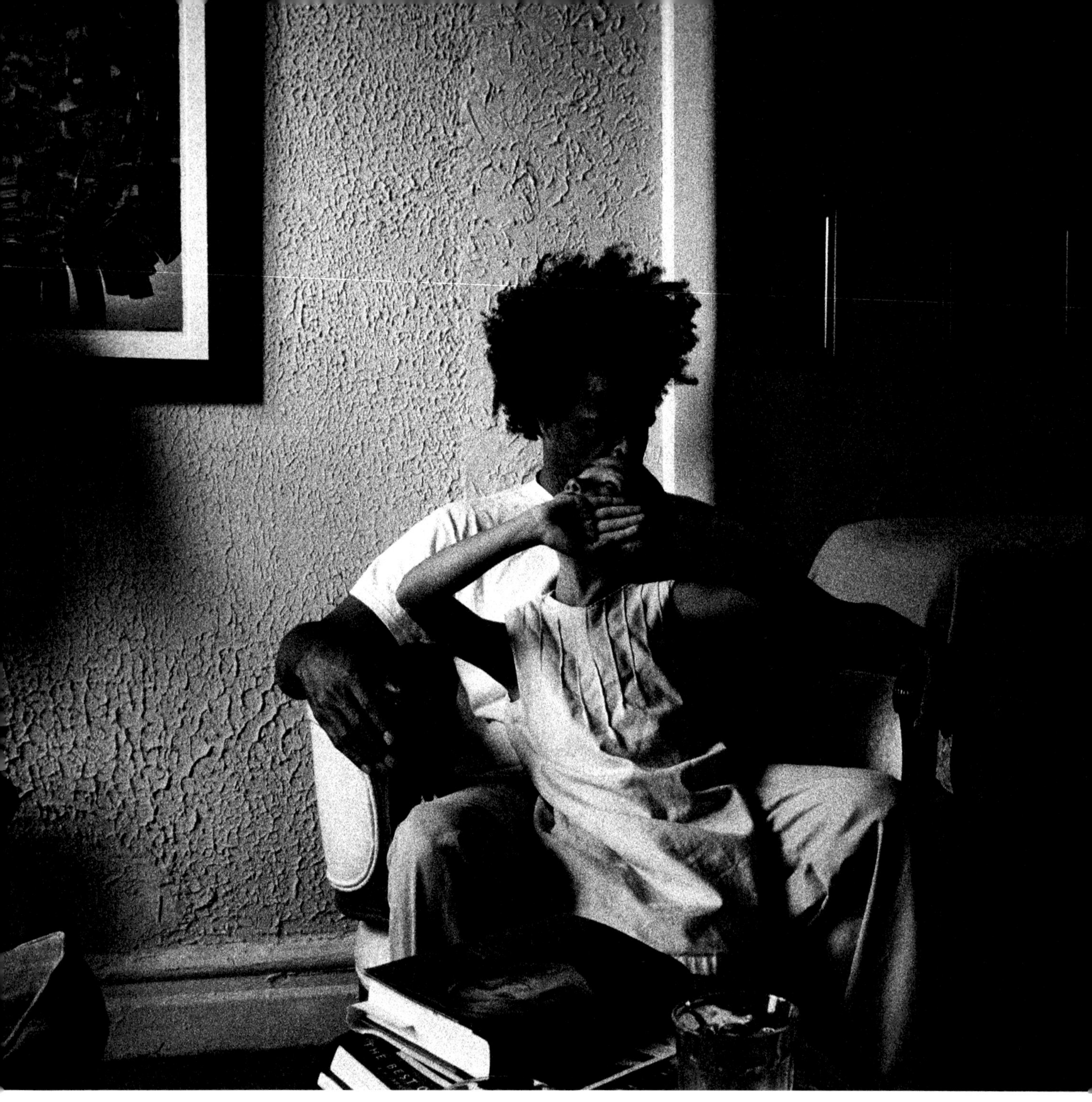

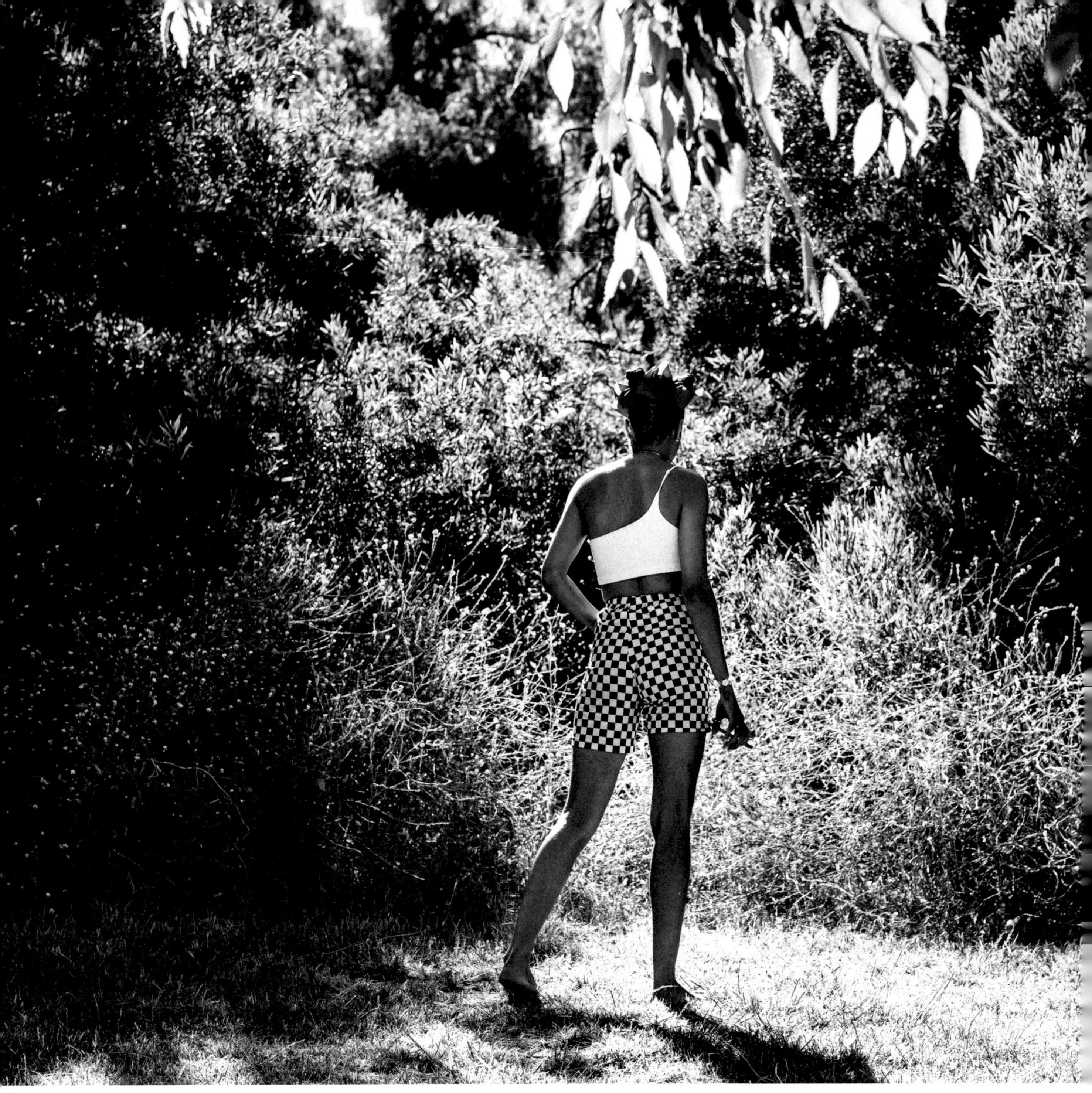

In memory of Jennifer Sterlin, Antoine Henri Bernard Sterlin, Andre Sterlin, Mami Denise Bolte, Marilynn Autherly Thompson, Leo Thompson, Lydia Jenkins, Chuck, Alex, Jancy and Camille. Let go. Let god. Be free.

✠

Afterword
Tessa Thompson

I can't recall if it was Kate who first placed a camera in my hand, or if she merely planted the seed that compelled me to find one. Either way, it amounts to the same thing.

She had come into my life as my father's partner, and I instantly found her relationship to photography captivating. I remember when she transformed the bathroom into a darkroom, and I felt it was one of the most romantic things I'd ever seen. I had pored over Kate's images for years, struck not only by their unassuming composition and honesty, but also for their enchanting intimacy. This was long before I knew I would spend much of my life trying to create the illusion of privacy in my own work.

One summer, I carried a camera with me everywhere in New York City as I explored it independently for the first time. I would leave California most holiday breaks from school to visit my father, and each time an indelible mark was left on me. It must have been the year before I graduated. I discovered that Manhattan is a nearly perfect place to take photographs. You can, at once, be entirely invisible and yet inside what feels like the very heart of humanity. I have long since lost the images I captured, and I can only vaguely place what they must have depicted. But, the sensation of shooting them still resides within me. It wasn't so much about the images I produced; instead, I was being introduced to a new way of seeing. I practiced a fervent observation of others, which remains, for me, one of the most thrilling aspects of being human: giving someone the gift of being seen.

Perhaps, in part, this is because I've never firmly believed in the continuity of personhood.

Of course, this may be an occupational hazard. My livelihood relies on my ability to shift what kind of person I am, and frequently. Instead of perceiving life as an arc, I often feel like I begin anew repeatedly. Living feels episodic, and the past often eludes me. It's no surprise, then, that I struggle to relate to some past version of myself when confronted with images of her. Although I've maintained a relatively similar physical appearance since childhood—retaining the plumpness in my cheeks, for instance—when I glance at old photos of myself, I sometimes struggle to recognize the humanity in the person staring back at me. I feel so profoundly altered by time, and while I cherish many moments from my past, I possess a persistent preoccupation with the present.

I've always marveled at the capacity of loved ones to recall dates and details, and I'm grateful for them.

Summoning someone else's story, however, is more than mere recall. It is perhaps one of the most essential acts of love. After all, aren't we all in need of someone else to bear witness to our lives, to help us remember later, in the fullest sense?

Who will recall the places I've gone?
Who will summon for me the person I used to be, if not you?
Remember for me, and I'll remember for you.

This brings me back to my subject, Kate. The one whose work helps to make a record. The one dedicated to remembrance.

There are those who see us with singularity and curiosity, with unwavering kindness, helping us see ourselves better, and more gently.

Then there are those who reveal themselves with such bravery and profound candor that they allow us to recognize our own truths. They whisper to us, reminding us that even in our most undecorated states, we deserve a warm gaze.

When I am moved by a photograph of a moment in time that might have otherwise been ignored, I feel indebted to Kate, the way her subject might be. Images are memory's faithful custodians. They preserve the ephemeral and fragile fragments of our existence. But images do more than guard memory: they give us portals into understanding the past so that we may live in a more unfettered, loving present. Ultimately, renderings of life—whether etched in pixels or on film, or strung together with words on a page—serve as tangible anchors for the evocation of our deeper selves.

To infuse the everyday with a sense of historical significance, poetry, and dignity is to affirm that the private lives we lead deserve inquiry, not only from others but from ourselves. To express the ineffable, to immortalize it in ink, is to prompt us to explore the things we've never dared to admit. Being interested in witnessing, summoning, and drawing close to those moments, as Kate has been for a lifetime, means being acutely aware that the fugitive present, in all its texture, will mostly be forgotten but always undeniably felt. With a loving, intimate record of it, we can begin to understand why.

Thank you, Kate, and all those who capture. It is a privilege to be seen by you.

In Conversation
Arooj Aftab

Your writing and your pictures show joy and pain in a very real and gentle way. It's beautiful, and as real as life is. I'm sorry for putting it so simply. Can you tell me about how you arrived at this gaze?

I've always thought that my drive to preserve memories and stop time was related to my dad's illness when I was growing up and in reaction, my mom's obsessive moving habits: every year, running to, running from. I think taking photographs was my attempt to create some permanence—a document I could later reference. And I was really young when I had my own kids, so I continued to document while also taking care of babies and a house and trying to act like an adult; so a lot of the images are of my family and friends. I think I am still learning the whats and whys of my lens and where I point it now, as I age and feel the weight of everything in a different way. The writing is a more personal exploration on love and intimacy, though it does feel related to the work of intimate portraiture: understanding the vulnerability intrinsic to that form, and experiencing it myself. In 2020, when everything stopped, I had time to dig through my inventory. I feel like I'd never slowed down long enough for the elements to separate— to see the shapes. The stories are like imprints or fossils. Excavating them, distilling them, and then releasing them just felt like an unfolding.

We hold memory in so many ways, and in all the senses. Photos can be like history, but they can also be like dreamcatchers. Did you capture some good ones? Tell me something no one knows about a photo you took.

It's so true: there's a layer of memory informing everything like a filter, reminding us that what we see is subjective to our own references. I've started cataloguing my negatives from the past thirty years and it's been like looking through a portal of who I was then, at fifteen, at twenty-five, thirty-five, etc.: the choices I made; how I saw; what I framed. I was such a purist in the beginning. I would pick out a few images that I thought were "the shot" and print them, and then never revisit the rest of the roll. Looking through them now, I've been finding so many images I can't believe I didn't

see at the time. I recently found a roll I developed and contacted but never printed from after 9/11 in NYC. I was living in Brooklyn at the time, and I went over to see the site when they started letting people near. I photographed everyone staring at the wreckage, and then I just put the film away. Finding it was like uncovering a lost file. I didn't remember being there or taking photos—kind of like a dream.

Where do we go when our forehead relaxes, and our eyelids close a bit? I call it the "chill thinking and dreaming face"—like when it's sunny and you don't have sunglasses. I'd love to know what happens to you when it sets in.

I'm a very anxious person, and I have a hard time relaxing in general, but I know what you mean— those in-between spaces of consciousness. I often wonder if this is all just a simulation. What the hell is déjà vu? I'm always debunking my own theories, and sometimes I feel like I know very little about what drives us or influences us, but I do think there's a thin veil between realms that falls away sometimes, especially when death is near in some way. When my dad died, I dreamt of him a lot and had the most vivid experiences with him. I felt like my unconscious dreamlife was where I felt more engaged, while during the day I was at a loss. And now those experiences are logged along with memories, so ultimately, what's the difference?

Yes—about consciousness, and how hard it is to interpret it, and then capture its complexity. Daily human life can feel a lot like a lemming game. But there is this incredible cosmic life force around us that is not human. How does your relationship to animals and nature play into your artistic sensibility?

I'm fascinated by animals and nature, even though I'm not really drawn to photograph them most of the time. I think that for me, certain types of beauty are best experienced in the flesh, that somehow a photo—or my kind of photo—won't do it justice. Like, a sunset is incredible to witness because it's happening in front of you and changing every second but on paper, who cares? Although, a few years ago, a friend upstate found a dead baby hawk and brought it to me, and I did photograph it and I really love the image. I think because it was both morbid and beautiful. The bird was so pristine and vibrant, but it was also dead, and soon it would rot. The beauty and serenity was there, but it was fleeting.

Are love and time the same thing?

Yes. I think love is a commitment to time. I think love is hard and beautiful and impatient and stubborn and time is mean and unforgiving and vast and yet so short. I just watched my mother fight for a little more time, and the last few months were a dance of hope and despair. But strangely, she arrived at a place of feeling joy and love in a way that I had never experienced with her. It was as though she finally felt loved and she could finally love freely. Maybe it was her "chill thinking and dreaming face." It felt like a gift; kind of cruel because it was so brief, but I'm still grateful to have it in the forefront of my mind now. I think that if we're lucky we can experience all the facets of love: not just the made-up fairytale version, but the complicated layers of unrequited love, forbidden love, platonic love, repaired love, forgiven love, lost love, unspoken love…

Do you allow yourself to be still? What happens then?

Photographing for me is about finding that stillness, which is something I can't otherwise access that easily. That sounds dramatic, but it's true. I channel my nervous energy into doing and making. I'm constantly moving, thinking, and worrying, but portraits require stillness. It's about finding the sweet space where we have decided to freeze time together and both be open (and a little nervous) to let each other in to see ourselves; my essence is as much a part of the expression reflected in the gaze in front as behind the lens. I'm not big on directing, and it makes for more awkwardness initially. But if we get through that, then I know that neither person is performing, that we are just trying to communicate something and make a moment. Like not being afraid of the quiet. Not trying to fill the space.

For helping me realize this book, thank you to: Maria Szabo, my constant—your unwavering love and support is immeasurable; Selenia Rios, for your giant heart and the magic of connection; Elise Durant, for your friendship and dedication to our art meetings when life was still; Sissy Onet, for showing me how beautiful change can be; Hallie Goodman, for helping me develop my knife skills; Taliesin Gilkes-Bower, for your enthusiasm and words; my Big Love Queens—Chan Marshall, Alana Lowe, Stella Yoon, Andrea Passarella, Michelle Buteau, and Bruce McNally—for sharing this beautiful life with me.

To Jesse Pollock, for believing in this book, for patiently guiding me through this process and always making it better, <3; to Mark Iosifescu, for your thoughtful and gentle hand; to Tanya Rubbak, for your ideas and considerate eye; to everyone at Anthology Editions.

Arooj Aftab and Isioma Chukwuani, for our adventure across the world and late-night talks and shoots in the ocean and what we wrote down.

Tessa Thompson, for seeing me—for appreciating what this came to be.

To Caleb, Miles, Treme, Michele, Ssanyu, Harolyn (where are you?), Suleika, Sarah, Molly, Amani, Lola, Dylan, Rick, Max, Devonte, DeVonn, and Jasper, for letting me get close enough to capture these moments.

To my mother, father, sister, and brother, for putting up with young teenage me clicking away at family dinners, learning how to tell a story.

To Mary Ellen Mark for mentorship, inspiration, and an endless dedication to the beauty of film.

Lastly, to my mother, Jenny, the most complicated love of my life— who taught me about fierce independence and emotional connection. I'll miss you forever.

THANK YOU.

Index of Images

Front and back cover: Free Box Fashion Show, Bolinas, CA, 2004

7:      Sissy in Pool 1, Mérida, Mexico, 2021

11:     Dad Seated, Boston, MA, 1989

12:     Zsela Upside-Down on Grandma Daisy's Rug 1, Los Angeles, CA, 1999

15:     Dad Seated, New York, NY, 2004

17:     Marilynn's Funeral, Hobart, Los Angeles, CA, 2000

20:     Sunday Morning, Harlem, NY, 2021

22:     Kids After a Flood, Treasure Beach, Jamaica, 2000

25:     Treme and Zsela on the Swings, Cambridge, MA, 2003

27:     Kate in New Orleans, LA, 1990 (photographed by Michael Manning)

28:     Kate in New Orleans, LA, 1990 (photographed by Michael Manning)

31:     Rain Storm 1, New York, NY, 2021

32:     After Hurricane Katrina, New Orleans, LA, 2005

35:     Kind of Tree, Miami, FL, 2021

36:     Marc Sleeping, Joshua Tree, CA, 2020

39:     Marc at the Lake, VA, 2004

41:     Marilynn and Leo in Doorway, Los Angeles, CA, 1997

43:     Driving up the Coast, Highway 1, CA, 2021

44:     Mami and Papi with My Father, Port-au-Prince, Haiti, 1944 (archival photograph)

46:     Christmas Dinner, Boston, MA, 1988

50:     Dad Seated at Christmas Dinner, Boston, MA, 1988

53:     Sissy Seated, Mérida, Mexico, 2021

56–57: Joshua Tree, CA, 2020 / Kids After a Flood 1, Treasure Beach, Jamaica, 2000

58:     Caleb in the Pool at Night, Hollywood, CA, 2022

60:     Miles at Halloween Party, Los Angeles, CA, 2022

62:     Staircase, Tangiers, Morocco, 2018

65:     Michelle Seated with Children Playing on Stoop, Fort Greene, Brooklyn, NY, 2003

69:     Performers at the Puerto Rican Day Parade, New York, NY, 2005

70-71: Self–Portrait, Los Angeles, CA, 2020 / Plane in the Sky, Juneteenth, Inglewood, CA, 2020

72-73: Tessa Twirling, Hudson, NY, 2002

75:     Sissy in the Pool 3, Mérida, Mexico, 2021

77:     Covered Street Light, Los Angeles, CA, 2020

78:     Cacti, Zuma Beach, Malibu, CA, 2019

82:     Eye on LA, Los Angeles, CA, 2020

83:     Queen, Mérida, Mexico, 2021

84:     Self-Portrait, Los Angeles, CA, 2020 / Palm Trees, Los Angeles, CA, 2000

88-89: Rain Storm 2, New York, NY, 2021 / Bed After Sleep, Los Angeles, CA, 2020 / Zsela Getting Dressed 1, Los Angeles, CA, 2020

90:     Zsela Getting Dressed 1, Los Angeles, CA, 2020

92-93: Zsela Getting Dressed 2, Los Angeles, CA, 2020 / Trees 1, Joshua Tree, CA, 2020 / Ssanyu Pregnant, Fort Greene, Brooklyn, NY, 2002

95:     Harolyn, Fort Greene, Brooklyn, NY, 2002

98:     Dad and Zsela Hospital 1, New York, NY, 2003

99:     Dad and Zsela Hospital 2, New York, NY, 2003

100:    Caleb in the Pool at Night, Hollywood, CA, 2022

103:    Mom at Home in Hell's Kitchen, NY, 2022

107:    Suleika at Sloan Kettering Hospital, New York City, NY, 2021

109:    Tessa and Malcolm X on the Beach, Malibu, CA, 2020

110:    Kids After a Flood 2, Treasure Beach, Jamaica, 2000

113:    Kids and Woman Walking By, Roxbury, MA, 1989

115:    Ssanyu Pregnant, Fort Greene, Brooklyn, NY, 2002

117:    Statues in the Backyard, Hobart, Los Angeles, CA, 2020

120:    Two Girls at the Puerto Rican Day Parade, New York, NY, 2005

122: Adrea, Tessa, Zsela and Jody Rome at Hobart on the Carpet 1, Los Angeles, CA, 2002

123: Adrea, Tessa, Zsela and Jody Rome at Hobart on the Carpet 2, Los Angeles, CA, 2002

126: Woman Seated in Front of Window, Manhattan Plaza, New York, NY, 2021

131: Caleb in the Pool at Night, Hollywood, CA, 2022

132: After Leo Died, Los Angeles, CA, 2006

135: Marc at the Piano, Los Angeles, CA, 2006

139: Marilynn Seated, Los Angeles, CA, 1999

140: Trees 2, Joshua Tree, CA, 2020

145: Zsela in Shadows, Los Angeles, CA, 2019

148: Harolyn Pregnant Seated, Fort Greene, Brooklyn, NY, 2002

151: Zsela in the Pool Turned Away, Los Angeles, CA, 2020

152: Harolyn Pregnant Lying Down, Fort Greene, Brooklyn, NY, 2002

155: Jody Rome Backlit, Los Angeles, CA, 2020

156-157: Dev Seated, Joshua Tree, CA, 2020 / Trees 3, Joshua Tree, CA, 2020

159: DeVonn Singing Karaoke, New York, NY, 2021

161: Zsela Upside-Down on Grandma Daisy's Rug 2, Los Angeles, CA, 1999

165: Jody Rome and Marc, Echo Park, Los Angeles, CA, 2006

167: Jody Rome Seated in Sunroom, Los Angeles, CA, 2020

169: Landscape, Joshua Tree, CA, 2020

170: Jasper Seated 1, Joshua Tree, CA, 2020

171: Jasper Seated 2, Joshua Tree, CA, 2020

175: Tessa and Jody Rome in the Crochet Museum, Joshua Tree, CA, 2020

176: Marc and Zsela Seated, Brooklyn, NY, 2004

178: Zsela in Elysian Park, Los Angeles, CA, 2020

Index of Stories

9: *Dad*, 2020

19: *Harlem*, 2021

29: *Montreal I*, 2020

37: *You*, 2021

45: *Untitled 01*, 2020

49: *Untitled 02*, 2020

55: *Halfway*, 2022

61: *Chuck*, 2021

67: *Brooklyn*, 2020

74: *2020*, 2021

81: *Alex*, 2022

87: *Los Angeles*, 2019

91: *Hudson*, 2022

97: *Until*, 2022

105: *The End*, 2023

111: *Montreal II*, 2020

118: *Us Again*, 2021

125: *Old Glass*, 2023

129: *New York*, 2023

137: *Sunny View*, 2022

143: *Jane*, 2023

147: *Han*, 2020

153: *Nightfall*, 2022

163: *Untitled 05*, 2023

173: *Sylvia*, 2021

First published in the United States of America
in 2024 by Anthology Editions

87 Guernsey Street
Brooklyn, NY 11222

anthologyeditions.com

Copyright © 2024 by Anthology Editions, LLC
Text and Images © 2024 by Kate Sterlin

All rights reserved under Pan American and
International Copyright Conventions. No part of
this publication may be reproduced, stored in a
retrieval system, or transmitted in any form or
by any means, electronic, mechanical,
photocopying, recording, or otherwise, without
prior consent of the publishers.

Editor: Mark Iosifescu
Assistant Editor: Jana Horn
Designer: Tanya Rubbak
Art Direction: Jesse Pollock
Retouching: Rachel Cabitt
Sales and Marketing: Casey Whalen
First Edition
ARC 129
Printed in China on FSC-certified paper
ISBN: 978-1-944860-62-2

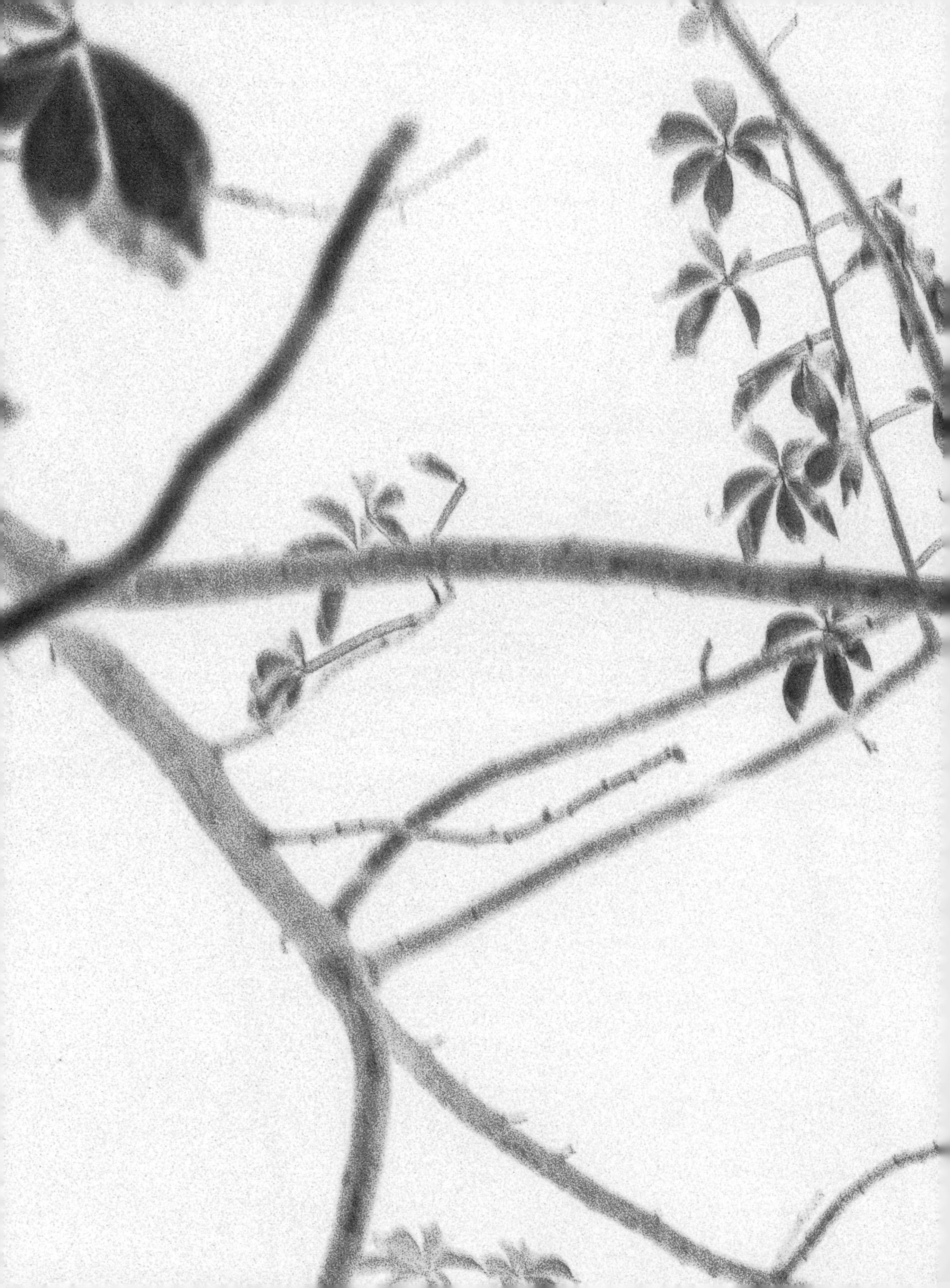

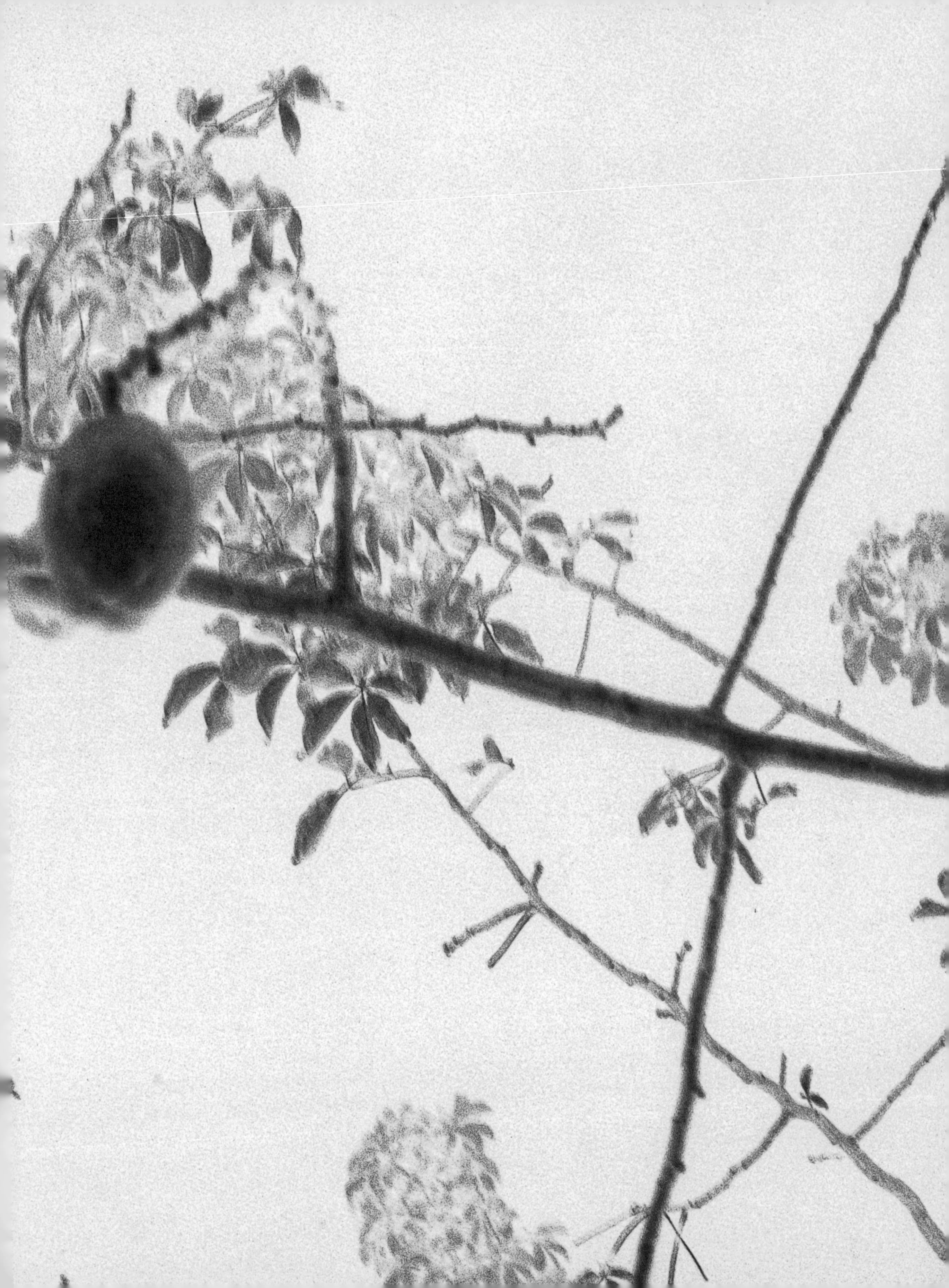